# Christian Thinking and Social Order

# Christian Thinking and Social Order

## Conviction Politics from the 1930s to the Present Day

**Edited by Marjorie Reeves**

Cassell
London and New York

Cassell
Wellington House, 125 Strand, London WC2R 0BB
370 Lexington Avenue, New York, NY 10017-6550

First published 1999

**British Library Cataloguing in Publication Data**
A catalogue record for this book is available from the British Library.

ISBN    0 304 70247 1 (hardback)
           0 304 70248 X (paperback)

Cover: the first issue of the *Christian News-Letter*, 18 October 1939, see p. 49.

Typeset by BookEns Ltd, Royston, Herts
Printed and bound in Great Britain by Biddles Ltd, Guildford and King's Lynn

# Contents

# Contributors

The Revd Keith Clements, PhD, General Secretary, Conference of European Churches

The Very Revd David L. Edwards, OBE, Provost Emeritus of Southwark Cathedral, London

The Revd Duncan B. Forrester, DPhil, Professor of Christian Ethics and Practical Theology, New College, University of Edinburgh

The Revd Daniel Jenkins, United Reformed Church Minister, formerly Professor of Theology

Dr Harry Judge, formerly Director of the Department of Educational Studies, University of Oxford

Dr Elaine Kaye, Lecturer in Church History, Mansfield College, Oxford

The Revd Eric Lord, MPhil, formerly Chief Inspector, HM Inspectorate of Schools

Professor W. Roy Niblett, CBE, formerly Professor of Higher Education, University of London Institute of Education

The Revd Ronald H. Preston, DD, Emeritus Professor of Social and Pastoral Theology, University of Manchester and Canon Emeritus, Manchester Cathedral

Professor Richard Pring, Professor of Educational Studies, University of Oxford

Dr Marjorie Reeves, CBE, FBA, Honorary Fellow, St Anne's and St Hugh's Colleges, Oxford

W. Salters Stirling, formerly Academic Registrar, Trinity College, Dublin

Sir William Taylor, CBE, formerly Vice Chancellor of Hull and Huddersfield Universities and previously Director of the University of London Institute of Education.

Dr John Wyatt, formerly Director of the Chichester Institute of Higher Education, University of Southampton

# Foreword

This book is a very valuable exercise in historical retrieval. It both chronicles and analyses a period when the churches were involved in a whole series of deep and contentious political issues: the search for social justice in domestic politics; the rise of the totalitarian states of the 1930s; the development of the Soviet Union as a society with an anti-religious ideology; the growth of the managerial culture in Western societies; the impact of the advent of nuclear weapons; and the pressures for decolonization.

Many of the thinkers and 'doers' whose activities are discussed in these pages made a significant impact on national life because of the seriousness of their engagement with these issues: J. H. Oldham, Archbishop Temple, Karl Mannheim, Sir Walter Moberly, T. S. Eliot to name just a select few. They were all agreed about the imperative need for the Christian churches to engage with these pressing issues of culture, society and politics. They were particularly concerned with the need to think about the nature of the new national and international order which the sacrifices of the Second World War seemed to them to demand and which had not emerged in a stable way after the Great War. They were also concerned with how Western societies could develop some kind of distinctive moral basis, as an alternative to the subjectivism and relativism which made them vulnerable to the challenge of more determinate and wilful belief systems of the sort that had dominated in the 1930s.

The individuals whose work is analysed in this book disagreed about many things, but that disagreement was itself fruitful. They did not think that it was possible to develop one authoritative view of the Christian attitude to politics and culture from the Bible or from the Christian tradition. The formulation and development of such views had to come from dialogue and discussion and from close engagement with the facts. This commitment meant that communication and discussion was at the heart of their enterprise, hence the role of the 'Moot' and *The Christian News-Letter*, both of which were sustained in the most adverse circumstances during the war.

An overarching concern was the question of what was the point and purpose of human life, and with the role of education, and in particular Higher Education, in developing a capacity to think seriously about such questions – questions which are a mark of our humanity. Education should not be reduced only to an instrumental and utilitarian preparation for life in the industrial and commercial worlds however important these things are. Rather, education should engage with the deep questions about value and purpose in the life of both individuals and institutions. Unless such questions about human purposes and the circumstances of human flourishing are constantiy raised, society will lose any sense of a transcendent and will become criterionless and prey to either managerial control or, more sinisterly, the blandishments of ideologies which claim to have the answer to human purposes in terms that liberal societies are in danger of not addressing.

Many of these issues which preoccupied this earlier generation of Christian thinkers are still with us. Social justice still seems to be both as salient and as elusive as ever, whether in national or international contexts. The scope for managerialism in a culture marked by relativism and moral subjectivism has been much debated recently following the publication of Alasdair MacIntyre's *After Virtue*. While the prospect of nuclear war between the West and the old Soviet Union has dissipated, nevertheless there are major problems about the proliferation of nuclear weapons and their development by other states, and the issue that this potential proliferation implies for international stability and, indeed, for state sovereignty. And, of course, the question of what education, and particularly Higher Education, is for. When our thinkers were active higher education was for a very small minority of the population. We are now in the world of mass and very expensive higher education. How far can such a system afford to devote time and effort to the questions that our thinkers believed to be so important? Equally, however, what are the implications for society if such fundamental questions are not raised within the university?

In our day, however, we face new challenges as Christians involved in politics: globalization, multiculturalism, the growth of narrow forms of nationalism which seem to have accompanied the growth of the global market, the growth of fundamentalism both within Christianity and within other religions, and the growth of the politics of difference, in which people want to bring to the political process their differences – whether of race, gender, culture or religion – rather than an emphasis on what they have in common as citizens. Grappling with these issues from a Christian perspective is a daunting task for us, as it was in their day and their context for the thinkers analysed in this book.

There is, however, a further problem in that the role of metaphysical beliefs in general and Christian beliefs in particular in the politics of a liberal society has become more acute than it was two generations ago. How far is it compatible with the values of a liberal society to argue about fundamental political issues and divisions from a religious standpoint? Most of the thinkers discussed were aware of some aspects of this problem but most of them adhered to a view of Christianity which would enable both Christians and non-Christians to work together, believing that they held certain principles in common. This assumption is now much more difficult to sustain, given the growth of what I have called the politics of difference and (for that matter) the growth of importance within Christian thought of narrative theology, which does emphasize the distinctiveness and irreducibility of the Christian understanding and perspective. Such approaches would see many of the strategies of this generation of thinkers as too accommodating to the secular. If, however, one does believe that there is the possibility of dialogue in Christian ethics and thinking about politics, then we can still learn a great deal from that committed generation whose struggles for Christian understanding are well-chronicled in this volume.

Lord Plant
Master, St Catherine's College, Oxford

# Preface

In 1960, at the age of 86, J. H. Oldham wrote a passionate exposition of 'The Frontier Idea' which he had served for much of his life. The frontier, was, of course, that between 'the church' and 'the world'. For Oldham the call was not so much for eager Christians to cross the line with a message from the church to the world, but rather for Christians, rejoicing in their secularity, to use all their individual competencies and experience to help solve the problems of their society. God was at work *equally* on both sides of 'the frontier', and 'the world', under God, had its proper autonomy as part of his creation. 'The crucial point,' said Oldham, 'was not the distinction between clergy and laity, but the question of their competence in the various spheres of secular activity.' The purpose of this book is to bring back to memory a network of Christians in Britain in the earlier decades of this century who, led by Oldham, found their vocation as thinker-doers in searching out 'the ways of God with man' inside the confused world of secular living. It is in no sense a comprehensive survey of Christian social thought through this period but rather aims to let certain voices speak again, voices which resonate with great clarity and urgency today. Broadly speaking, the theme of the whole book turns on the responsibility of 'intellectuals' to follow through the transmutation of theological and philosophical ideas into social policies, precisely through their involvement in 'the world'. Intellectuals often agonized over the charge of élitism and the limitations of the leadership they could give in a mass democracy. Yet today there is still a necessary role for thinkers: in this age of one-issue propaganda and quick fixes, we still need the intellectual contribution of wide perspectives and deep reflection.

Textual accuracy takes precedence over political correctness. We apologize to all those readers for whom the male language habitually used by our writers touches a sensitive nerve. In the common usage of the day man = the inclusive homo of Latin. In fact there were several key women closely involved in 'the network', notably Amy Buller, Eleanora Iredale, Dorothy Emmet and Kathleen Bliss.

# Acknowledgements

We are grateful for permission from the author, editor and publisher to include here a shortened version of Sir William Taylor's essay 'The Moot and Education', first published in R. Aldrich (ed.), *In History and in Education: Essays presented to Peter Gordon* (Woburn Press, 1996), pp. 156–86. We have endeavoured without success to trace any surviving owner of *The Christian News-Letter* copyright. We acknowledge with gratitude the encouragement and advice given in the preparation of this book by the Rt Revd Richard Harries, bishop of Oxford and the commendation of it by Lord Plant, master of St Catherine's College, Oxford. Our thanks also go to the Education Services Trust for a grant towards the editing of this book. The editor wishes to thank the sub-editor, Dr Elaine Kaye, for much assistance, for a wise judgement and an eagle eye, and also all the contributors for their enthusiastic collaboration and for the stimulating dialogue which has ensued.

M.E.R.

# Abbreviations

| | |
|---|---|
| BCC | British Council of Churches |
| *CN-L* | *The Christian News-Letter* |
| HEF | Higher Education Foundation |
| HEG | Higher Education Group |
| HMI | His/Her Majesty's inspector |
| ICE | Institute of Christian Education |
| LEA | Local education authority |
| LSE | London School of Economics |
| PEP | Political and Economic Planning |
| PPU | Peace Pledge Union |
| SCAA | Schools' Curriculum Assessment Authority |
| SCM | Student Christian Movement |
| *TES* | *Times Educational Supplement* |
| TUC | Trades Union Congress |
| UGC | University Grants Committee |
| UTG | University Teacher's Group |
| WCC | World Council of Churches |
| WSCF | World Student Christian Federation |
| YMCA | Young Men's Christian Association |

# Part I

*Chapter 1*

# Themes of the 1930s

Eric Lord and Marjorie Reeves

## Christianity and Crisis*

Is a 'state of crisis' endemic in modern society? The word punctuates the decades of this century. In 1933 a symposium entitled *Christianity and the Crisis*, edited by Percy Dearmer, canon of Westminster, was commissioned by the publisher Victor Gollancz. Financial collapse in America and Europe in 1931, economic depression and rising unemployment, ominous mutterings of political turbulence in Germany – these formed the gathering crisis which prompted Gollancz's title and his commission for a book which would 'go all out for immediate and practical socialism and internationalism'.[1] Dearmer had a reputation as a theological radical; Gollancz was later well known for his sponsorship of the Left Book Club. In the event, the 32 lay and clerical contributions did not concentrate their attack sufficiently to be very effective. Nevertheless, amid some nebulous writing, there were those prepared to get down to the concrete. Lay contributors in particular grappled with such specifics as the deficiencies of laissez-faire economics and the strain unemployment put on the domestic rating system. The style of their thinking was prophetic, for the solutions they offered tended to occupy the political 'middle ground', with government action supplying the corrective to market forces.[2] What was emerging was that feeling after consensual solutions with a collectivist tinge which became a feature of wartime politics. *Christianity and the Crisis* was in fact a pointer towards a whole series of initiatives which form the core of this book.

\* The first half of this chapter is by Eric Lord.

Other reformist groups in the 1930s shared the same character-istics. They were by no means all under Christian influence, but William Temple was involved both in PEP[3] and in the group called The Next Five Years, the, the League of Nations Union drew much support from the churches, while Lloyd George's Council of Action for Peace and Reconstruction had a great Nonconformist following. In what Arthur Marwick later called the 'middle opinion' of the 1930s the Christian social conscience played an important part, with a deep concern for peace in Europe and for social reconstruction at home.[4]

## Theological Encounters: Liberal Protestantism, Barth and Niebuhr

The main theological position which underpinned this social and political concern was liberal Protestantism. There were, of course, variations ranging from a more leftish position, theologically and politically, among Free Churchmen to the theologically radical but politically conservative stance of, for instance, the Anglican Modern Churchman's Union.[5] In essence, however, the underlying convictions which united this diverse company included the belief that the Christian faith could, and must, be commended in ways that took account of modern scientific knowledge; that God was indwelling in all humanity and therefore human beings could be responsive to goodness and truth; and that the theme of the Kingdom of God in the teaching of Jesus was a call to men and women to work for 'the steady encouragement of all that is good in the world'.[6] But liberal Protestantism's endemic optimism too glibly translated the concept of the Kingdom of God into notions of fraternity and social betterment which human beings could reach if they put their minds to it.

A counterbalance was provided by two theological 'movements' of this period. First the New Testament scholar, C. H. Dodd, was leading a call to attend more closely to the message of the New Testament. The theology which flowed from this spoke of God's intervention in the world rather than humanity's progressive discovery of God: 'The Kingdom was the work of God rather than of human efforts.' The emphasis in 'biblical theology' was on the themes of judgement and promise, and upon divine disclosure, not human discerning.[7] At the same time a stronger, harsher proclama-tion of the transcendence of God was coming from the German theologian, Karl Barth. God is 'the Wholly Other', not reachable by the intellect or knowable apart from the revelation given in Jesus Christ. In Barth's words, 'God is to be distinguished qualitatively from men and from everything human, and must never be identified with anything which we name or experience or conceive, or worship as God'.[8] Barthian 'neo-orthodoxy' received a better hearing in Scotland than in England, where pre-war theologians found it hard to take.

A new voice coming from America was that of Reinhold Niebuhr, holding the tension between Barthians and social reformers. On the one hand, he shared Barth's judgemental view of man and society, yet he earthed this in a powerful social ethic. In 1933 the publication of *Moral Man and Immoral Society* in England[9] made a great impact. In fact the title was somewhat misleading, for he had no illusions about the deeply sinful nature of individual human beings, but it was the collective evil of power-seeking groups in society that aroused his passions. In his diagnosis he was Marxist rather than liberal but he joined the crusade for social justice and peace. His peculiar position made him a powerful prophet among students. For many of these the 1930s was a time of urgent questioning about social morals and a desperate searching for panaceas. Douglas Credit, the Peace Pledge Union and the Christian Left were among those on offer. The inevitability of human progress was viewed with a growing disbelief which made Niebuhr's argument that we must fight for social justice even while recognizing that all our efforts are deeply flawed all the more convincing. We were bound up in a sinful society from which we could not seek 'purity of conscience' by withdrawal. Yet the ideal of perfection was always relevant. It was Niebuhr's phrase 'the relevance of an impossible possible' which struck home so revealingly. The SCM issued a study outline, *Reinhold Niebuhr: An Introduction to his Thought*, by David Paton, which admirably reflected the cross-currents of social thinking in the 1930s.[10]

## The Student Christian Movement

In a period before denominational societies began to play an active role among students, the Student Christian Movement was seen (and saw itself) as an interdenominational agency in the service of the churches. In contrast to the Inter-Varsity Fellowship, the SCM endeavoured to encompass liberal, catholic, and evangelical in its capacious 'Aim and basis'.[11] It laid special emphasis on Christian responsibility in social and international affairs and the search for a theology adequate to meet the contemporary situation. With international links through the World Student Christian Federation (WSCF) its intellectual discussions were vigorous and alive to the latest theological trends – so much so that in 1937 the joke was circulating that the SCM had rewritten a summary of the commandments: 'Thou shalt love the Lord thy Dodd ... and thy Niebuhr as thyself.'[12] In study groups and conferences the movement grappled with the demands for 'holy worldliness'. Many years later Lesslie Newbigin recalled his sense of 'sharing in a world-wide Christian enterprise which was commanding the devotion of men and women whose sheer intellectual and spiritual power was unmistakable'.[13]

## Political Groups: Christian Left to Peace Pledge Union

In the international arena the attraction of communism and the rising menace of fascism challenged Christian political thought sharply. The Christian Left offered one path of action but the pacifism of the inter-war years, combining political humanism and religious elements in its amoeba-like formations and re-formations, presented an alternative. Here pure pacifism – the belief that all war is wrong and should never be resorted to – must be distinguished from what A. J. P. Taylor called pacificism, the view that war, though sometimes necessary, is always an irrational and inhumane method of trying to solve disputes.[14] The churches' strong support for the League of Nations Union expressed the latter view, as also did many of the eleven million affirmative answers in the unofficial Peace Ballot of 1934 to the question 'Should Britain remain a member of the League?'[15] But as the international scene darkened the absolutist stance of the pacifists came to the fore. Christian pacifism was represented in the international Fellowship of Reconciliation and in denominational groups such as the Methodist, Baptist and Anglican Pacifist fellowships. In 1935 the Peace Pledge Union (PPU) was inaugurated by Dick Sheppard[16] who wrote a letter to the press in October 1934 inviting people to indicate their support for the pledge 'We renounce war and never again, directly or indirectly, will we support another'. When the PPU was formally launched in May 1936 its list of sponsors from various shades of rationalist and religious belief included Bertrand Russell, Vera Brittain, Siegfried Sassoon, Aldous Huxley, Donald Soper and George Macleod.

## Scientific 'Imperialism' and 'the primacy of the personal'

By the 1930s the long battle between science and the conservative forces of religion was, to a large extent, over. Scientific method had rightly won the middle ground in large areas of academic research and the Baconian assertion of the 'Adam-right' to rule over the natural world was finding full expression in the burgeoning new technologies. In the scientific world-view, it could be claimed, humanity was 'ordained to possess the Earth'. Scientific method was now invading the social sciences. One spin-off from this outlook was to view society, not in terms of human beings with personal needs, but as 'cohorts' whose functioning could be studied scientifically. Thus the influence of science led to more and better surveys of social conditions, while from 1937 the views of the citizenry began to be analysed statistically in Gallup Polls.[17]

Yet in the same year a poet, Charles Madge, and an anthropologist, Tom Harrisson, founded Mass Observation,[18] a social survey which emphasized what actual people said and did rather than the quantification of social trends, and Ronald Gregor Smith published his translation of Martin Buber's *Ich und Du* (I and Thou).[19] Buber's influence was already pervasive in some Christian circles and will be detected again and again in this book.[20] Here was a philosophy of persons-in-relationships which acted as a powerful counterbalance to the prevailing philosophical stance which viewed human beings as individual objects. The gifts to humankind which flowed from scientific investigation were undoubted, but science represented only one half of the picture. The 'primacy of the personal' was in danger and must be rescued. With others, this was the viewpoint of J. H. Oldham and John Macmurray.

## Three Prophets*

### *J. H. Oldham: 1874–1969*

The essence of Joe Oldham might be expressed as thought-in-action. In many ways he serves as a perfect example of Macmurray's continuum between thought and action. At any one time in his long adult career he would be spotting what he deemed to be the most urgent problems for human society which Christians ought to be confronting and then moving into action to bring together the wise and experienced in a deep, probing exercise of discussion which might lead towards solutions. There were no quick fixes on the way: the lives of men and women in society formed too delicate a web of relationships to be roughly reordered but there was always a vision

* The following sections of this chapter are by Marjorie Reeves.

at the end. 'Oldham was a prophet, looking out on the world with a keen eye for the acceptable moment at which a blow could be struck against oppression and for justice.'[21] Here we can only mention briefly the early exercise of his skills: in the SCM, with the YMCA in India, as secretary to the first World Missionary Conference (Edinburgh 1910) and of its continuation committee until, after bitter war experience in 1914–18, the International Missionary Council was born. By this time Oldham was seeing 'mission' in terms of 'One World', marking the impact of its increasingly common economic and political problems on the lives of human beings everywhere. Influenced by Graham Wallas's *The Great Society*[22] he had published in 1916 *The World and the Gospel*,[23] and after the war this widening concept of Christian mission led to his long concern with Africa. 'Shall the African peoples be enabled to develop their latent powers, to cultivate their peculiar gifts and so enrich the life of humanity by their distinctive contributions?'[24] he asked. He devoted himself to obtaining the British government's recognition of the paramountcy of native rights in Kenya; with his friend, Lord Lugard, he got established the Advisory Committee on Education in the colonies and drafted its first policy statement in 1925. Later, again with Lord Lugard, he created the International Institute of African Languages and Culture, working for it from 1931 to 1938. But the process leading to such practical steps was always based on what he called 'thinking things together',[25] gathering representatives of all concerned into co-operative problem-solving discussion. His own thinking in this field was crystallized in his widely influential *Christianity and the Race Problem*, published in 1924.

By the 1930s Joe Oldham was moving into a new field. In an address to the International Missionary Council in 1929 on 'The New Christian Adventure' he remarked that more books worth reading that took account of the realities of the modern world were being written from the standpoint of scientific humanism than by Christians.[26] Christians must now seek this 'new adventure' boldly by grappling with the problems raised for humanity by the new science, emphatically not rejecting its benefits, but probing its inadequacies. His method of attack, as before, was to gather key thinkers together in a first conference of young theologians at York.[27] He then repeated a similar exercise in the States. The point at which the British churches first seriously took up the challenge of secular society together came in 1937 when the two ecumenical conferences on 'Faith and Order' and 'Life and Work', with the theme 'Church, Community and State', met in Edinburgh and Oxford. Not surprisingly, Oldham was one of the prime movers behind the latter, organizing thorough study papers beforehand and acting as one of the secretaries to the conference itself and the follow-up. The actual conference was dominated by the clash between the German Confessional Churches and the Nazi state and the key problem of church and state continued to occupy Oldham. With some of his most intimate friends he debated the future relationship of the nation states to the 'European vision'. Following the Oxford Conference the Council on the Christian Faith and the Common life was set up, with a membership of twelve clergy (including William Temple) and twelve laity and Oldham as secretary. The conference papers were published and had a certain impact but almost immediately the country was swept into pre-war crisis.[28] The vision would appear to have vanished behind war clouds but the astonishing thing was that long-term, wide-ranging thought on the real goals of society went on collaterally all through the war. Joe Oldham's flair for gathering leading thinkers together provided a major resource already to hand: in the Moot, which is the subject of the first essay in Part II, the urgent question of how to rebuild a better society after the war was kept alive. The Moot first met in 1938. This could be seen as a think-tank of élites, but Oldham's second initiative, *The Christian News-Letter* was certainly not élitist. Throughout the war and after we can track Oldham's particular style in stimulating thought and action.

For Oldham, as for Macmurray, the basic question always was, where is secular society by itself inadequate? In one of his later works, *Life is Commitment* (1953), he echoes Macmurray to a remarkable degree in his own language. For instance he expresses the dualism that haunted Macmurray in a different way as 'two half circles which need to be joined in such a way that they combine to form a full circle'. 'I experience the world as a world of objects open to my observation. That is the world with which science is concerned. But I also experience life as an inner awareness of being alive.'[29] 'Life is full of situations to which I can respond not with part of myself but only with the commitment of my whole being.'[30] There are some things in life – and they may be the most important things – that we cannot know by research or reflection, but only by committing ourselves. We must dare in order to know. Oldham acknowledges his debt to a range of philosophers. Most importantly he says that a 'radical change in his outlook resulted from reading Martin Buber's book *I and Thou*', and behind Buber he cites Ludwig Feuerbach and the contemporary Eberhard Grisebach. In this context he also names Macmurray who 'helped about the same time to open my mind to the same truth'.[31] It would be interesting to know more about the relationship between these two.[32] Macmurray almost uses Buber's language but without citing him. Oldham read Buber's original *Ich und Du* before it was translated into English and published his first expression of Buber's ideas in the little book *Real Life is Meeting* in 1941.[33] Later he gave a more refined version of this philosophy in *Life is Commitment*. Both Macmurray and Oldham felt themselves to be at a turning-point in Western civilization. The dominant view, they felt, was of 'man as an individual standing over against an external world which it was his aim (singly or collectively) to explore and subdue to his purposes'.[34] Pushed to its logical conclusion, this denied the 'otherness of persons and ended up in a solitary, unreal wilderness'. For 'the real is what limits me. ... It is when I find myself confronted by another person than myself ... another independent centre'.[35] One must either destroy the other person by using him as an object or go out and meet him. Both Macmurray's call to transcend the dualisms and Oldham's to bring the two half-circles together constituted what was for them a new vision of life in their time. It was bound, as Oldham said, to have in the long run a transforming influence on politics, industry and social activities generally.

One might sum up J. H. Oldham's life as that of a frontiersman. At the age of 86 he was still defending the 'Frontier Idea', the creative point of meeting (or tension) between Christian faith and secular vocation.[36]

## John Macmurray: 1891–1976

In the early 1930s John Macmurray attended an ecumenical conference organized by J. H. Oldham on 'What is Christianity?' Although their methods of work were very different, these two men both had their attention focused at this time on what they diagnosed as a crisis situation for Christians. They saw that old authorities in church and state were being questioned and that the threat of financial and social instability was leading to a frantic search for new answers. Where did the church stand? It must find a message for an increasingly secular society. This led Oldham to throw his energies into preparation for the Oxford Conference on Church, Community and State in 1937. For Macmurray the earlier conference had sparked a political interest in Marxism and the communist solution. Philosophically, he found Marxism shared with Christianity a basic belief in the unity of theory and practice. As a leader in the 1930s of the Christian Left movement, he followed to some extent the political path, but his main role in relation to the rising generation was as a philosophical prophet and guru.

It is important to note that Macmurray was brought up in a deeply religious family of Scottish Calvinist persuasion. His family heritage was an overwhelming sense of the reality of God.[37] As a student at Glasgow he was strongly influenced by the SCM but his student career was broken by war experience which left him 'radically disillusioned' with contemporary culture. 'By the end of the war we soldiers had largely lost faith in the society we had been fighting for.'[38] He was also moving away from the institutional church. In contrast to Oldham, he never again worked from inside a religious organization until, late in life, he became a Quaker. Yet his whole life was spent in teaching a philosophy which, while openly critical of 'externalized' religious establishments, was passionately committed to the search for 'reality' in religious experience. In this he spoke directly to the perplexities of a whole generation of students, as well as to other thinking people. From 1928–44 he held the chair of the Philosophy of Mind and Logic in London. This writer, then a research student, still retains vivid memories of the packed lecture-room at University College where, in his inimitable Scottish accent, he developed his arguments. At the same time he was broadcasting twelve radio talks on 'Reality and Freedom' and, in 1932, another series on 'the Modern Dilemma'. Together they were published as *Freedom in the Modern World*. These must have been among the BBC's first experiments in getting a philosopher on 'the wireless'. The letters which poured in afterwards 'made broadcasting history'.[39] In fact Macmurray's success in translating philosophy into the vernacular formed part of a 'miniature renaissance', focused on adult education and stimulated by a new Central Council for Broadcast Adult Education. This organized the publication of supporting pamphlets and the formation of 'listening groups' which flourished during the 1930s. But opposition, for a complexity of reasons, developed within the BBC and the enterprise faded out in the early 1940s.[40]

The general sense of rising crisis was most obviously felt in the political and economic spheres but, said Macmurray, 'we shall never solve our economic troubles till we have solved the dilemma in our spiritual life'.[41] In his inaugural lecture at London, published in April 1929, he had said:[42]

The unity of modern problems is the problem of discovering or constructing ... a new schema of the Self, which will transcend both the mechanical and organic schema; and which will enable us to construct

... a civilisation where mechanical and organic structures will be at the service of a personal life, whose meaning and essence is friendship.

In the broadcasts he sought to convey this philosophy to a wider public. He diagnosed the root of our dilemma as a 'detachment of our emotional life from our intellectual conclusions'.[43] In its long battle with religion science had rightly won much of the intellectual ground but 'disinterested science' cannot of itself fuel action because 'action cannot be disinterested'. 'Science cannot provide a faith for the modern world. It can only provide the means for achieving what we want to achieve.[44] 'What we want' implies a choice which is rooted in the emotions, that is, in Macmurray's phrase, in a faith. He defines a faith as 'a person's ... supreme principle of valuation' whereby we decide what is 'most worth having'.[45] So, when we lose faith, 'we lose the power of action'.[46] Elsewhere,[47] he contrasts our common use of 'faith' as a 'statement of beliefs' with Jesus' use of faith as 'trust in living', a confident, as opposed to a fearful, attitude towards life. Here he embraced what he called the Hebrew philosophy, that is, involvement in life as a doer, rejecting what he saw as the Greek idea of the thinker as observer of life. He saw the crippling divorce of science from religion as one manifestation of a fundamental dualism which, he believed, afflicted our civilization: the material was divorced from the spiritual, mind from emotion, the thinker from the doer. Thus he rejected decisively the prevailing 'Greek' stance of contemporary philosophers. Against Descartes's famous *Cogito, ergo sum*, he set his own version, 'I do, therefore I am'.

Macmurray's message, therefore, to his contemporary society, and particularly to the rising generation, was essentially focused on his concept of what it means to be a 'whole person'. A person is an agent (a doer) and since an agent must have an 'other' he or she is 'necessarily in relation'.[48] Thus a person finds true identity by responding in open encounters to the 'reality' of the world of nature and humanity outside the self.

Thought and knowledge are necessary parts of this response and Macmurray defines action as a unity of movement and knowledge.[49] The highest response is that of person to person: 'the unit of personal existence is not the individual but two persons in personal relations' and here Macmurray echoes Martin Buber when he says that the unity of the personal is not the 'I' but the 'YOU and I'.[50] This doctrine of 'openness' to what Macmurray believed profoundly was God's world carried a proclamation of freedom. Experience of 'reality' (the 'Other') could, of course, carry pain and disappointment, but by this faith men and women broke out of an iron-bound individualism in which self stood over against the world in suspicion and fear. 'That sense of individual isolation which is so common in the modern world, which is so often called "individualism" is one of the inevitable experiences of fear ... [it is] fundamentally on the defensive permeated by the feeling of being alone in a hostile world.'[51] By contrast, to move outwards with spontaneity and courage brings a freedom which reaches its climax in love. 'The final basis [of human freedom] lies in real friendship. All reality, that is to say, all significance, converges upon friendship, upon the real relationship of one person with another independently real person.'[52] For Macmurray the courage to do this came from God. False religion offers us spurious security but

> real Christianity stands today ... for spontaneity against formalism, for the spirit of adventure against the spirit of security, for faith against fear, for the living colourful multiplicity of difference against the monotony of the mechanical, whether it be the mechanization of the mind which is dogmatism or the mechanization of the emotions, which is conformity.[53]

Given the continuity of thought and action, the truly personal extended itself to the making of true community. At a conference in 1938 which issued a pamphlet, *The Christian Answer to Fascism*, Macmurray called urgently for a social and political commitment to 'reality'. As Christians our business in the historic crisis was 'to intend equality and freedom in all human relations and to resist any effort to assert or achieve superiority ... equality and freedom in the social field' rested upon the intention of equality and freedom in the field of personal relationships.[54]

The collapse of peace buried Macmurray's political idealism but his doctrine of the person as agent relating freely to the 'Other' remained powerful. In 1929 at an SCM quadrennial conference, he had made an indelible impression on a student audience, preaching from John 15: 15: 'Henceforth I call you not servants, for the servant knoweth not what his lord doeth; but I have called you friends.'[55] 'Love and fear are the two primary personal motives.'[56] Release from the slavery of fear is only possible through the power of love: 'There is no fear in love but perfect love casteth out fear'.[57] So the 'friends of Jesus', in seeking 'to intend what Jesus intended',[58] would be empowered to respond freely to the realities of God's creation.

## Reinhold Niebuhr: 1892–1971

For the student generations of the 1930s and 1940s – as well as many older intellectuals – 'Reinie' was a major prophet from America. He was a disconcerting one, for he spoke in paradoxes. Indeed, physically and metaphorically, his utterances were often Delphic. For the impatient student who wanted a clear distinction between black and white this could be maddening, especially in relation to the pacifist/ non-pacifist debate which had suddenly become an issue of agonizing immediacy. His first major book, *Moral Man and Immoral Society* hit the Christian reading public, both American and British, in 1932/3.[59] In 1937 the SCM published his *An Interpretation of Christian Ethics* and David Paton, as SCM study secretary, prepared a study outline: *Reinhold Niebuhr: An Introduction to his Thought*,[60] which was argued over in universities up and down the country, from Edinburgh to Oxford. In the 1940s his close involvement in the testing experiences of his British friends found expression in six important 'supplements' published in *The Christian News-Letter*. (*CN-L*). These included 'Christianity and Political Justice' (S.11), 'The Providence of God and the Defence of Civilisation' (S.82), 'The Religious Level of the World Crisis' (S.246) and 'We are Men and not God' (S.323).[61] His supplements and other pronouncements were discussed in more than twenty issues of the *CN-L*.

After a period as a Lutheran pastor in Detroit, Niebuhr became Professor of Applied Christianity at Union Seminary, New York. He came from a background of American liberalism with its easy assumption that if we were only reasonable enough war and industrial conflict would go away. But his German roots were Lutheran. From this tradition he derived his sense of the gulf between God and humanity which was reinforced by Barth's insistence that God stands in judgement over against all human achievements, all human philosophies and all human ideals. In Detroit Niebuhr came up against the power of capitalism in society and, reflecting on this crucial fact of our times, turned to Marxism. In his belief that the problem of power was fundamental and that social justice demanded power for the workers, he embraced Marxist theory. Thus he gradually moved theologically 'right' and politically 'left' of the bland liberalism from which he had started. He developed what Paton calls a 'Theology of Tension'.[62] The innate sinfulness of human beings means that there is a fundamentally irrational element, both in individuals and groups. Human nature is a compound of idealism and self-seeking, of creativeness and destructiveness, closely bound together. Yet, he insists, 'prophetic Christianity' must continually struggle for more justice in society, since 'man is a child of God and has aspirations towards goodness which impel him to seek some kind of just society'.[63] The irrationality of the individual is enormously magnified in the group. This means that love is an impossible ideal for large social groups, an ideal which yet judges our miserable compromises and spurs us to further efforts. Full justice, the derivative ideal of love, is also impossible but we can use it to measure our failures. We may not hope for perfection but must desire to realize in society these ideals of love and justice.

Thus Christians must be independent of the temporal, as well as involved in it: they must, in loyalty to the eternal divine perspective, recognize how far individuals and societies fall short of God's purposes, yet, precisely because of their obedience to the transcendent, they have a vital part to play in building a new society which endeavours to move nearer a perfect justice. But they will always have an ambiguous relationship to this new society and this will never be understood by the secular devotees of the new society. Christians must be clear that the new society will stand under the judgement of God as much as the old one, that classes in society which were the instruments of God yesterday may become the enemies of God tomorrow.[64]

It was this paradoxical mode of thought – the tension of holding together a sense of eternal perspective and a passion for righteousness on earth – which gripped the attention of disillusioned liberals in the 1930s and 1940s, people who had seen all their complacent dreams of a world getting better and better rudely shattered. The very complexities in which good and evil seemed to be intertwined in the experiences of those years confused loyalties and rendered all choices ambiguous. In July 1939, Niebuhr gave an address at a SCM conference. Dorothy Emmet recalls:

> He had just come back from the Continent and, bilingual as he was, had been talking to people in Germany, and sizing up what was going on. He painted a terrifying picture ... but the text of his address was 'we are perplexed but not unto despair'.[65]

'What is God doing?' was the cry in October 1939,[66] and later, 'Where is the divine will in reconstruction?' Reinhold Niebuhr's message that behind all the confusions was still 'the impossible possibility of acting under the ultimate love of God' was immensely relevant then and still is. 'To keep the transcendent reference can save us ... from swinging between pride in what we can achieve and despair about what we cannot.'[67] Emmet points out that the Kennedy administration listened to him and since then both Edward Heath and

Lord Hailsham have acknowledged his influence; most recently, David Owen too, it seems.

Dorothy Emmet compares Macmurray and Niebuhr. 'They were', she says, 'the two major moralists who mattered most to us in the 1930s.' Both were concerned with the crisis of their civilization and both in different ways spoke to the condition of those caught up in the uncertainties of a world of unemployment, Nazism, the threat of war. John Macmurray was speaking of the need to discover one's real self through sincerity in immediate personal relations. Reinhold Niebuhr was saying that the morality of personal relations did not meet the problems of group conflicts of power and interests, especially international and class conflicts. Both were attacking a kind of idealism which set up a simplified theoretic or moralistic view instead of facing 'reality'. Both saw the world first and foremost as a place where practical decisions had to be made.[68]

## Notes

1. R. D. Edwards, *Victor Gollancz: A Biography* (Gollancz, 1987), p. 211.
2. A. Marwick, 'Middle Opinion in the Thirties: Planning Progress and Political "Agreement"', *English Historical Review*, 78 (Apr. 1964), pp. 285–98.
3. Political and Economic Planning.
4. For Marwick, see above, n. 2; see also S. Koss, *Nonconformity in Modern British Politics* (Batsford, 1975), pp. 195–215.
5. A. R. Vidler, *Twentieth-Century Defenders of the Faith* (SCM Press, 1965), p. 124.
6. A. M. Ramsey, *From Gore to Temple* (Longman, 1960), p. 133.
7. Three influential books from the biblical theology school in the 1930s were C. H. Dodd, *The Parables of the Kingdom* (Nisbet, 1935) and *The Apostolic Preaching and its Development* (Hodder & Stoughton, 1937); E. Hoskyns and N. Davey, *The Riddle of the New Testament* (Faber, 1936).
8. K. Barth, tr. E. Hoskyns, *The Epistle to the Romans* (OUP, 1933).
9. R. Niebuhr, *Moral Man and Immoral Society* (Scribner, London, 1933). This had American spelling. The SCM ed of 1963 was called 'the first British ed.' On Niebuhr and his influence in England, see below, pp. 14–16.
10. For Paton's outline, see below, p. 14.
11. Tissington Tatlow, *The Story of the Student Christian Movement of Great Britain and Ireland* (SCM, 1933).
12. J. B. McCaughey, *Christian Obedience in the University* (SCM, 1955) refers to the first use of this much-quoted saying.
13. J. E. L. Newbigin, *Unfinished Agenda: An Autobiography* (SPCK, 1985), p. 13.
14. See M. Ceadel, *Pacifism in Britain 1814–1945: The Defining of a Faith* (OUP, 1980), pp. 163–8; for A. J. P. Taylor's remark see p. 3.
15. C. L. Mowat, *Britain Between the Wars 1918–1940* (Methuen, 1988), pp. 541–2.
16. H. R. L. Sheppard's most widely read book was *The Impatience of a Parson* (Hodder & Stoughton, 1927).
17. G. H. Gallup (ed.), *The Gallup International Public Opinion Polls: Great Britain 1937–1975* (Random House, NY, 1978).

18. T. Harrison and C. Madge, *Britain by Mass Observation* (Penguin, 1938).
19. Martin Buber, *I and Thou*, tr. R. Gregor Smith (T. & T. Clark, 1937).
20. See below, pp. 9–10 and index.
21. K. Bliss, 'The Legacy of J. H. Oldham', *Bulletin of International Missionary Research* (Jan. 1980), p. 18. KB also wrote the article on Oldham in the DNB.
22. Graham Wallas, *The Great Society: A Psychological Analysis* (Macmillan, 1914).
23. J. H. Oldham, *The World and the Gospel* (United Council for Missionary Education, 1916).
24. Quoted from *The World and The Gospel*, by Bliss, 'Legacy', p. 21. See also the account of Oldham's influence on colonial policies and his work with Lord Lugard in Africa, pp. 21–2.
25. Ibid., p. 19. See also D. Bates, 'Ecumenism and Religious Education between the Wars: The Work of J. H. Oldham', *British Journal of Religious Education*, 86/3 (1986), p. 132, quoting J. W. Cell; (he was) 'the single most influential individual in the shaping of British official thinking and colonial policy towards Africa between the wars'.
26. Bliss, 'Legacy', p. 22.
27. Ibid. This included Visser't Hooft, later a key figure in the WSCF, and Michael Ramsey, future archbishop of Canterbury.
28. The early part of this paragraph draws on a long personal letter from Dr K. Bliss to Dr Birgit Rödhe, a Swedish friend, to whom I am indebted for the loan of material on Oldham by KB. Oldham edited the conference report: *The Churches Survey Their Task. The Report of the Conference at Oxford, July 1937, on Church, Community and State* (Allen & Unwin, 1937).
29. J. H. Oldham, *Life is Commitment* (SCM Press, 1953), p. 20 quoting C. F. von Weizsacker, *The History of Nature*, p. 157.
30. Oldham, *Commitment*, p. 24.
31. Ibid., p. 28, cf. Macmurray's works. Oldham mentions especially *Freedom in the Modern World* and *Interpreting the Universe*.
32. It is curious that Macmurray apparently never took part in the Moot deliberations. He appears in *CN-L*, S156, S192 and L209.
33. This is based on *CN-L*, S112, 17 Dec. 1941. The joke that made the round of his committee-involved friends, first voiced by Christopher Dawson, was that 'real life is meetings' (see *Commitment*, pp. 27–8).
34. *Commitment*, pp. 26–7.
35. Ibid., p. 30.
36. Idem, 'The Frontier Idea', *Frontier*, 4/3 (1960), pp. 247–52.
37. On John Macmurray's early life, see D. Ferguson, *John Macmurray in a Nutshell*, Nutshell series, no. 2 (Handset Press, 1992). In preparing this 'profile' I am much indebted for advice and material to Mrs Jeanne Warrenne and Mr P. Hunt.
38. Ferguson, *Macmurray*, p. 2, quoting Macmurray, *Search for the Reality of Religion* (Allen & Unwin, 1965), p. 19.
39. J. Macmurray, *Freedom in the Modern World* (Faber, 1932), preface by C. A. Siepmann, p. 7. The introductory pamphlet became a best-seller. *Reason and Emotion* (Faber, 1935) followed, repub. 1995.
40. This brief account is drawn, with the kind permission of the author, from an unpublished paper by Philip Hunt, 'A Public Philosopher: Macmurray and the BBC, 1930 to 1941', which throws a fascinating light on aims and attitudes in the BBC at this formative stage. Macmurray's final broadcast series on 'Persons and Functions' (1941) remains unpublished in the BBC archives, see below for a reference to this series, p. 12.

41. Macmurray, *Freedom*, p. 18.
42. Quoted by Hunt, 'Public Philosopher', p. 6.
43. Macmurray, *Freedom*, p. 26.
44. Ibid., p. 32.
45. Ibid., p. 21.
46. Ibid., p. 20.
47. Macmurray, *The Philosophy of Jesus* (Friends Home Service Committee, Friends House, Euston Rd, London, 1977, first publ. 1973), p. 8.
48. Ibid., p. 10. In the 1941 broadcast series 'Persons and Functions' Macmurray took what some saw as an alarming line on the old problem of religion and politics. The organized functional life of economic and political organization has no value in itself, he said; its value lies only in its contributions to personal life. He formulated his basic principle thus: the functional life is for the personal life, the personal life is through the functional life.
49. Macmurray, Gifford Lectures: I. *The Self as Agent* (Faber, 1957, repub. 1995), p. 128.
50. Gifford Lectures: II. *Personal Relations*, pp. 60–1. Jean Warrenne tells me that she gave Macmurray a copy of M. Friedman's book, *Martin Buber: The Life of Dialogue*, and that she has a letter in which Macmurray speaks of his knowledge of Buber's works.
51. Macmurray, *Freedom*, p. 55.
52. Ibid., p. 169.
53. Ibid., p. 62.
54. Macmurray, *The Christian Answer to Fascism*, p. 17.
55. This address has been published under the title 'Ye are my Friends', together with 'To save from fear, 4 lenten talks on the BBC 1964' by the Friends Home Service Committee (see n. 47 above) in 1979. The SCM address was given in 1929, not 1943, as stated in this pamphlet.
56. Macmurray, *Philosophy*, p. 11.
57. 1 John 4: 18.
58. Macmurray, *Christian Answer*, p. 17.
59. For this work, see above, n. 9.
60. The author possesses what may now be a rare copy of this. It is illuminating on the theological issues under debate in universities in 1937.
61. For this last supplement which formed part of a debate with Karl Barth, see below, pp. 55–6.
62. See D. Paton, *Reinhold Niebuhr: An Introduction to his Thought*. Study Outline p.1 (SCM Press, 1937), pp. 16, 22, based on Niebuhr, *Does the State and Nation belong to God or the Devil?*, p. 43.
63. D. Emmet, 'Persons and Community: John Macmurray and Reinhold Niebuhr', a paper given at the Higher Education Foundation Conference on 'Contemplation and Action' in March 1984.
64. Paton, *Niebuhr*, p. 22.
65. Emmet, 'Persons and Community'.
66. *CN-L*, S1 (1 Nov. 1939).
67. D. Emmet, *Philosophers and Friends: Reminiscences of Seventy Years in Philosophy* (Macmillan, 1996), p. 60. Ch. 6 (pp. 50–61) deals with Macmurray and Niebuhr as major influences in the 1930s. Both published key books in 1932, *Freedom in the Modern World* and *Moral Man and Immoral Society*. Both acknowledged the influence of Marxist theory, though in different ways.
68. Emmet, 'Persons and Community'.

# Part II

# Introduction

In the 1930s and 1940s a network of people emerged who shared certain characteristics: they were thinkers but also doers; they were predominantly Christian but not exclusively so; they had a variety of commitments, ecclesiastical and political, but no one 'party line'. 'Network' indicates the informality of their associations: out of a group of some 40 people in different walks of life, any one would be in contact with a number of the others, some with many. One can see J. H. Oldham, for instance, rounding up his flock like a faithful sheepdog. They came together largely through the sense of gathering crisis. The roots of this are too complex to dig up here, but would include disillusionment with the Europe created after the First World War, concern with the rate and direction of social change (a legacy of the 1937 Oxford Conference), alarm at 'that hideous strength' revealed in totalitarian leadership, and, in reaction to this, a desperate inquiry into the sources of true leadership and responsible power.

Sir William Taylor, reflecting on the nature of the Moot, the first of the initiatives examined here, stresses the importance of informal discussion as the seedbed from which policies for action spring: 'Neither ideas nor experiences,' he writes, 'start life at political congresses, let alone in the offices of parliamentary draughtsmen or administrators. Critical and imaginative thoughts flow into the policy pool from distance sources, after much underground filtering'.[1] Frequently they rise among the foothills of academic discourse or other intellectual debate. Discussions go on in common rooms and around dining tables, in working groups and during conference coffee breaks. The stream of thought gathers force as the books, published papers and speeches of members flow into it. So theoretical perceptions gradually become focused on specific problems of human living and the actions needed to solve them. As John Macmurray teaches, thinkers must become doers.

Significantly, all the groups under discussion here were 'inter-disciplinary' – not only academically, but in the broader sense of cutting across divides of professions, faiths and experiences. Four aspects of their working style stand out. First these groups were predominantly the expression of a deep Christian concern about the nature and health of secular society. These concerns were certainly grounded in a theology of human beings within creation, but the focus of attention was outside, rather than inside the church, nor did they adopt the official stance of any church organization. Thus *The Christian News-Letter* spoke with a Christian voice to the whole nation. Moreover, the contributions of fellow-thinkers who shared their concerns were always highly valued. Karl Mannheim was a key member of the Moot – much to the puzzlement of LSE colleagues;[2] Herman Bondi savoured the free air of Cumberland Lodge discussions. Secondly, great importance was placed on open and unconstricted dialogue, rather than confrontational argument from predetermined positions. Complex problems of social behaviour, for instance, needed deep probing and shared reflection. Preparatory analytical papers were important features of the Moot and Christian Frontier Council, while the editor of the *CN-L* habitually circulated drafts of an important supplement, such as one on 'The Free Society'. Later, the Higher Education Group offered a no-holds-barred forum where no form of academic political correctness operated. Thirdly, the goal of discussion was to stimulate further thought leading to action on the part of members or readers, rather than to cobble together resolutions or hasty manifestos. The main harvest was reaped in pamphlets, articles and books sparked off by these dialogues. The *CN-L* published a series of small books, including Fred Clarke's seminal *Education and Social Change*;[3] under the auspices of the Frontier Council a number of larger studies appeared, such as Daniel Jenkins's *The Educated Society*;[4] out of the University Teachers'/Higher Education Group came both conference reports and individual monographs. Fourthly, the structures which carried these activities were largely informal fellowships, with fluid memberships and changing leadership, rather than those of organized parties or pressure groups. Cumberland Lodge, as a permanent organization, is the exception here, but it shared the general ambience of informality.

Professor Jose Harris has characterized what she calls 'the reconstruction movement' of this period by three principles: first, a belief that social problems needed to be considered as a whole instead of in piecemeal compartments; second, a belief that social reconstruction required a more extensive use of coercion through governmental and legal powers than had traditionally been thought tolerable; and thirdly, the belief that such coercion need not necessarily entail the abrogation of personal freedom.[5] In general, these principles apply closely to much of the thinking described here, with the qualification that the implicit tension between the second and the third often led to much anxious debate.

The real influence of these initiatives is impossible to measure accurately. Some books were undoubtedly influential; some thinking was translated into official statements and policies of church and state; in some councils and senates of higher education echoes of these debates were heard; some voluntary experiments arose out of their concerns. Certainly many persons found their professional lives illuminated through these conversations and their official activities expanded. Joe Oldham's creed of 'Real Life is Meeting' bore many fruits, recognized and unrecognized.

### Notes

1.  William Taylor, 'Education and the Moot' in Richard Aldrich (ed.), *In History and in Education. Essays presented to Peter Gordon* (Woburn Press, 1996), p. 159. The following sentences further summarize Taylor's words.
2.  See below, p. 43, for the question of Mannheim's religious position.
3.  F. Clarke, *Education and Social Change: An English Interpretation. CN-L* books, 3 (Sheldon Press, 1940).
4.  D. Jenkins, *Equality and Excellence: A Christian Comment on Britain's Life* (SCM Press, 1961); *The Educated Society* (Faber, 1966). For both these books, see below, ch. 4, s. 2.
5.  J. Harris, 'Political Ideas and the Debate on State Welfare', in L. Smith (ed.), *War and Social Change* (Manchester University Press, 1986), p. 239.

## Chapter 2

# Intellectuals in Debate: The Moot

William Taylor and Marjorie Reeves*

### Meetings and Membership of the Moot

In the discussions which followed the Oxford Conference of 1937 J. H. Oldham, as we have seen, was a prime mover. One idea central to his thinking at this time was that of an order of Christian lay people. The group he gathered to consider this became the basis for the Moot. It met in various residential conference centres within easy reach of London, usually from Friday evening to Sunday evening. Papers for discussion were circulated in advance, as were commentaries upon them that some members produced ahead of the meeting.[1] J. H. Oldham served as convenor and organizer throughout the life of the group.[2] All Moot discussions were 'highly disciplined affairs'. Oldham was deaf. Each member had to speak in order, so that Oldham 'could position himself alongside each in turn'.[3]

The Moot's most active period was from 1938 to 1944. After the first two gatherings in 1938, four meetings were held in 1939, three in 1940, four in 1941, two in 1942, then three in each of 1943 and 1944. In 1945, 1946 and 1947 there was only one annual meeting. Oldham was remarkably successful in maintaining a pattern of residential weekend meetings during the worst of wartime conditions. Air raids were frequent. Travel was difficult. Food was rationed. Yet members of the Moot continued to gather throughout the war years, undertaking what were sometimes long and difficult journeys to do so.

Oldham's main achievement, however, was in the intellectual distinction of those whom he persuaded to participate. Among them were T. S. Eliot, poet and playwright; Karl Mannheim, sociologist;

\* The main part of this chapter is by William Taylor and is a shortened version of his essay 'Education and the Moot' (see Acknowledgements section).

Walter Moberly, Chairman of the University Grants Committee (and former vice-chancellor); Fred Clarke, director of the University of London Institute of Education; John Middleton Murry, Christian pacifist, social and literary critic; Eric Fenn, director of religious broadcasting at the BBC; Alec Vidler, theologian, later dean of King's College, Cambridge, and prominent broadcaster; H. A. Hodges, philosopher; John Baillie, theologian; Walter Oakeshott, then high master of St Paul's School, and Geoffrey Shaw. Others who from a predominantly but not exclusively Christian standpoint made important contributions to social and educational ideas in this period attended on a regular or occasional basis. Oliver Franks, Philip Mairet, Reinhold Niebuhr and R. H. Tawney were among those who took part in a special meeting shortly after the outbreak of war in September 1939.[4]

Present at nine or more of the meetings held between April 1938 and July 1945 were Baillie, Clarke, Eliot, Fenn, Hodges, Eleanor Iredale, Mannheim, Moberly, Murry, Oldham, Mary Oldham, Shaw and Vidler. Kathleen Bliss joined in 1943. Adolf Löwe of Manchester University was a regular member until he left for the United States in 1940.[5] Among occasional visitors were Frank Pakenham (Lord Longford), Geoffrey Vickers, industrialist and organization theorist, and Christopher Dawson, Catholic theologian. Michael Polanyi's position is discussed below.[6]

The Moot held its last meeting in January 1947. Oldham explained that he had encouraged the Moot to end because he disliked the way in which many institutions were unwilling to conform to the universal principle of death and rebirth. The decisive factor, however, had been the death of Karl Mannheim.[7] Mannheim's role in the meetings was of great importance. In many respects he was, as Vidler put it 'the central figure in the Moot'. He attended every meeting held between September 1938 and December 1944, an attendance record equalled only by Oldham. He contributed a large number of papers. He played an active part in every discussion. He secured a large measure of agreement to his ideas about social planning in a democracy as an alternative to bureaucratic totalitarianism.

H. E. S. Woldring has explained why Mannheim's commitment to the Moot was so strong:

> Various friends and colleagues criticized him for participating in this group of religiously oriented thinkers. ... Yet Mannheim remained a member because, in his opinion, the Christian tradition was one of the great supporting pillars of Western civilization and would remain so

indefinitely. He found the discussions between sociologists and theologians to be of genuine importance, because he wanted to interrogate Christians about the essential values of their faith and about the utility of these values in the process of social change. On the other hand, he was willing to learn from theologians, because he acknowledged as sociologist that no society can function without norms and values; he found he needed to look at religion to find the essence of these norms and values. Also, his own position in this group was not threatening for him. Precisely by inviting him and other non-Christians, the group displayed the broad-mindedness which improved the quality of the discussions.[8]

## Fellowship or Order?

A focus on post-war reconstruction was clear even before war was declared. At the second meeting in September 1938, Adolf Löwe commented that the trouble with Britain was that, having won the First World War, she had lost the peace. Plans must immediately be made to collect together a nucleus of sane people who would prepare for the peace. The role of the church in the process of post-war political and social reconstruction was seen as crucial and especially the part that Christian laymen must play.

For the meeting in September 1939 Oldham circulated a 26-page typescript paper entitled 'A Reborn Christendom', produced for the Council on the Christian Faith and the Common Life. He proposed the establishment of a Christian 'Order'. Participation in its work would not require the taking of vows. The order would not even have a registered membership. Its main purpose would be to emphasize the conscious dedication of its members to the cause of the new Christendom and to their fellow members.[9] Such a group would require the guidance of people with high ability and experience who occupied influential positions in public life. Oldham envisaged subgroups concerned with politics, public administration, local government, the social services, industry, labour, commerce, the press, and education – elementary, secondary and tertiary.

A minority of members saw the proposed order as a political organization, perhaps even the basis of a new political party. The majority were more concerned with prophetic matters. Like Oldham, they wanted the order to embrace people from the left as well as from the right. In a commentary which summarized the problems, Löwe expressed the view that the Moot should not be simply another discussion group. But he did not believe that it was feasible to set up an organization across the political spectrum that could commit itself to anything more than the most general propositions or undertake an effective programme of political action. The breadth and catholicity of opinion represented among the group was of enormous benefit to the quality of its discussions. It did not make for an effective political role.

Löwe was sceptical concerning Oldham's hopes that the Moot would itself become the basis of an order. Much remained to be thought out.[10] The co-option of more members should be approached with caution. The principles proposed for the constitution of an order were admirable. But the group based on these principles should not be called an order. Löwe thought that its name should be as colourless as possible, as general as the term 'Moot' itself.

In other commentaries, Walter Oakeshott queried whether the proposed order should be within or outside the church, while Alec Vidler stressed the importance of personal fellowship within whatever pattern might emerge, but also advocated a cautious approach. Members should be content for the present to work through the Moot, the value of which had already been proved, unless it was felt that no further progress could be achieved without creating another organization.[11]

Oldham did not press the issue of an order. Nor did he let it go. His ideas were discussed at a number of meetings over the next two years, notably in March 1942 on the basis of his paper advocating a 'Fraternity of the Spirit'.[12] He held to the view that while the function of the Moot was not to take corporate action, still less to act as a general staff for the churches, there was still a great deal that a small group of committed people could do to influence those in power.[13]

The Moot continued to agonize about its role throughout its existence. Mannheim frequently returned to the notion of an order. Oldham supported his ideas on democratic planning as the most positive and coherent line of thought that the Moot had pursued, behind which members should be prepared to unite. Some members were content for the Moot to continue to function as an informal discussion group for intellectuals. In response to a query by Oldham as to whether there was anything worth saying to public audiences about Mannheim's alternative to totalitarianism, one member feared that this sounded dangerously like action. Members of the Moot could only act as individuals, advising and clearing their own minds.[14]

Despite all the external and internal uncertainties to which members were subject, Moot discussions and papers display a measure of cultural confidence that would be unlikely to feature in similar exchanges today. In his paper for the March 1943 meeting, 'The Crisis in Valuation', Mannheim was in no doubt concerning the meretricious influence exerted by leisure activities characteristic of the machine age. While democratic in their nature, and able to offer new stimuli for humble lives, the cinema, the radio and the gramophone were all disintegrative rather than integrative of human character.[15] There was similar confidence, at least on the part of some members, concerning Christian truth. Christianity was the only true religion, not one religion among many. Such truth as there was in other religions was itself Christian.[16]

Geoffrey Vickers, in a paper prepared in December 1939 and considered in April 1940, stated what can be taken as the *credo* of the reconstruction movement. The war-to-peace transition might take even longer than that from peace to war. Waiting until the war's end would be too late. At such a time there is little vision or energy. A beginning had to be made while old habits had been shaken, while it still seemed worthwhile to make common purpose, and while active efforts were being made to spell out the type of society which it was worthwhile fighting to create.[17]

## Reconciling Economic Realism with Human Potentiality

Education in one form or another came up in almost every Moot discussion, but it was only occasionally the central focus of a meeting. Post-war educational organization, which featured strongly in the deliberations of some other groups within the reconstruction movement, received systematic attention by the Moot on only two or three occasions. One was at the meeting planned for November 1939.

The keynote paper was by Fred Clarke. 'Some Notes on English Educational Institutions: in the light of the necessities of "Planning for Freedom" in the coming Collectivized Regime' had been written in the summer of 1939 while Clarke was on a ship travelling to Canada.[18] Like so much of social policy discussion at the Moot, it showed the influence of Mannheim. 'Planning for Freedom' in Clarke's title came from a paper by Mannheim discussed at the second meeting of the Moot in April 1939.

In a memorandum written soon after Mannheim's death in 1947, but not published until nearly twenty years later,[19] Clarke recalls having been invited at 'some time in 1939' to 'join a small private

discussion group of which Mannheim was a member' and goes on to
say:

> At the first meeting of the group that I attended the subject for
> discussion was a paper in which Mannheim had set out his conception
> of the relevant principles. .... In the course of discussion it was suggested
> that the practical bearing of Mannheim's ideas could be more clearly
> seen if they could be worked out in some detail in application to one or
> other of the particular fields in question. The suggestion was accepted,
> the field of education was chosen for the purpose, and I was asked to
> prepare a paper, translating as it were, Mannheim's principles into the
> concrete terms of a possible educational policy.

The 25 pages of single-spaced typescript that Clarke circulated to
members of the Moot contained a closely argued mixture of
philosophical ideas, sociological analysis and practical proposals,
with particular reference to the relations between different types of
post-elementary education.

Clarke did not propose that a common primary education be
provided in a single type of state school. But both state and
independent preparatory schools should be subject to common
inspection. As far as curriculum was concerned, this would be easier
to deal with when the overdue reassessment of the old classical
curriculum had been completed.[20] Nor was Clarke opposed to an
appropriate form of selection at the age of 11. This should not,
however, be based on the results of a one-off examination. Instead,
there should be a period similar to the French *année d'orientation*,
which might be as short as six months and could extend to two
years.[21] The technical high school that had been proposed by the
Spens Report of 1938 should be given the opportunity to develop a
distinctive character. It should be *sui generis*, neither given workshop status in an educational corner, nor treated as a mere variation
on the grammar school.[22]

Clarke saw the ending of the 'cultural–vocational distinction' as a
priority. He was concerned that the separate technical high schools
recommended by Spens were already threatened as unnecessary. By
adaptations of curriculum and co-operation with technical colleges,
secondary schools could meet the need. Another danger was that
new school types would be assimilated to the existing grammar-
school model, in the same way as the schools that developed after
the 1902 Act were based on the public school. Strong vested interests
had to be reckoned with, and the conviction that only 'academic'
courses were culturally worthwhile. Clarke felt that modern society
had not yet recognized the full significance of vocation.[23]

Clarke's paper followed the well-established English tradition of focusing on structural issues such as selection and institutional missions. Mannheim responded in a paper circulated for the November 1939 meeting. Some of his concerns coincided with Clarke's, such as the uses and advantages of education as a social ladder. Other topics emphasized the gap between the style of his thought and that of many of his British contemporaries. They included the creation of a new common culture, means for democratizing and enlarging the social basis of education, the co-ordination of education with other social agencies in terms of planning for freedom, and reinspiring the aims of education. To these four, Mannheim added the need to emphasize the role of education for change, as against education for security, and the importance of educating for humanized bureaucracy, on the grounds that in planned societies, bureaucracy would be bound to increase.

Clarke wrote a longer than usual manuscript note on his copy of this paper, which he headed 'Relation to the Economic Order'. It is of particular interest in relation to the cultural/vocational issue that he had already identified.[24] Clarke wondered if the effect of enlarging access would be merely to broaden the basis from which were drawn potential capitalists or to add to the supply of every sort of dutiful careerist-technicians. He asked if the aim should rather be to reduce the *differentials* of social advantage and of culture that arose from economic conditions, requiring simultaneous attempts to emphasize 'non-economic values' in education alongside improved public provision of opportunities in the field of culture.[25]

Clarke did not, however, exclude economic considerations. Non-economic and economic values were not opposed to each other. Non-economic values needed to extend beyond the purely economic, perhaps even incorporating them. In this context, he returned to the importance of the Spens Committee proposals concerning the technical high school, and feared the possibility of reform being overlaid by the prestige of the existing public schools. The relation of these schools to the political and social order he saw to be a matter of great importance.[26]

The issues to which Clarke refers in his note are still on policy agendas today. The alleged failure of the schools to give sufficient emphasis to economic values and to the development of marketable skills has been a mainstay of right-wing criticism of educators over the past three decades. Politicians who seek electoral advantage by berating 'trendy sixties values' often fail to recognize that these values have deeper roots than the fashions of 30 years ago.

Wartime aspirations to give all children opportunities hitherto enjoyed only by a fortunate minority, to counter through schooling the evils of totalitarianism, and to offer the elements of a common rather than a class-related culture, reflected a very mixed bag of influences. These included the perceived impact of early industrialization on social conditions and civility, revulsion at the human costs of the First World War, world recession at the beginning of the 1930s, anxieties about declining birth-rates, the rise of the European dictatorships and the growth of child study and psychometric testing.[27]

Clarke's apparent lack of logic in suggesting that non-economic values might *incorporate* the economic should not obscure the essential point that he, in common with many other educators, did not wish to suppress but to *transcend* purely economic considerations. The Christian message that man does not live by bread alone has always had to confront attacks from the left on the grounds of its quietism, and from the right because of its anti-commercial and anti-entrepreneurial implications. The task of reconciling economic realism with the fullest development of human potentiality, especially in its spiritual dimension, did not begin in the 1930s or after the 1944 Education Act or with the Thatcher premiership of the 1980s. It is an endemic problem of educational policy.

The technical high school movement in which Clarke and others invested so much hope did not succeed. A three-tier system offered even less chance than a two-tier one for the secondary modern schools established in the 1940s and 1950s to define a role for themselves alongside the established secondary grammar schools.[28] More recent efforts to create a distinctive type of school that would transcend the vocational/cultural divide, which would neither be pushed into what Clarke had called a 'workshop corner' nor seek to emulate the curriculum of existing high-status grammar schools, have been little more successful. The city technology colleges on which the Conservative government of the 1980s pinned their hopes have failed to attract the private funding needed to create an effective challenge to the existing pattern of secondary provision.

By 1943 Clarke was expressing disappointment at an apparent failure to deal with fundamentals. Deeper changes were needed to deal with the entrenched position of the public schools and 'the Elementary School dump'. Without more fundamental change Britain might become a 'historical museum'. Ways had to be found of preserving what was valuable in the public schools while getting rid of their position of privilege.[29] By January 1944, and having seen the text of the new Education Bill, Clarke was more optimistic. The

Bill's proposals displayed a welcome note of *authority* and *orderliness*. They seemed to recognize that education was potentially a very effective instrument for social control. Perhaps outlooks and entrenched modes of thinking could still be changed.[30]

## Schooling and Values

If criticism of the economic effectiveness of education is not new, nor are doubts about schools' success in civilizing the young. There is a venerable tradition – to which Bede himself contributed – of nostalgia on the part of the middle-aged and elderly for a golden age (often coinciding with their own youth) when children were polite, orderly and hard-working, respected their elders, and were seen and not heard. It is proper to distrust such a historical assessment. It is neither proper nor wise to despise or neglect the civilizing tasks which schools and other social institutions must perform for each generation. It was these, rather than structural and organizational issues, that featured most frequently in the Moot's discussions of education.

In a paper on 'The Sociology of Education' circulated to the Moot as a follow-up to his earlier 'Planning for Freedom',[31] Mannheim emphasized the importance of those forms of experience which arise in face-to-face contacts and determine how people will spontaneously respond to both the trivial and the important objects of life. Whether they will shrink from cruelty, attempt to settle disputes through argument rather than with their fists, seek to establish loving relationships or to keep their emotional distance, turns on the examples with which they are presented in their surroundings.

Mannheim was concerned that to neglect the cultivation of these sentiments and attitudes, or to take them for granted, especially in circumstances where social control by family and community was lacking, might rebarbarize society. The history of fundamental virtues had a place in the study of basic attitudes. Some such virtues would need to be re-established. New ones, appropriate to the age, would need to be discovered. Without attention to such virtues, society would lack that minimum of social conformity without which it could not continue. A study of basic attitudes might also reveal the educational techniques by means of which fundamental virtues could, directly or indirectly, be fostered and developed.[32] In chapter 4 of *Diagnosis of our Time*, based on papers presented to the Moot, Mannheim again stressed the need in the planned society to:

... establish a set of basic virtues such as decency, mutual help, honesty and social justice, which can be brought home through education and social influence, whereas the higher forms of thought, art, literature, etc., remain as free as they were in the philosophy of Liberalism.[33]

In March 1941 Fred Clarke gave a paper under the title 'Some Notes on Religious Education'. He drew attention to the implications of the growing tendency for subject boundaries to break down in the hands of the 'interpreter teacher'. Taking religious education seriously and according it the status of a school subject were not the same thing. Nor was it sufficient to go along with glib phrases about religion being caught rather than taught. Effective religious instruction needed religious schools, although not in the sectarian sense of that term.[34] Clarke was critical of the motives of some of those who sought to impose religious education on the schools by law. This was less a concern for the future of religious education than a desire to retain the influence of the clergy, something opposed by the long memories of the teachers' organizations. At a later meeting, Walter Oakeshott returned to the role of education in general, and Christian education in particular, in putting across explicit principles of conduct. He conceded that it would be difficult to do so by means of an education that was doctrinally Christian, but that it was possible to teach objective human values for which the Christian doctrine of God might be the ultimate sanction.[35]

Members of the Moot found it easy to agree that the question of values was paramount. It was harder to identify particular values on which they agreed. As Oldham put it at the December 1941 meeting, if he went to see the Minister of Education [*sic*] he would have to admit that no two people, even members of the Moot, really agreed on the question of values.[36] Yet many saw such agreement as essential to their purposes.

Mannheim was not alone at this time in his concern that, outside the public boarding schools, little explicit attention was being given to the development of attitudes and dispositions congruent with life in an industrialized urbanized democracy.[37] During the post-war decades, however, such concerns were to be muted. The sociology of education that Mannheim helped to found focused on issues of access and opportunity. The 'new sociology of education' of the 1970s did give more attention to both the formal and the hidden curriculum, but for the most part in a context of new-Marxist criticism of existing economic and educational institutions. 'Moral education' was a field in which philosophers and religious educators held sway, and from which most sociologists steered clear.

Mannheim had emphasized that to counter the effects of bureaucratic totalitarianism it would be necessary for a militant democracy to agree on certain basic values, which would be put across with all the means that the educational system could command. He contrasted for this purpose the basics essential for democratic government and those more complicated values which should be left open to free experimentation, individual choice or creed.[38] The validity of Mannheim's distinction is doubtful. There are few things more complicated than the application of basic virtues to the conduct of everyday social and political life in family, community and work group. Much more is involved than 'recipe knowledge', capable of being learned from a manual or from classes in personal and social relationships. The existence of families and communities which disseminate core values through their social practice is every bit as important today as it was when discussed by the Moot half a century ago.[39]

In the early 1990s, Conservative politicians, alarmed by the growth in Britain of what was becoming known as the Underclass, attempted to reinstate what Mannheim had referred to as fundamental virtues under the slogan 'Back to Basics', with particular reference to the importance of the family in child-rearing. By this time education had become so politicized that such an attempt, although supported by many non-political and some left-leaning educators (including distinguished sociologists of education) proved to be a political albatross. 'Back to Basics' was soon thrown overboard. Yet the issues to which Mannheim had drawn attention in his papers for the Moot were and are real. They cannot be dismissed as one of Britain's periodic fits of morality, or as signs of a so-called moral panic. It is unfortunate that the class associations of 'character training', the unwillingness and inability of the élite to be seen to be offering, let alone imposing, any kind of positive educational lead, the decline of religious belief and the priority that the left attaches to structural reform, all militate against the committed discussion of 'fundamental virtues' that went on in the Moot and elsewhere.

In April 1940 most people in Britain had more immediate things to worry about than what would happen after the war. What is surprising is the extent to which post-war social planning did feature in the thinking of groups such as the Moot. For example, at the July 1940 meeting – held at a time when a German invasion seemed to be imminent – members considered how a Christian élite could be organized which might influence key persons in government and administration in planning for a post-war world. (References were made to the possibility of O. S. Franks[40] being recruited to lead this movement.) Perhaps it should not be a matter of surprise that intellectuals' eyes were on the longer term future. As Moberly put it, to plan on the basis of the Germans winning was, at least for him, unreal, since he would be either in a concentration camp or dead.[41]

## Revolution or Reconstruction?

The Moot returned to the structure and organization of education at meetings of its subgroup on education in 1941 and 1942.[42] In February 1942 Mannheim set out a syllabus for the consideration of ideas he had already put before the Moot itself.[43] While discussion of eternal aims was important, it must also be recognized that education was linked to the social situation for which and in which it worked. Educational thinking should be based on social diagnosis. A reorientation of education would only be possible if there existed a more concrete knowledge of society. The desirable broadening of the basis of selection for membership of élites had immediate consequences for the shape of secondary, adult and technical education.

Clarke followed up Mannheim's 'Syllabus' with a paper headed 'Notes on Secondary Education in England'.[44] Secondary education for all would require the provision of forms of secondary education appropriate to the variety of pupils' aptitudes and needs. Clarke stressed that this was primarily a *curriculum* issue. Variety could exist in either a multilateral school or in a number of separate schools. Sheep-and-goats selection for secondary education should be replaced by a process whereby children were allocated for forms of education suitable for their needs as a result of a period of special observation, a form of the *année d'observation* to which he had referred in a paper already mentioned.

The President of the Board of Education, R. A. Butler, clearly attached importance to ease of transfer between types of post-primary schools. In February 1943 he asked one of his officials, 'How do we propose to arrange for a re-switch between 11 and 13 if we don't have multilateral schools?' On being told that the allocation at age 11 would be no more than 'a rough shake-out' and that the 11 to 13 age group would constitute a distinct entity within every type of secondary school, he expressed himself 'much comforted'.[45]

Many of these ideas on the future of secondary education were widely held during the war, and were to be reflected in the reforms that followed the 1944 Education Act. The proposed period of special observation did not, however, become a general reality. The continuing sheep-and-goats consequences of the 11-plus examination were eventually to swing a large body of moderate public and political opinion behind the comprehensive school idea.

The Moot's group on education met again in May 1942 in Oxford. In addition to Clarke, Mannheim, Moberly and Oldham, the participants included Marjorie Reeves, John Trevelyan, Sir Richard Livingstone and Kathleen Bliss.[46] A paper on 'Reform in Education' by Harold C. Dent[47] had been circulated, together with an extract from Mannheim's paper 'Towards a New Social Philosophy', the full version of which had been considered earlier by the Moot and would be included in *Diagnosis of Our Time*.

Dent's paper began with a call for an educational revolution. Nothing less could save the democracies. The present divided system of education could not be retained. Palliatives were not enough. The only valid educational model was that of the nursery school. Junior and secondary schools were excessively academic, sedentary and competitive. Dent wanted to rethink the stages of education – up to 7 as the infant stage, from 7 to 13 or 14 as the primary, and from then to 21 as the post-primary. From 16 onwards education would be offered through industrial, commercial and professional training establishments under the direction of the local education authority. For academic children, public libraries and archives would be an important training site. Compulsory National Service from 18 plus until 19 or 20 would require a period of residence in a university-like hostel. University studies would be integrated with adult education. All workers would be entitled to periods of sabbatical study.[48]

At the outset of the subgroup's discussion, Mannheim took a stand on the importance of *content* as distinct from *structure*. Too much attention was being given to such matters as raising the school-leaving age, not enough to what an extended educational period should contain. Greater social justice in education was needed, but not at the expense of diversity; gradations in society were not in themselves harmful. Many members of the subgroup thought that Dent's paper went too far. It seemed to suggest that the educational system could be scrapped and a fresh start made. Furthermore, too great a role was being given to the state. Discussion ranged over nursery, primary, secondary, vocational and higher education and apprenticeships. Towards the end of the meeting it was agreed that the education of the adolescent was the crucial area of concern, but Sir Richard Livingstone also made a forceful defence of adult education in all its forms. Moberly acknowledged its importance, but felt that the fire had gone from the University Extension Movement and the Workers' Educational Association, which had become rather conservative institutions and lacked a sense of direction.

Dent's call for revolution did not secure many adherents. Most members took a more meliorist approach, of the kind that was later to be reflected in the 1944 Education Act and post-war educational developments. Several members of the subgroup saw signs of hope in recent 'reconstruction' efforts. Clarke had been impressed by the work of the Committee on the Training of Teachers – of which he was a member – set up by the Board of Education (from which came the McNair Report of 1944). In response to a point from Oldham about the dangers of indifference and fragmentation of effort, Clarke suggested that one way of dealing with enemies was to give the impression that you were not doing very much until one day you suddenly appeared in the middle of their camp.

## A Crisis in the Universities?

Most members of the Moot came from an academic background. This was reflected more in the scholarly character of their contributions than in a concern for university reform, but in 1940 two major papers, which reflected ideas that were to have a continuing influence, were presented to the Moot.

One was by Sir Walter Moberly, chairman of the University Grants Committee since 1935. The substance of his paper would later be included in his *The Crisis in the University*.[49] The other paper, equally substantial, was by Professor Adolf Löwe of Manchester University, soon to depart for an academic appointment in the United States. His *The Universities in Transformation* appeared in 1941.[50]

Clarke's copy of Moberly's paper is liberally embellished with approvals, queries and demurrals. Over the next few years the ideas in its 22 single-spaced foolscap pages were to be extended and refined through meetings of the Student Christian Movement and the Christian Frontier Council. But the argument in Moberly's 1940 Moot paper remained at the core of what he was to publish nine years later. After restating the Oxford and Cambridge ideal of liberal education, with many references to Newman, Moberly went on to interpret the ethos of Scottish and 'Modern' universities, and then to identify what he felt to be wrong with university life. Utilitarianism, specialization and lack of opportunity to live in an academic community mocked many features of the liberal ideal. This led to a neglect of such major issues as the nature of man and of the universe and the principles by which life should be lived. Under a cloak of specious 'neutrality' universities were abdicating their responsibility to provide direction and guidance. Some of the necessary changes which Moberly envisaged are discussed below in relation to the ideas behind the establishment of Cumberland Lodge (chapter 6). He also emphasized the case for extending opportunities to more mature candidates. Arguments for the exclusion of certain subjects from university studies on the grounds of their illiberality were flawed; what mattered was the manner of the teaching, whether the syllabus and the style encouraged students to think for themselves (for which many exciting courses were too short) or merely to acquire tricks of the trade. Moberly felt that changes were unlikely to be achieved by state intervention. Better to convince small groups of the abler university teachers to take the initiative; hence the importance of discussions of the kind that went on in the Moot.

Löwe's paper emphasized what he saw as the settled character of university values in the nineteenth century, and the difficulties that the university faced as a consequence of social change in the twentieth. He shared Moberly's concerns about lack of guidance and direction. Both cultural and moral education had lost their reality for most students. As to the future, Löwe saw an increase both in specialization and in vocationalism. A heavy burden of responsibility would fall upon those subjects which could offer continuing cultural and interpretative education. Student life must offer more opportunities and experience and initiatives that would contribute to moral education. The example of Kurt Hahn's school at Salem was praised. The dangers of what would later come to be called a 'meritocracy' were explored. To avoid these dangers would probably require a reform of the school system. The argument was put for one or two years of general education to precede specialized study – an idea later to be embodied in the work of the new University College at Keele – and for a reform of teaching (fewer lectures) and examining (greater variety of methods). Löwe wanted to see the establishment of an experimental college which would attempt cultural synthesis at postgraduate level.[51]

The record of the discussion on the two papers[52] showed a large measure of agreement on essentials between Moberly and Löwe. Clarke observed that, as Professor of Education at McGill, he had been expected to be a source of information about the value system of the university as a whole. Moberly commented adversely – and not for the first time – on the record of university education departments in this country. In his view they focused on potted psychology and tips for teachers, and failed to deal with more basic issues.

In December 1940 a paper by Mannheim was circulated which, *inter alia*, drew attention to the way in which the war was sharpening the gap between the generations, and in particular underlining the difference in attitudes towards personal security that existed between older and more 'vital' younger people. Mannheim argued that one of the functions of the proposed order should be to revitalize the country's leadership.[53] The capacity of the élite to assimilate new groups and new ideas had been declining. The order could draw on insights and ideas from sources beyond the existing parties and power groups. Britain did not require a revolution. Social reconstruction could be achieved by revitalizing existing historical groups and extending the basis on which their members were selected – a principle that was to find wide acceptance in years to come.

This paper was considered in January 1941. A paper by T. S. Eliot had been circulated before the meeting in which he disagreed with some of Mannheim's points, especially those relating to the gap between the generations, and discussion turned to the attitudes of students in the pre-war and wartime periods. H. A. Hodges, Professor of Philosophy at Reading, thought that student interest in fundamental issues had diminished as a consequence of the economic depression at the beginning of the 1930s, leaving the political running to those with extreme views, such as the communists. The war was enhancing interest in the aims of life and in the insights that could be obtained through the social sciences. Other speakers emphasized the lack of trust on the part of the young in those who held political power.[54]

## The Influence of the Moot

How influential was the Moot on wartime thinking? There is little evidence of anyone claiming to speak on behalf of the Moot attempting to bring systematic pressure to bear on politicians or administrators. As the record of the meetings shows, members found it hard to agree on very much beyond the importance of the issues under discussion, the need for a robust Christian response to the threat of totalitarianism, and the inclusion of certain basic values in any kind of worthwhile post-war educational programme. This very lack of agreement was testimony to the width of opinion represented among the members and the freedom with which views were expressed.[55] Both Mannheim and Oldham had hoped that the Moot would become more directly involved in political and social action. This was not what the majority of members wanted.

The Moot's influence was to be found rather in its effects on the thinking of individuals. Many members were what today would be described as 'active networkers'. In Vidler's words: 'If [the Moot] exerted influence, it was by its effects on the thinking and writing and actions of its members, not by issuing any statements as a group'. Writing in 1977, he went on to say:

> Hardly any of the regular members are still alive but I think they would all testify that they learned an immense amount through the Moot, not least from those members who started with presuppositions far removed from their own. For instance, I was constantly struck by the sympathy that grew up between T. S. Eliot and Karl Mannheim and by the way they impressed and influenced each other.[56]

Mannheim was active in political circles. The title of the paper that he presented at the Moot in 1939, 'Planning for Freedom', became a widely used political slogan. Following meetings with the President of the Board of Education, R. A. Butler, it was reported that their views on reconstruction 'were in full accord'.[57] Both Walter Oakeshott and Fred Clarke were members of the Conservative subcommittee on educational reconstruction.[58] Its chairman was Geoffrey Faber, chairman of the publishing firm of which Eliot was a director. Oldham had the ear of many influential men and women, such as A. D. Lindsay, who was to become head of Britain's first new post-war university, the University College of Keele. Through his work at the Institute of Education, Clarke helped to shape the educational thinking of a generation of teachers and administrators – not only in this country but in Australia and elsewhere in the Commonwealth.

Many of the papers discussed by the Moot were later incorporated by their authors into books, sometimes amended in the light of members' written and oral comments. Other works by members – such as T. S. Eliot's *Notes Towards the Definition of Culture* (Faber, 1948) – show the influence of discussions at the Moot. *The Christian News-Letter* (*CN-L*) drew on discussions in the Moot, as did a series of *Christian News-Letter* books. Members of the Moot were active in other informal groups with political connections within the 'Reconstruction movement'. Kathleen Bliss took over the editorship of *CN-L* from Oldham, and organized a series of talks that Archbishop Temple held with influential people on the shape of post-war society. Several members of the Moot were also involved in the All Souls Group founded in 1941 with the encouragement of Dr W. G. S. Adams, then warden of All Souls, and which after more than 50 years continues to meet. Alec Vidler became secretary of the Christian Frontier Council, which was (in his own words) 'another prong' of the 1937 Oxford Conference. Like the Moot, the CFC owed a great deal to J. H. Oldham, but had a more practical and less intellectual focus, with government ministers, industrialists and scientists among its members.

Participants in the Moot contributed significantly to the Student Christian Movement's Commission on Higher Education which stimulated Moberly to write his *Crisis in the University*. The Commission itself was responsible for starting the Dons' Advisory Group which – successively known as the University Teachers' Group and the Higher Education Group – still exists in the Higher Education Foundation.[59] Post-war conference series such as the Foundation Conference (1947 to 1962) were also influenced by the Moot. The series of books issued under the title *Educational Issues of Today* which appeared between 1947 and 1952 under the general editorship of Professor W. R. Niblett included Fred Clarke's *Freedom in the Educative Society* and Marjorie Reeves's *Growing up in a Modern Society*, both of which showed Moot influence.

The Moot was only one of a large number of formal and informal groups which helped to form the consciousness of those who played a part in the formation and execution of educational policy during and after the Second World War. Its founder and *animateur*, J. H. Oldham, was expressly concerned to bring together people of differing views. The clashes of opinion and juxtapositions of viewpoint that occur in such groups helped to create the common understanding that facilitated the emergence of policy and the implementation of educational change.

The post-war consensus may be behind us, but without some level of bipartisan agreement on how things are, what needs to be done and how it can best be achieved, educational change is unlikely to be educational progress. Such agreement does not easily emerge in the heat of public debate. Groups such as the Moot and their contemporary equivalents have played and can continue to play an important part in establishing the moral and intellectual basis for long-term social and educational improvement.

# Additional Note on the Moot*

## *The dynamics of the Moot*

The Moot worked as a catalyst for the thinking of an extraordinarily diverse group of people. It worked because Oldham infused it with a sense of loyalty to a group of friends who – however sharply their views differed – shared a common commitment to the rigorous exploration of beliefs and a strong concern with the crisis of their times. It worked because, as Michael Polanyi wrote, 'these things [i.e. Moot discussions] changed our lives'.[60] Part of this dynamic was due to the thoroughness with which Oldham planned the meetings. Thus for the meeting in December 1944, he asked Mannheim and Polanyi to give a critique beforehand of a paper by Eliot on 'Clerisy and Clerisies'. He then organized the programme around Eliot's paper, the two commenting responses and Eliot's reply. Further discussion was to be focused on a new publication by Eliot, *Cultural Forces in the Human Order* and Polanyi's *The European Crisis*, as well as a paper by Donald Mackinnon on 'Christianity and Science'.[61] A weekend spent by such a group pondering on such an agenda must indeed have been a mind-stretching exercise!

The papers certainly were no trifles. In July 1945 Mackinnon submitted the following problems for the Moot; 'absolutism' versus 'relativism' in political thinking; the claims of democracy; the nature of the state; the Christian in politics. This sparked off discussions on problems of creating the free society which are reflected in several *CN-L*[62] supplements. In November 1945, H. A. Hodges presented a 40-page paper on 'Christian Archetypes and Paradigms' which gave a wide survey of Christian theology in relation to other twentieth-century belief systems.[63] When, on 6 August 1945, the first nuclear bomb was dropped on Hiroshima, Oldham and his friends instantly saw this as a cataclysmic event, a great turning-point in history requiring that 'The Human Mind Must Jump'.[64] Oldham chaired the commission on the era of atomic power, set up by the British Council of Churches, which produced a massive report. This became the basis for further study in the Moot, under such headings as 'The Influence of the Bomb on Men's Minds and Outlook'; 'Science and Society'; 'Power and Law'; 'The Atomic Bomb and World Community'.[65]

The cerebral level of the Moot was, indeed, pitched high but crucial to the binding quality of the underpinning fellowship were

---

*   This section is by Marjorie Reeves.

the acts of worship and meditation which formed part of the usual weekend programme. This may seem surprising in view of the differing positions of the members. Geoffrey Vickers, for instance was described by Oldham as 'not a member of any church',[66] while both Mannheim's and Polanyi's religious positions are unclear. In a revealing correspondence between the two, Polanyi at one point writes 'as Christians and Westerners we are dedicated to seek and uphold human interpretations more especially in terms of our own moral tradition' (2 May 1944).[67] Yet, giving an account of his spiritual pilgrimage, he confesses 'My faith in God has never failed me entirely since 1913 but my faith in the divinity of Christ (for example) has been with me only at rare moments' (19 March 1944).[68] Later (31 May 1948), writing to Oldham about Moot discussions on the 'new atheism', Polanyi says:

> Our meeting leaves me increasingly with the feeling that I have no right to describe myself as a Christian. So perhaps I may play the part of the outsider in the discussions. But my dominant sentiment is really this: whatever meeting you may call and invite me to, I shall certainly attend. I don't think the subject will make much difference to the benefit which I will derive from such a meeting.[69]

Such was the compelling force which drew those who might well call themselves 'outsiders' to an emphatically Christian think-tank.

## Three refugee thinkers in the Moot

It was perhaps this unusual combination of commitment and openness which made the Moot an intellectual home for the three refugee scholars: Adolf Löwe, Karl Mannheim and Michael Polanyi. Löwe and Mannheim appear in the Moot deliberations from the second meeting onwards. Löwe's concern at that time centred partly on the dangers of extreme individualism in education, drawing a cautionary lesson from German university experience:

> Never in history did an educational system formally rely to such a degree on intellectual liberty ... as did the pre-Hitler university system in Germany. Its basic idea was the absolute freedom of self-education for every individual student. ... Yet in actual fact social conduct and the patterns of life were entirely pre-formed by the feudal and military standards of Prussian tradition.[70]

His argument for a truly democratic social education exercised a considerable influence not only in the Oldham circle but more generally among educationists who were already moving away from an extreme individualist philosophy.[71] More broadly, as an economist and political thinker he saw the war as 'a political and moral judgement on the past' and therefore as presenting 'our only opportunity for action'. Writing in the *CN-L* in June 1940, he was clear that we must lay down the 'conditions of peace' from the start. His conditions are starkly expressed as two overriding principles: (i) 'Peace cannot be secure until national sovereignties in Europe are contained in a higher political unit'; (ii) 'the new international order must be balanced by an internal order of social democracy'. The urgency of this refugee voice was impressive. After he departed for the States in 1940, he continued to write on world affairs with great effect.

Karl Mannheim played, after Oldham, one of the largest roles in the Moot, both in his unfailing attendance and in his powerful contributions on paper and in discussion. His part in developing the young science of sociology in this country is well known through his lectures and books. What has only recently received attention is the vital part the Moot fellowship played as his intellectual home in this country.[72] Professor Kudomi, studying Mannheim in Britain, writes 'For Mannheim the Moot was a body whose importance cannot be over-estimated. For the Moot, Mannheim was indispensable. Already in 1948 he had circulated a 19-page paper on 'Planning for Freedom'. This became a key theme running through Moot deliberations, finding expression in a whole series of supplements in the *CN-L*. Apart from the books he published in English before his death in 1947, Mannheim contributed a vital *CN-L* supplement on 'Popularisation in a Mass Society'.[73]

Polanyi came late to the Moot. In 1944 Mannheim, who had known him in Vienna, asked Oldham to invite Polanyi to the June Moot meeting, but it appears that he did not attend until the December meeting, when he gave a paper on 'The European Crisis' (a chapter from a book he had just finished).[74] It is not clear whether Polanyi came to later meetings as a member or a guest but he was certainly a congenial participant who, as already indicated, responded with enthusiasm. Oldham became his close friend and this was crucial to Polanyi's thinking at a fundamental level. He gave Polanyi his first book on theology by John Oman. In 1948 Oldham wrote in a letter to Polanyi of 'our conversations in the Moot about God approached from the standpoint of modern atheism', to which Polanyi replied in an extensive series of notes on 'Forms of Atheism'. Much of Polanyi's thinking finds its full expression in *Personal Knowledge*,[75] which Oldham read in draft, writing in 1957:

Of all the books I have read of recent years, none has taken so powerful a hold on me – you have, by the comprehensiveness of your thought brought to the birth in me a way of seeing things as a whole that up till now has existed only in a very embryonic and incomplete stage.

Surely this tribute could be taken as encapsulating the way the 'chemistry' of the Moot had so often worked between its members.[76]

## Notes

1. For help in identifying sources I am grateful to the Revd Keith Clements, Professor John Dancy, Professor David Kettler, Professor W. R. Niblett, Dr Marjorie Reeves and Professor Clive Whitehead. Mr Gordon Brewer, Librarian of the University of London Institute of Education made available the Moot archive, and Professor Duncan Forrester kindly granted access to the J. H. Oldham Papers in the Library of New College, Edinburgh.
2. On J. H. Oldham, see above, pp. 7–10. A series of Moot papers was deposited by Sir Fred Clarke in the library of the University of London Institute of Education (ref. here FCMA, followed by a three-part code). Papers in the J. H. Oldham archive, University of Edinburgh, are referred to as JHOP, followed by the university's numerical ref.
3. See Keith Clements, 'John Baillie and "The Moot",' in D. Fergusson (ed.), *Christ, Church and Society: Essays on John Baillie and Donald Baillie* (T. & T. Clark, 1993), p. 201.
4. See index for the people mentioned here. After this meeting Moberly, Mannheim and Shaw circulated a note suggesting that membership should be limited to this original group.
5. See below, p. 43.
6. See below, pp. 42–5.
7. JHOP 13:3:47. R. Kojecky, *T. S. Eliot's Social Thought* (Faber, 1971), gives a copy of Oldham's attendance list up to July 1945, but this does not distinguish between members and visitors and omits two meetings. A full list of meetings is given in Taylor, 'Education and the Moot'.
8. H. E. S. Woldring, *Karl Mannheim: The Development of his Thought* (Van Gorcum, 1986), p. 60.
9. FCMA I:2:17.
10. Ibid., I:3:3.
11. Ibid., I:4:2; 5:2.
12. Commentaries on Oldham's paper came from Vidler, Murry, Micklem, Mannheim, Fenn, Vickers, Eliot and Shaw.
13. See especially the 18th meeting, 29 Oct.–1 Nov. 1943 (JHOP 13:3:22).
14. FCMA XII:76:2; 76:18.
15. Ibid., XII:76:19.
16. Ibid., XII:76:19.
17. Ibid., II:13:9. In fact much of the thinking that contributed to the 1944 Education Act took place before and in the early years of the war, see R. G. Wallace, *History of Education*, 10/47 (1981), pp. 283–90. Oakeshott, a founder member of the Moot, dropped out at an early stage, perhaps because he had direct access to the top and in the official discussions which led up to the 1944 Act; see J. Dancy,

*Walter Oakeshott: A Diversity of Gifts* (Wilby, Norwich, 1995), pp. 112–13. For G. Vickers, see below, p. 58.

18. F. W. Mitchell, *Sir Fred Clarke: Master Teacher, 1880–1952* (Longman, 1966), p. 105.
19. Mitchell, *Clarke*. See appendix 132.
20. FCMA II:7:20.
21. The Hadow Report of 1926, *The Education of the Adolescent*, had included evidence making suggestions along similar lines but the Committee had not agreed with these proposals.
22. FCMA II:7:22. See *Secondary Education: with special reference to Grammar Schools and Technical High Schools* (The Spens Report).
23. FCMA II:7:24.
24. Anxieties about the dominance of economic values in reconstruction were expressed by Canon Demant in FCMA VII:41, for whom, see below, p. 63.
25. See later discussions in this area in *CN-L* below, pp. 68–9 and the Christian Frontier Council, ch. 4, s. 3.
26. FCMA II:7:24.
27. Many of these points recur below, see chs. 3, 4 and 5.
28. See William Taylor, *The Secondary Modern School*, (Faber, 1963).
29. JHOP 13:3:22.
30. F. Clarke, 'Some Notes on National Re-equipment in Relation to Fundamental Decisions', paper discussed 14–17 Jan. 1944 (JHOP 14:7:58).
31. FCMA II:11.
32. For Mannheim's views on the relation of education to social planning, see C. Loader, *The Intellectual Development of Karl Mannheim: Culture, Politics and Planning* (CUP, 1985) esp. pp. 162–73.
33. K. Mannheim, *Diagnosis of Our Time* (Routledge & Kegan Paul, 1943), p. 100 and n. 110.
34. For similar discussions, see below, ch. 5. See also J. Drewett and M. Reeves, *What is Christian Education?* (Sheldon Press, 1942).
35. FCMA X:66:15.
36. Ibid., X:66:20.
37. This concern was also voiced by J. Middleton Murry, see *The Price of Leadership* (SCM Press, 1939) and discussions below, ch. 5, s. 2.
38. See Mannheim's paper 'The Diagnosis of Our Time', FCMA XI:72:5.
39. At a teacher level these issues were being discussed in the same period by the Auxiliary Movement of the SCM, see below, ch. 5, s. 2.
40. Sir Oliver Franks, later Lord Franks, philosopher, academic, one-time British Ambassador, Washington and chairman of various post-war commissions. He did not take up Oldham's invitation to lead the movement.
41. FCMA V:28:7.
42. Ibid., XIII:80; JHOP 13:3:204; 13:4:212; 13:4:219.
43. FCMA XI:73:2.
44. Ibid., XI:74.
45. Quoted from PRO documents in Wallace, *History of Education* (1981), pp. 287–8.
46. Kojecky, *Eliot's Social Thought*, attendance list, pp. 238–9.
47. Editor of the *TES* and later Prof. of Education, Sheffield University, and dean, University of London, Institute of Education.
48. FCMA XIII:81.
49. See below, ch. 7.
50. FCMA III:17/18.

51. For Löwe's views, see below, p. 43.
52. FCMA III:15.
53. Ibid., VI:32:6.
54. FCMA also includes a MS letter from Eliot to Clarke enclosing a paper on 'The Christian Concept of Education', emphasizing that this is much more than extending equal opportunities of education to every child. This to Eliot was a matter of social justice. Educational questions had to do with what part of knowledge was desirable. Humanist criticism of the fragmentation of knowledge was welcome, but not enough. Humanist values failed to touch the deeper sources of human conduct, lacked roots in any dogmatic system of belief and were unlikely to provide an adequate basis for a way of life for more than a minority of educated individuals. See also Eliot's *Notes Towards a Definition of Culture* (Faber, 1948) and further discussions on the concept of Christian education in ch. 5.
55. Commented on specifically by Eliot, see Kojecky, *Eliot's Social Thought*, pp. 187, 195, 197.
56. A. Vidler, *Scenes from a Clerical Life* (Collins, 1977), pp. 118–19.
57. J. Harris, 'Political Ideas and the Debate on State Welfare', in H. L. Smith, *War and Social Change* (Manchester University Press, 1986), p. 240.
58. Ibid., p. 242.
59. For the history of this body, see M. Reeves, 'From D.A.G. to H.E.F.', *News Letter of the Higher Education Group* (1983), pp. 19–29. See also below, ch. 8.
60. I owe references to the correspondence of Michael Polanyi and Karl Mannheim to the generosity of Professor Jose Harris who has worked on the Polanyi/Mannheim papers. These include some general Moot papers.
61. Ibid.
62. See *CN-L*, S2, 8 Nov. 1939; L&S 4, 31 Jan. 1940; S43, 21 Aug. 1940; S88, 1 July 1941; S274, 27 Nov. 1946; S280, 5 Mar. 1947; S284, 30 Apr. 1947; S257, 3 Apr. 1946.
63. See n. 60.
64. *CN-L*, L260, 15 May 1946.
65. See n. 60 and also below, pp. 56–7.
66. *CN-L*, L2, 8 Nov. 1939.
67. See n. 60.
68. Ibid.
69. Ibid.
70. A. Löwe, 'The Task of Democratic Education', quoted M. Reeves, *Growing Up in a Modern Society* (Univ. of London Press, 1946), pp. 29–30. Löwe had been Professor of Economics and Social Sciences in the universities of Kiel and Frankfurt. In England, he lectured at Manchester and later, in the States, became director of the newly established Institute of World Affairs. The 1940 quotation is from his supplement, 'Social Transformation and the War', *CN-L*, S29, 15 May 1940. The 1944 ref. is quoted by JHO from Löwe's address at the inauguration of the new Institute, *CN-L*, L211, 28 June 1944. See below, p. 117.
71. See below, pp. 117–18.
72. See above, Taylor, p. 25.
73. Quoted with the author's permission from Professor Kudomi's paper 'Karl Mannheim in Britain: An Interim Research report', *Hitotsubashi Journal of Social Studies*, 28/2 (Dec. 1996), p. 51. *CN-L*, S227, 7 Feb. 1945, in which Mannheim discusses the ways in which 'creative personalities' activate society at various levels. The *CN-L* also reviewed his *Man and Society* (S104, 22 Oct. 1941) and *Diagnosis of Our Times* (S174, 24 Feb. 1943).

74. This was entitled 'Full Employment and Free Trade' when published in 1949.
75. M. Polanyi, *Personal Knowledge: Towards a Post Critical Theology* (RKP & Univ. of Chicago Press, 1958).
76. See n. 60.

## Chapter 3

# Tracts for Wartime: *The Christian News-Letter*

Marjorie Reeves and Elaine Kaye

## A Prophetic Idea

On 18 October 1939, the first issue (No. 0) of *The Christian News-Letter* appeared – less than six weeks after Britain declared war.[1] How could this have happened? An alert group of Christian thinkers had been reading the signs of the times and preparing this agency of moral leadership for the nation in its approaching crisis. It was sponsored by the Council of the Churches on the Christian Faith and the Common Life (set up after 'Oxford 1937'), but it was the initiators who mattered – the friends who had been 'thinking together' in the Moot and elsewhere, with Joe Oldham who undertook the editorship of *CN-L* at their centre. Among those closely associated with the launch were William Temple, Alec Vidler, Philip Mairet, T. S. Eliot and a redoubtable SCM campaigner, Eleanora Iredale,[2] who not only raised the funds for this venture but, foreseeing government restrictions on paper, bought in a large supply in advance. The list of collaborators on the first page[3] was varied enough to excite instant attention, ranging from the archbishop of York (William Temple) and the master of Balliol (A. D. Lindsay) to R. H. Tawney, Sir Alfred Zimmern, and G. D. H. Cole.[4] Oldham stresses that they are active collaborators, gathered by him from his 'large number of friends of different outlook and different types of experience', but all concerned about 'the fundamental problems of modern society'.

*The Christian News-Letter*, Oldham announced, aimed at 'bridging the gulf which exists at present between organised religion and the general life of the community'. Each number would have a news section and a supplement on a more extended theme. The first supplement presents three marks of the fundamental Christian message, a message which is far more radical than merely a 'religious flavour' added to 'generally accepted humanitarian ... aspirations'. First, 'it must always reflect the acute *tension* between the world as it is and the new divine order which broke into the world in Christ'; secondly, 'it will never lose sight of the universal character of the Christian society ... (which) transcends the bounds of nationality'; thirdly, 'it must fasten attention on the redemptive and constructive tasks that are possible even in times of war'. Oldham warns that the 'existing order of things is at an end', but to be ready for a 'drastic transformation of values', we need to be delivered from 'black-out of mind'. 'The functions of a Christian News-Letter in war-time are to encourage the free exercise of the imagination and intelligence' and 'to strengthen in ourselves and others the belief in life'. A notable feature was the care with which its judgements were tested. Oldham later wrote: 'Very little appears in the News-Letter that has not been criticized in draft at the weekly meeting of our editorial board, and drafts are also in many instances submitted to experts for criticism'.[5]

The perspective informing the whole enterprise focused on the great social upheaval, underlining the clear duty of Christians to turn outwards towards the nation, Europe and the world. The *CN-L* did, indeed, offer spiritual guidance and comfort to the faithful inside the churches, but its whole thrust was towards the future of social and world order. It followed that contributions from sympathetic people who stood partially or wholly outside the church establishment were freely invited.

The venture took off immediately. By the end of November there were nearly 5000 subscribers.[6] Local discussion groups had already sprung up and by February 1940 there were 9081 subscribers and 45 local groups.[7] The pace of growth was astonishing. By April membership passed the 10,000 mark.[8] As early as the beginning of March 1940, a companion enterprise had been launched in the form of little *CN-L* books – tracts for the times – each costing 1*s*. The first five titles were: J. H. Oldham, *The Resurrection of Christendom*; Middleton Murry, *Europe in Travail*; Fred Clarke, *Education and Social Change*; W. Paton, *The Message of the World-Wide Church*; O. C. Quick, *Christianity and Justice*. At its peak there were *c*.11,000 subscribers, which implied many more readers within the *CN-L* discussion groups. Although German occupation cut off considerable parts of Europe, there were more than 1500 overseas subscribers, scattered through all the continents. Among many others, the Abbé Couturier wrote appreciatively in 1945 that the *CN-L* had 'given much light, opened up many perspectives, rectified many judgements' and that he hoped 'from time to time to republish some of your News-Letters in one of our big daily papers here in Lyon'.[9] The *CN-L* appeared, first weekly and then fortnightly, right through the war and on until 1949.

Bombed out of its first premises at Balcombe Street, London, it moved to Oxford and for a time inhabited the Arlosh Hall at Manchester College. Barring a few holidays when T. S. Eliot and others took over, Joe Oldham carried the editorship until January 1945, when Kathleen Bliss joined him as co-editor, assuming entire responsibility in May when Oldham wrote: 'There has never been any doubt or hesitation about who should take over the editorship of *The Christian News-Letter.*' The regular plop of *CN-L* through the letter-box heartened many vicarages and manses in town and country during the war and it followed combatants all over the world – even to the Arctic Circle where there was a discussion group.[10] A bishop, who described himself as a 'Journeyman Christian', said he relied on *CN-L* 'to keep our minds focused on really significant issues'; another reader, who said 'My approach to religion is unorthodox', was equally appreciative.[11]

The last number (341) appeared on 6 July 1949. There was instantly a great storm of protest from all quarters, at home and abroad. The decision, taken for a variety of financial and personal reasons, was indeed a most reluctant one. Hopes for a revival were momentarily strong but remained unfulfilled. There has never been anything like *CN-L* since.[12] The moral seems to be that a group of inspired friends can achieve what organizations cannot.

## Confronting aggression

In the supplement to the second issue,[13] the editor tackled head-on the most troubling question of all: 'What is God doing?' 'Dare we make the tremendous act of faith to say that God is working His purpose out not merely in spite of, but actually through, the tragedy of the war itself?' This supplement was the outcome of discussion by a group who did not reach a collective mind. Precisely because the subject is of 'supreme importance' the article aims at being an 'honest dealing with great issues to the shaping of which different minds and different types of experience have made their contribution ... for we can learn much from those with whom we disagree'. Thus, at the outset, Oldham defines the characteristic method by which so much of *CN-L* was hammered out. He goes on: 'Our conviction is that war is the utmost contradiction of God's purpose for man. It is humanity's greatest collective sin.' Yet, on the other hand, 'the evil forces at work in human society are, through the outbreak of war, being laid bare as they would not have been if we had gone on in the existing state of peacefulness which we ought to have known to be no real peace'. He expounds five ways in which he sees the judgement and purpose of God being revealed: (1) the unmasking of evil forces ('God is answering the prayer: "From sleep and from damnation deliver us, good lord"'); (2) destruction of false peace ('There is, therefore, danger in prayer ... just for the cessation of strife, without prayer ... for the destruction of the deeper evils of which war is a consequence'); (3) God's judgement on idolatries ('God showing ... that this idolatry of political power which we see in the enemy is a reaction from a more disguised but no less real idolatry of commercial and financial values that have deeply infected the democratic peoples'); (4) the disclosure of false values ('war is giving many people a livelihood and status of which they [had been] deprived ... God is thereby putting to us a searching question. Money can be found in any quantities to discharge shells *gratis* to the enemy; shall we again be fobbed off with the plea of poverty when the more modest demand of social decency again becomes clamant?'); (5) charity, penitence and forgiveness ('God is offering to those who have faith, the insight and power which will enable them to fight the foreign, the domestic and the interior enemy all at once').

In the issue of 10 January 1940, Reinhold Niebuhr, writing as a 'foreign observer', added his voice in a supplement entitled 'Christianity and Political Justice'.[14] He first noted the hesitations among his British friends about the motives for going to war: 'Many ... have expressed embarrassment that the same slogans are being used for this war as for the last' – would the future justify them any more than by hindsight they were seen to be justified after the last war? Although the differences are obvious between the 1914 situation and that of 1939, the trap of self-righteousness must still be avoided: '"Judge not that we be not judged" does not cease to have validity for us even when we are called upon to make historic judgements.' Niebuhr continues:

> In all history we are constantly called upon to defend such justice as we have against flagrant forms of injustice. Yet every scheme of human justice is not only a mere approximation of justice but invariably contains elements of injustice. We must contend for the truth against the lie but also recognise that the truth is not in us and that there is no human truth which is not tainted with the 'ideological taint', ... This double perspective is of the very essence of Christianity ... Christianity believes that man, despite his finiteness, has the possibility of serving the

will of God. But ... it knows that this ideal possibility is corrupted by sinful self-interest. ... This double perspective of the Christian faith demands, on the one hand, fateful historical decisions and, on the other hand, the contrite knowledge that all historical decisions remain ambiguous. ... This double perspective may be termed 'dialectical' in the modern sense. ... For it requires both a 'Yes' and a 'No' upon every historical action'.

Two opposite errors are then exposed. The first is the so-called 'Barthian' emphasis in modern Protestant thought which 'discourages Christians from dealing responsibly with the "nicely calculated less and more" which is the very stuff of historic justice and ordinary decency'. The second, opposite, error is that of 'religious perfectionism' which rests on the belief that the contest of powers can be renounced, that 'it would be a simple thing to purge politics of this element of power and make it an exercise in pure moral persuasion'. Running through the whole essay there is an urgent sense that, if our Christian scruples prevent us from wholeheartedly resisting the monster of evil while there is yet time, 'it would be "tragic" in the narrow and exact sense of the word. It would reveal the possibility of evil emerging from our highest good.'

The next number[15] records the numerous letters received on the Christian attitude to war. In introducing an anonymous supplement on the pacifist position, the editor again strikes the key-note of *CN-L:* 'if the Christian witness is to be effective in the reshaping of the world in days to come, it is of the highest importance that those who on Christian grounds take pacifist and non-pacifist positions should understand one another'. Supplement 15[16] gives extracts from a letter by Karl Barth to a French editor which expresses in agonizing terms the cruel dilemma facing one who acknowledges 'how much I am bound to Germany, its Church and its people'.

> The Church of Jesus Christ cannot and will not make war .... It will therefore not identify the cause of Britain and France with the cause of God and will not preach a crusade against Hitler. He who died upon the Cross died for Hitler too, and for all the confused people who are willingly or unwillingly standing under his flag.
> Yet the Churches must ... tell every people that it is necessary and worthwhile to fight and to suffer for just peace. They must certainly not persuade people of the democratic states that they are fighting for the cause of God; they must, however, say ... that we have in God's name a right to be human and must defend ourselves with the strength of desperation against the invasion of open inhumanity.

Barth implores his friends to consider what is to happen to the German people which is

> not a bad people. ... All nations have their bad dreams. Hitlerism is at present the bad dream of German pagans, whose Christianization in a Lutheran form conserved and strengthened certain elements in their paganism. ... Those nations resisting it must keep in view the fact that in this enemy they have to do with a sick man. Very firm but merciful hands will be necessary.

Continuing the dialogue, Niebuhr, in February 1940[17] spells out the fundamental evils inherent in Western civilization which have led to the present crisis: the worship of power for its own sake; the combination of extreme nationalism with radicalism; the weaknesses of economic structure at variance with the necessities of inter-dependence.

> There are tendencies in all modern democratic nations to drift towards totalitarianism. We are faced at once with the necessity of resistance to this and the need for repentance. The Christian faith has to fight on two fronts. Against all forms of moral complacency it must sharpen the sense of the Kingdom of God as a relevant alternative to every scheme of human justice .... But against all forms of Utopianism the Christian faith must insist that sinlessness is not a possibility of historic existence.

A different note was struck by John Baillie out of the centre of conflict. In the early part of 1940 he was in France in charge of YMCA educational work, evacuated back to England only just before the French collapse. Later in the year he raised the desperate question which haunted 'the minds of numberless people' besides himself: 'Does God Defend the Right?'[18]

> In those days [in France] the most fervent of all our petitions was that God would champion the cause of justice and true religion before it was too late. ... And how men prayed during those terrible days. Frequently I heard the remark 'I pray these days as I've never prayed before.'

Baillie was reading the Psalms and was astonished to realize that their problem was his problem:

> Their cause, they protest, is God's cause; why, then, does God not champion it? ... 'Awake, why sleepest thou, O Lord?' – this to the keeper of Israel 'who neither slumbers nor sleeps'. These words are from the forty-fourth psalm, and I confess that the day I lighted on it in France God seemed to me to have gone sound asleep.

The New Testament, he noted, had

much less to say about the triumph of *right in this world.* Does this mean that ... we can no longer, like the psalmist, trust in God for the victory of right over wrong on the battlefields of earth? ... One cannot pray without faith and how can one pray for the triumph of the right cause on the earthly scene if one is not allowed to believe that God is in some way working to bring this triumph about?

In attempting to reach a balanced view, Baillie makes several points: (1) Christian prayer never dictates the terms of its own answer but must always be content to leave the issue in God's hands; (2) our purposes, however noble they may appear to us, are never His purposes; (3) we must not seek to identify the temporal within the eternal order: it may be His purpose to make us pass through the discipline of humiliation and defeat; (4) nevertheless, we need assurance that God's plan does include some triumph of righteousness in the historical order of events.

He sums up:

> The solution to our problems, appears to lie in some combination of the witness of the ancient Hebrew prophets with the witness of the later apocalyptic (i.e. other-worldly) period. Must we not believe that we shall have some foretaste of the blessed Kingdom), not only in our individual souls but also in the ordering of our earth's society ... ?

The period immediately after the war brought sharply into focus the different approaches of the so-called 'continental' and 'Anglo-Saxon' schools of theology to the role of Christians in relation to the nuclear power struggle. This was mirrored in the *CN-L.* Under the title 'We are Men and not God',[19] Niebuhr sought to modify the uncompromising stand Barth had taken at the first gathering of the World Council of Churches[20] declaring, as reported by Niebuhr, 'we have no systems of economic or political principles to offer to the world. We can present it only "with a revolutionary hope"'. In other words, says Niebuhr, it is not ours to present a kind of 'Christian Marshall Plan', and he comments:

> a wholesome warning but does it not annul the Church's prophetic role to the nations? It is certainly not right for Christians to leave it to the 'pagans' of our day to walk the tight rope of our age which is strung over the abyss of war and tyranny, seeking by patience and courage to prevent war on the one hand and the spread of tyranny on the other, while they rejoice in a 'revolutionary hope' in which all these anxieties of human existence are overcome proleptically.

He finds a 'special pathos' in the position of German Christian leaders who 'yesterday discovered that the Church can be an ark in which to survive a flood' but today

> seem so enamoured of this special function of the Church that they have decided to turn the ark into a home on Mount Ararat and live in it perpetually. . . . With the fullest appreciation of what this theology did to puncture the illusions of church men . . . one must insist that it did not expound the whole Gospel. . . . Belief in the final inadequacy of every form of human justice must not lead to defeatism in our approach to the perplexing problems of social justice in our day. . . . We cannot deny that this 'continental theology' outlines the final pinnacle of the Christian faith and hope . . . [but] it has obscured the foothills where human life must be lived. . . . It started its theological assault . . . with the reminder that we are men and not god. . . . The wheel has come full circle. It is in danger of offering a crown without a cross, a triumph without a battle . . . in short, a too simple and premature escape from the trials and perplexities, the duties and tragic choices which are the condition of our common humanity. The Christian faith knows of a way through these sorrows, but not of a way around them.

There is no space here to pursue the dialogue which ensued,[21] but it highlights, against the background of dramatic world change, the perpetually ambiguous position of Christians in power politics.

In the post-war period, the problem of confronting aggression takes a new shape. In November 1948,[22] writing on 'The Nature of Modern War' in response to the churches' report on 'The Era of Atomic Power', Oldham says: 'Many see in the modern methods of mass destruction . . . the emergence of something fundamentally new in human history.' One's first reaction is the extreme one:

> only by an uncalculating, passionate revolt of the human spirit against the evil hideous thing that is dragging it down to the sub-human, bestial level, can humanity hope to survive. . . . There is only one thing open to us – an uncompromising refusal to have any part in indiscriminate massacre, in large-scale senseless destruction.

But, as Christians, are we free to take this uncompromising 'bold leap into the world of freedom?' 'I long to take this leap', Oldham says, 'but can I?' We cannot think simply from the standpoint of the individual conscience. We must consider the collective responsibility for the prevention of war.

> Suppose that we were to elevate conscientious objection on the part of the individual into a principle of general application and that the Churches were to instruct their members to withdraw their support from

their Governments' measures, even of self-defence, they would be taking political action ... that might defeat the efforts of statesmen to avert war. ... Suppose that the statesmen who direct foreign policy ... taking on their shoulders the burden of political responsibility and working in the only context open to them – armies and navies and atomic weapons – do succeed ... in averting from God's creation the awful fatality of modern war, may not the great and good God who loves His creation, say to them: 'Well done, good and faithful servants', while He looks with a less approving eye on those of us who in the desire not to soil our garments slip out from under the load of real political responsibility.... What if the very essence of the Christian ethic is that it is an 'ethic of the situation'; not conformity to abstract principles but a direct response to the living God in the demand which He makes in a concrete situation?

While differences will remain, 'those who truly respond are united to one another by a common loyalty, a common humanity and a common dependence on divine forgiveness'.


## The Search for a 'Free Society'

In Trinity term, 1941, William Temple, then archbishop of York, spoke to a packed congregation at the University Church of Oxford.[23] His theme was the urgent need for a Christian social philosophy. In the face of deep social change, a new consciousness was needed. In social management, as in education, British life had been based on tacit assumptions and passive consensus which were grounded in a more-or-less accepted class system. The First World War had shocked thinking people out of complacency but the seismic waves of change travelled slowly and it took a decade or more for searching questions to surface: was it acceptable that 'the masses' should simply be educated for and allotted functions as 'industrial fodder' and most cynically, 'cannon fodder'? Then to a disillusioned intellectual élite came the 1930s challenge of planned societies based on an enforced ideology, both from the left and the right. In August 1940, T. S. Eliot wrote[24] 'When a nation is engaged in a vital struggle which revives the sense of community, social injustice is more patent and more intolerable and demands control of the actions of some in the interests of all.' Did this mean that we were perforce moving to a planned society? If so, what about the freedoms of which Sir Norman Angell had written a recent Penguin special: *Why Freedom Matters?* A great concerted effort of thought and feeling was needed. In a later paper Oldham declares:

'something must come into existence which the historian of the future will recognise as having comparable importance in history with the rise of the Communist and Nazi Movements'.[25]

*CN-L* provided a debating arena in which thoughtful people wrestled with Temple's challenge. Geoffrey Vickers asked: 'Where are we going: it would take a book to do justice to this stupendous wild-goose chase, which has provided more and more techniques for doing things and left fewer and fewer criteria for deciding what is worth doing'.[26] Vickers was a friend of Oldham's, a lawyer 'who is not associated with any church'.[27] He focused attention at once on the central problem: 'There is no order without purpose; there is no force without will ... The only sort of common purpose which will hold people together is one which makes them responsible both for the future and for each other'. Such a purpose must be 'national', 'educative' and 'social', but how would it be found?

On 31 January 1940, Oldham devoted a whole letter and supplement to the subject 'Educating for a Free Society'.[28] Characteristically, he had prepared this after 'much private discussion among an influential group'.

> We cannot have a society which binds men to one another in mutual respect without a specific common faith ... people are ceasing to believe that societies ... are kept on any road of 'progress' by any automatic 'harmony of interests'. Only a conscious act of educational planning will arrest the drift. But does not planning for a common purpose endanger the concept of the free society?

Could a 'common faith' any longer be based directly on Christian ethics? These were the problems with which writers in *CN-L* wrestled throughout and after the war.

H. A. Hodges, writing on 'Standards in a Mixed Society',[29] articulated the theological basis for a Christian social philosophy, but warned that this could not be applied simplistically in a mixed society.

> What reasonable grounds are there on which some part at least of the Christian social philosophy can be commended to the non-Christian? ... For everyone alike (whether he realises it or not) it is better to work for a good outside himself, to recognise a duty which claims him, and in whose fulfilment his life finds its meaning.

Christians historically have justified such an assertion of 'good' on grounds of 'natural law', but Hodges realizes that this will no longer wash with many non-Christians. The need is for a subtle persuasion to a kind of moral wisdom:

We have to get people to think seriously of forms of life and experience which may hitherto have been outside their horizons. We have to persuade them that these new forms of life are real possibilities for them, and are richer and better than their present modes of life.

This picks up what a lawyer, Owen Barfield had been saying a few weeks earlier.[30] Writing on social change, he doubts the effectiveness of *any* appeal purely to reason to *move* people. 'You have to start from the feeling of something good which potentially exists already and which it is our true nature to make to happen.' Can we, by this second method, produce 'a widespread conviction in the minds of English people that it is their urgent business to create a new society?' Barfield's complex argument on the relation of freedom and individualism to collectivism cannot be summarized here, but he concludes:

> a man must be free, not because he is a trader, but because he is a spirit. ... Nor is such freedom a necessity for his individual moral well-being only. ... For the forms of society are the products of creative thought and moral imagination; and these are functions of the individual human spirit in its sacramental relation to the Holy Spirit.

Here Barfield shows how an imaginative appeal to a latent potentiality can, in a mixed society, be traced to its hidden theological root – the Holy Spirit at work in creation.

In the ongoing debate on the new society, one approach was to identify the 'universals' of a potentially 'good' society in terms that would ring true to humanists as well as Christians. 'A free society', wrote Oldham,[31] 'has a particular kind of unity – namely, the unity of people who have developed a sense of responsibility for each other and for the future.' Lionel Curtis defined the 'object of human life' as the perfecting of that instinct in human beings 'to put the good of others before their own'.[32] But, commenting on Curtis's supplement, Oldham juxtaposes Christian realism to this liberal/humanist vision: 'Man's freedom ... is a limited freedom. This combination of infinite possibilities with inescapable finitude gives to human life its *tragic* character. ... When he acts in defiance of these limitations his creativity becomes demonic ...' Indeed, both Oldham and Eliot felt deeply that only a society with Christian insights at its core could put the brake on unreal utopianism. In the autumn of 1939 T. S. Eliot had published a controversial book, *The Idea of a Christian Society*, which J. H. Oldham analysed critically in February 1940. He believed a 'Christian Community' is still possible in which 'for a great majority ... religion would be largely a matter of behaviour and habit'. But within it there must be an active 'community of Christians' to act as the leaven and the salt. This, in Oldham's words, would be 'a body somewhat indistinct in its boundaries, of conscious, thoughtful and practising Christians, possessing spiritual and intellectual gifts beyond the ordinary, which enable them to exert a formative influence on social life. It would include both clergy and laity ...'.[33] Here in a nutshell, we see the vision which inspired the spiritual drive of Eliot, Oldham and others in the Moot and elsewhere. But was there still a sufficient residue of Christian 'presuppositions in general society' to give Eliot's 'Core Christian group' any real substance? Furthermore, was the concept of a 'community of Christians' as an élite leadership (whether of intellect or class) still acceptable in a fast-changing society?

For John Middleton Murry, member of the Moot and contributor to the *CN-L*, this question posed an acute problem. In his *Price of Leadership* (1939), which he wrote at Oldham's instigation, he dwelt lovingly on the virtues of his own 'Public School' education and the Arnoldian ideal of responsible public service behind it, but he now saw, with a sharp new awareness, the implications of universal suffrage.

> It was at this moment of paramount importance that the members of the new society should be educated to their new responsibilities ... and, above all, that this new education should be based on a deep consideration of the ends of society and the ends of man in society ... members of a democracy must be educated – not simply for some particular economic function but genuinely educated into a sense of their new responsibility, as fellow-rulers and fellow-members of a new kind of society. They must be educated in the capacity for deciding what is the purpose of man's existence in society.[34]

The sharp end of the debate turned on the question of whether social justice could be achieved (full employment, etc.) without authoritarian management. For some thinkers the paramountcy of social justice propelled them towards a modified Marxist model. Middleton Murry was among those who defended free choice with passion. Yet he saw the dilemma. In a later *CN-L* supplement,[35] 'Can Democracy Survive?', he characterizes the emotive term 'democratic socialism' as a society of full employment, social security and educational equality. In such a society the traditional motives for working hard – to keep the wolf from the door and improve opportunities for the next generation – are absent. Ultimately, the indispensable condition of successful democratic socialism is that labour should be willing to discipline itself. This will involve 'taking the workers representatives into full and responsible partnership on the job'. It is 'imperative that there should be a revolution in trade union mentality'. We have to find the 'practical *via media* between the regimentation required by economic planning and the personal initiative required for general progress and individual fulfilment in a harmonious society'.

In *CN-L* Supplement 280,[36] Ian Crombie (a philosophy don at Balliol) picked up the continuing debate on the pros and cons of the Russian system. If we leave the realm of ideas, he says, and get down to actual situations, it is often the case that

> human affairs consist in getting one thing right at the expense of something else. ... Therefore the question 'What is possible now?' is always as important as the question 'How could human affairs be arranged if only men would behave reasonably?' ... Marxism expresses some truths about human relationships, liberalism expresses others; actual situations are too complex to allow the exact expression of any principles.

But the fact that counts most for him is that 'poverty' is more unpleasant for the poor than being regimented: 'people, do, in fact, want economic justice and security ... In this situation you cannot have democracy until something is being done about these demands.' Social justice comes before political freedom.

Middleton Murry immediately came back at Crombie with a sharp sense of political danger in Supplement 284:[37] 'If there is one task above all others to which Christians are called today, it is to spread awareness of the potentialities and the predicament of the free society'. In the 'fully free political society' we see

> a new kind of moral being, a new form of society which is dedicated to discovering what social justice really is ... this conception we have to pit against the individualistic and atomistic 'liberalism' of the bourgeois political society ... and against the totalitarian solidarity of the Communist social organisation.

Political freedom is an

> essential part of social justice. ... It is the indispensable condition of discovering by the processes of the free society what the real (as distinct from the ideal) content of social justice is. ... It is the free society only which can discover – by its openness and receptivity to experience – what is humanely beneficial and what is not in the very abstract and still largely doctrinaire idea of Socialism. The free society itself is infinitely more important than any 'ism'.

In declaring his belief that political democracy is crucial, Middleton Murry maintains that it is 'a novel, experimental and highly vulnerable form of religious – and specifically Christian – society' and that it is urgent that this should be understood by all Christians:

> first because it gives Christians common ground on which to stand in active religious fellowship with non-Christians, which I believe is a necessity today, if the free society is to be preserved and the radical economic crisis of the country overcome; secondly, because the free society is, in itself, a more Christian society than any specifically Christian society of comparable magnitude and thirdly, because I believe the future of the Christian Church itself depends on whether the free society can be kept alive.

A different approach had been heralded in a Christmas supplement of 1943,[38] when William Temple said that the crisis of our modern society was a cultural and not a moral or directly political one. Starting from the proposition that 'it is no longer possible to maintain "the naïve spontaneity" of proclaiming the Gospel of redemption without any sense of incongruity with the ordering of life in the world outside', he said: 'Our problem is to envisage the task of the Church in a largely alien world.' To go back to the catacombs, or conduct the church as 'an evangelistic enterprise in a heathen country', was today a 'shirking of responsibility'. The task was to 'make sense' of the world, not meaning that we can show that it is sense, but with the more literal and radical meaning of making *into* sense what, until it is transformed, is largely nonsense – a disordered chaos waiting to be reduced to order as the Spirit of God gives it shape. In seeking to highlight where this responsibility lay, Temple focuses attention on 'Neighbour': 'Personality is inherently social; only in social groupings can it mature, or indeed fully exist. These groups must be small enough to enable each individual to feel ... that he can influence the quality and activity of the group.' The characteristic of much present-day democratic thought, he maintained, is 'that it seeks to eliminate or depreciate all associations intermediate between the individual and the state'.

These, as the foci of local and other departmental loyalties, are obnoxious in the eyes of the 'prophets of progress'. Because the state is too large, Temple sees 'limitless individualism' as defeating its own end and leading to totalitarianism. Christianity has always favoured those lesser units, but Descartes's disastrous deliverance *Cogito, ergo sum* 'became the basis for the mechanistic type of thought in which individual self-consciousness becomes central and the individual relates only to a world of things'. He can even organize 'psycho-logical things' to suit his own ends, treating persons as things. His relation to them is an 'I–it', not an 'I–thou' relation. Temple expands the two relationships in terms which echo Buber and Macmurray, concluding: 'A decision for sociality as the basic truth of human existence would create an outlook and temper so different from that which has been dominant in the modern era now drawing to its close as to create a new epoch in humanity.'[39] This summary only covers one aspect of Temple's immensely realistic and profoundly theological essay.

In Supplement 257[40] V. A. Demant picked up this key statement in a close examination of how societies actually work. The search for real community involves the 'problem of how to give the mass of men the right to existence, to function or to status without making them undifferentiated cogs in a society organised as a mechanism'. The key to the problem lies in Temple's word 'culture', which he defines as 'the ways of life that the members of a community can count on'. The inner life of human beings has two parts: the spirit and the soul. The spirit is 'the clear, deliberative, active force which reasons and wills'; 'the soul is the less conscious complex of emotions, attitudes and habits which provide the energy of life. The first gives direction, the second, power.' There is here an analogy with society which has both its aims and its culture. 'The former is what it stands *for*, the latter what it stands *on*. When these two work together, society is in a creative stage.' The core of Demant's argument was that the culture or 'soul' of European civilization over the past three centuries had, in large measure, withered. Its unsupported ideals (such as ideas of truth, right and wrong, law and metaphysical equality of all men) remain, but virtuous ideals unrooted in a real culture are simply 'incompetent'. Under a heading 'The Uselessness of Better Behaviour', he argues that you cannot arrest the disintegrating effect of the technological revolution by plastering on moral injunctions or political expedients: 'In fact our moral and political problems largely arise out of the failure of progress to meet man's fundamental needs. What is the good of preaching community when the nurseries of community in the family and region are enfeebled?' So the task to which Demant calls all Christians is the recreation of our culture. Here he strikes a note of hope: 'There are still remnants of an older, sounder culture. They were our stand-by in war.'

*CN-L* writers, starting from grass-roots experience, sought to interpret and build on these indigenous local democracies. In 1944[41] Oldham had reported the remark of a refugee from Nazism that 'after more than five years study of British society' he believed that 'the most remarkable difference between the social life of this country and of the Continent was the number, variety and vigour of our voluntary organisations'.[42] In 1941 W. G. Symons, a factory inspector, writing on 'Ecumenical Christianity and the Working Class'[43] showed the 'social significance of Working Class Non-conformity in the closely-knit local community where chapel, trade union and co-op, were all of a piece'. Ironically, war had revitalized local community through such necessary efforts as civil defence associations and an issue of *CN-L* in January 1945[44] focuses on hopes of capitalizing on wartime experiments in post-war reconstruction by experiments in spontaneous sociability. 'The essential thing', wrote Kathleen Bliss, 'is to keep alive the tiny plants of a desire for a less atomised, more corporate community. The range and richness added to personal life by free association with others in some worthwhile activity can only gauged by experiencing it.'

The cultural problems of a mass democracy had already been highlighted by G. D. H. Cole in his supplement 'Democracy Face to Face with Hugeness':[45]

> In the long span of human history only quite lately ... have ordinary men been placed in a position in which they are called upon to take part in decisions which ... require a capacity for reasoning in generalisations which far transcends the limits of their practical knowledge and acquaintance.

The problem was compounded by rapid social change.

> Under the leadership of science, things ran away with men and the social mind was left groping further and further behind. Modern representative democracy was atomistically conceived in terms of millions of voters, each casting his individual vote into a pool which was somehow mystically to back up a General Will.

But this was not how 'persons' function: 'they find their common will through relationships in manageable societies'. So individuals who could not cope with democracy in the state, created social groups which they could manage democratically because the decisions made in them could be taken on the basis of real collective experience (e.g. Co-ops, trade unions, Friendly Societies, etc.). Cole prophetically sees the state as hostile to 'these natural growths of the spirit of democracy': dangerous enemies of a democracy which was conceived atomistically, whereas they were in truth the embodiment of a democratic spirit in the form in which its realisation was most within men's grasp'. Our problem now 'is to find democratic ways of living for little men in big societies', or, in another phrase, 'to create new social tissues'. Writing in the midst of the black-out, with difficulties of communication, Cole ends with a great plea 'to find ways of getting together and of making contact with . . . the countless little groups which are learning to practise democratic fellowship'.

Finally, in an early key supplement (December 1941),[46] Oldham had expounded what he believed was the crucial issue underlying the whole debate on society. 'All Real Life is Meeting' was sparked off by the last of Macmurray's broadcast series on 'Persons and Functions' in 1941. Oldham's essay was an exposition of the ideas of Macmurray and Buber. Far from people being subordinate to jobs, Macmurray argued, the true and Christian view was that men and women are essentially 'persons', meant to live in personal fellowship with one another, and that the services they have to perform in society are incidental and subordinate to their personal lives. 'The functional life is *for* the personal life; the personal life is *through* the functional life.'[47] This philosophy is fortified by Buber's distinction between 'I–Thou' and 'I–it' relationships – the world of people and the world of things. Is there any escape, Oldham asks, from the increasing domination of the world of things? Is not a man a hopeless captive in the prison-house of his organizations? The world of things is not inherently evil but by itself 'It' is a word of separation, while 'Thou' is a word of union. It is only the recovery of the experience of 'meeting' that can once more infuse our 'petrified world' with the 'creative living spirit which is God': 'Those who meet . . . are already sharers of eternal life.' In 1947 Oldham returned to this theme in a supplement 'Life is a Dialogue'[48] to mark the publication of Buber's *Between Man and Man*:

> Address and Answer, demand and self-forgetting response: these are the creative experiences that make up the 'whole person'. They stand in stark contrast to the confrontational exchange between individuals or collectives where there is no 'meeting' and no 'dialogue'.

These brief notes cannot adequately convey the richness of this vein of thinking in the 1940s but perhaps they can hold a mirror to today's social crisis.

## Educating the Next Generation

The writers of *CN-L* put education at the forefront of their concerns, for the education of its citizens would determine the character of the free society of the future. It was a matter of urgency to them to work out a common purpose, for however tragic a time of war might be, it did provide the opportunity to rethink the values upon which post-war society would be constructed. Above all, these writers issued challenges for change, appealing to imagination, understanding and will in order to create the kind of society in which Christianity might, for those who so chose, take root.

Underlying these challenges was a theology of both creation and redemption, and no one expounded this more clearly or profoundly than the first editor, Joe Oldham:[49] 'The two fundamental assertions of Christianity are that God created the world and man and that He sent Christ to redeem them.[50] On the basis of the first, Christians and non-Christians could find common ground in formulating 'a good human education, that takes account of the true nature of man as understood in the light of the Christian revelation',[51] and in recognizing 'the right of each individual to develop the capacities which God has given him'.[52] The values of humanity, freedom and social obligation were not the exclusive preserve of Christians, but were shared by all who now united to dethrone fascism and the claims of an all-powerful totalitarian state. 'The main, specific task of the school is the perfecting of the human in accordance with the law of its own nature.'[53]

In one of the earliest issues of *CN-L* Oldham urged that 'in the transformation of society which lies nearest to the heart of Christians is the status, growth and welfare of persons and the kind of relations they have with one another'. The deepest need of every human being 'is to be redeemed from his ego-centricity'.[54] The Christian therefore challenges the view that education can be seen solely in terms of the individual on the one hand or the state on the other, for that disregards the fact that an individual person lives and only achieves fulfilment in relation to others. A person cannot evade responsibilities to other persons, and cannot escape the religious question – 'What is it all for?' Oldham saw education as 'social philosophy in action', for it reflects the priorities of each generation. He listed three major educational issues which had to be faced in the immediate future: the equalizing of opportunity; the extension of the period of education from 14 to 15 (immediately) and ultimately to 16; and the need to deepen the purpose of education, by integrating three educational traditions – the critical, the instructional and the individualist.[55] A point constantly stressed was that education was not to be identified exclusively with schooling. The home and the local community were just as significant as the school and the church for the transmission of values from one generation to another, and unless what the school taught related to the values of society at large, it would have little effect. Oldham had asked, 'What effect can the teaching of the Sermon on the Mount as a moral code to guide daily conduct in a society, whose practices follow for the most part the rules of the skin-game, have upon young people except to convince them that Christianity is quite irrelevant to life?'[56]

In July 1941 the Conservative R. A. Butler was appointed President of the Board of Education, with a Labour MP, James Chuter Ede, as his Parliamentary Under-Secretary. The evacuation of inner-city children to more prosperous parts of the country had revealed to those hitherto in ignorance how poor was the quality of education in many schools, not only those provided by local authorities but also those provided by the churches. There was general agreement on the need for radical reform, but also a fear of the difficulties. The last major reform, in 1902, had generated bitter controversy between Anglicans and Nonconformists, and the potential for conflict was still strong. No new reform could be carried out without tackling the question of church (Anglican and Roman Catholic) schools, and that was bound to revive the resentment of Nonconformists and others at the support of such schools from the rates. Nevertheless Butler and Chuter Ede were prepared to surmount the difficulties, and in August 1941 they took a first step by receiving a deputation of Anglicans (including both English archbishops, Lang and Temple) and Nonconformists, who were prepared to co-operate with a scheme which guaranteed Christian teaching and worship in schools. Negotiations with church leaders and others were pursued energetically over the following period; one of the most creative thinkers was Walter Oakeshott, then high master of St Paul's School in London. By July 1943 a White Paper on 'Educational Reconstruction' (on which the subsequent Education Act of 1944 was based) was published. Church schools were retained, but had to submit to more control in return for partial funding.

It was against the background of these and similar discussions that the contributors to *CN-L* wrote in the years 1941–4.[57] While they recognized that the issue of religious education was important, none of them wanted denominational issues to become predominant, and all wished education to be set in a broader context than schooling alone. Oldham in particular recognized that no previous society had ever attempted to educate all its citizens in the way that many in Britain were now planning to do; secondary education for all was a bold new vision. It involved a transformation of attitude and purpose, and in particular, a new understanding of the lives of the majority of young people, of their needs and of their potential. Before 1944 this majority was not offered secondary schooling, but usually remained in all-age schools until the leaving age of 14, while those who won scholarships or whose parents were able to pay fees went to grammar or private schools, and the more socially privileged to public schools.

The existence of public schools posed a challenge. Butler, and many others, wanted to integrate them into a national system of education. In June 1942 he appointed a committee of inquiry under Lord Fleming to 'investigate how the facilities of a boarding school education might be extended to those who desired to profit by them, irrespective of their means'. Oldham had already drawn attention to the need to examine the purpose and values of public schools,[58] and later Michael Clarke, the former headmaster of Repton, writing in support of the Fleming Committee's report which recommended widening the opportunities for attendance at a public school, argued that they could pass on to others the 'profound sense of community' which he claimed was one of their strongest virtues.[59] However, a warning note had been sounded by A. D. Lindsay in 1942: 'Our educational reforms up till now have mainly been directed to the construction of educational ladders by which the clever boy can escape from the rest.'[60] He deeply regretted the class division in education.

All the writers in *CN-L* recognized that the biggest changes would have to come in the attitude towards that majority who were not offered the opportunity to climb one of these ladders. There was 'an irresistible case' for raising the school-leaving age to 15, and extending part-time education to 18, but that only touched part of the issue. A report in 1941 on the position of young men between the ages of 18 and 25 in South Wales[61] presented findings which related, in fact, to experience between 14 and 18. It revealed a depressing picture of mass unemployment, a society whose youth had no jobs and little hope of ever having one, of poverty and an altogether unacceptably poor quality of life. In response, A. D. Lindsay, who with Sir Humphrey Milford had started an Oxford branch of *CN-L*, convened a small group of teachers, industrialists and psychologists to consider that report's implications for planning for the future. While they favoured the raising of the school-leaving age to 15, they felt that it was just as important to consider the need of young people between the ages of 15 and 18 for work, and work which trained them in a skill and inculcated a sense of responsibility. Oldham had already written that no greater step could be taken towards creating a *real* new order ... than that the nation should accept its responsibilities for making the good life possible for all its members and determine that every future citizen should have the chance of making his fullest contribution to the common good.[62]

Both Oldham and Lindsay showed enthusiasm for the 'County Badge' scheme, based on the ideas of Kurt Hahn, founder of Gordonstoun (and similar to the post-war Duke of Edinburgh's Award Scheme). Oldham predicted that, through working together the young people would discover in the experience of mutual service an ethos which would open the way for Christian worship and teaching: 'Those who have learned in the experience of life to love their fellow-men are on the road which leads to the knowledge of God.'[63]

It followed that what the young person did after leaving school should be educative, though it would take the form of paid employment. Marjorie Reeves wrote, a year after the end of the war, that 'we ought ... to be fighting hard for the principle that up to 18 the experience of all juveniles must be weighed for its educational not for its productive value'. As the work itself was to be perceived as giving a meaning and purpose to life, any forms of education offered to young workers must be integrated into it; 'we must teach the young worker, not as little as he needs to know to perform an unskilled operation, but as much as he can absorb as a person about the implications of his work'.[64]

Throughout the war, church leaders and others had pronounced on the widespread ignorance of Christianity within society and the need for more effective Christian education. While the delicate negotiations on church and state schools were proceeding, writers in *CN-L* warned that 'religious education' divorced both from the life of the churches and from the actual experience of children would be quite ineffective, and it was not to be regarded as a panacea for society's ills. T. S. Eliot wrote that religious education divorced from any church connection would result in some kind of 'national Christianity', 'free from the control of any theological authority'.[65]

In January 1944 Marjorie Reeves wrote of religious education as 'nurture in the faith by which a group (or an individual) really lives', which inevitably pervades the whole of life. It takes place through personal relations, and is 'apprehended emotionally and actively before it is understood intellectually'. She listed six experiences which might form the basis of values which could be shared by Christians and 'a significant number of others': perceiving the natural world as a universe of law and order; living in societies which seek to express this principle in their own life; being loved as a unique person and responding to others similarly; understanding and undertaking one's work as 'a significant and worthy service' to the community; comprehending where one belongs; and solitariness. These experiences would provide the atmosphere in which the Christian Gospel might be heard and responded to.[66] While the Christian message of redemption and the call to faith and obedience were the specific business of the church, the raising of questions, and the study of other people's answers, was the business of education. On school worship, about which many church people were much concerned, the writer pointed out that real worship could never be imposed from above. 'I am not sure it would not be better to abandon the "daily dose" and concentrate on particular services of worship planned carefully for certain high-lights of school life and general festivals.'

The writers of *CN-L* had a particularly acute insight into the problems and challenges of the education of young people, and Oldham especially had a profound understanding of the theological foundations of Christian education. In their concern for moral education as the total experience of young people growing up in society they have much to teach us today.

## Britain and the World

Throughout the war *CN-L* maintained a vigilant world-watch and enlisted contributions by writers from all quarters of the globe. At the level of sheer human sympathy, the theme of sufferings and privations in occupied Europe and elsewhere among the world's peoples runs right through to the stark reports of post-war chaos. Food shortage in Britain gets few mentions, but 'Hunger in Europe' occurs again and again. An issue of January 1943 gives a telling little report:[67] conditions in Europe following the first war were appalling but we were largely ignorant of this and when Austen Chamberlain was asked to increase a parliamentary grant of £100,000 for relief work, he had replied: 'it is not our bounden duty to become a kind of Mrs Jellaby among the nations'. Now, Oldham notes, 'in marked contrast to this indifference is the present attitude both of public opinion and government policy'. In August 1940, Churchill had said: 'We shall do our best to encourage the building up of reserves of food all over the world', while in 1941 Eden declared government policy to be 'social security abroad no less than at home'. Oldham comments: 'We are committed to succour Europe. Human Issues have taken precedence. This change of attitude is something for which to be thankful.'

In spite of communication restrictions, Oldham was determined to keep his readers as accurately informed as possible on human situations throughout the world. As early as the end of November, 1939[68] he was able to give a sympathetic account of China's fight against Japanese occupation. How he could contact so many observers is a marvel.

From India he gets 'A War-time View' from J. Z. Hodge;[69] from a Russian theologian in Paris, 'A Russian View;[70] George Bell, Bishop of Chichester, supplies information gathered from a visit to Sweden and other European contacts; Nicholas Zernov writes on Britain and the Balkans; Margaret Wrong on Africa.[71] Other voices – of C. L. Hsija and Francis Wei – come from China.[72] William Paton writes on 'The World-Wide Christian Society'.[73] In June 1941 Oldham reports on a meeting in Westminster where British Christians actually met with representatives from a number of European countries; a symbol he comments, 'of the future and the rich universality of the Church of Christ'.[74] Throughout 1941 to 1943 he reports on the political situations, sufferings and resistances of occupied countries in Europe. In March 1941 he writes movingly about Britain's relationship to Europe: 'There is never any doubt that we are bound to Europe by fundamental ties of kinship.'[75]

Discussions on the tortuous evolution of Indian independence were reported throughout the war, while Britain's responsibility for the nations of the Commonwealth was recognized. In March 1940 Oldham reports on the Colonial Development Fund and the government's 'acceptance of its trusteeship for the colonies'.[76] In November that year *CN-L* gives an account of a meeting in Delhi of representatives from eleven British Commonwealth countries which called forth the observation that 'the war is being fought to save the destruction of some of the essential values of western civilisation, but the ultimate problems of human society are not merely European but world problems'.[77] William Paton gave a sensitive analysis of Britain's relations with India, emphasizing the difficulties of overcoming 'the barriers of misunderstanding' and calling on the 'Christian world community, which is alive in India as it is in Britain, to play a decisive part in the creation of a new under-standing'.[78] In *CN-L* 126 and 130, the 'positive initiative' of the British government in opening up talks with Indian leaders is seized upon as a first sign of that new understanding and Oldham hammers home its full meaning:

There are only two ways in which a society can be held together. The one is by force and the other by free consent. If we want the latter, there must be a readiness of each party to pass beyond insistence on the full satisfaction of its own claims to the discovery of how that satisfaction can be combined with the satisfaction of other claims in a common higher good. If this is not achieved ... there can be no escape from chaos except in dictatorship. This respect for other points of view and concern for the good of the whole is at bottom a religious view; it has its roots in religious faith.[79]

It was a Russian refugee, Professor Fedorov in Paris, who saw the British Commonwealth as called to a leading role in the creation of a new world order: 'The radical transformation of the British State from the empire to the Commonwealth makes it particularly well prepared for understanding and undertaking a new international order ... The temptation of Great Britain is not to do too much but too little.'[80] The fall of France, which immediately followed, heightened this sense of world responsibility, leading at once to a statement in *CN-L* in July 1940 that the British Commonwealth of Nations now bore the brunt of the war to defend free institutions. Since it included 'most diverse races and peoples ... we have to use to the full the talent that has been given us'.[81]

Yet, right from the start, discussing 'Preliminaries to Peace Aims' in November 1939,[82] Oldham strikes a note of stark realism:

It is essential to remember how precarious is our hold on the values we are defending. We do not own them; they are the gifts of history and of grace. We are no more immune than others from succumbing to the temptation of power. We must see the world and ourselves as we really are. ... It is quite unreal to plan for an international order unless there is some body of commonly accepted ideas about the ends for which society exists. ... Our expectations of what may be immediately achieved must be modest. We are not yet ready to build a true international order; the foundations have yet to be dug. We must not evade this reality.

From the beginning of the war peace aims are at the forefront of concern. In 1941, church leaders, Catholic and Protestant, laid out in a letter to *The Times* five agreed peace principles, while the pope promulgated his own five points.[83] There was a remarkable convergence between these statements, as summarized in *CN-L*. They included the equal dignity of all, the solidarity for good or evil of all nations, recognition that the exercise of any kind of power, political or economic, must be co-extensive with responsibility and the right of every nation to independence, protection of minority rights, the abolition of extreme inequalities in wealth and equal educational opportunities for all. How far could such broad principles be applied in the chaotic situation envisaged in post-war Europe?

Already in August 1941, Oldham was writing a closely argued *CN-L* on the future of Germany within a changed Europe, which he based on several influential publications of the moment, including a PEP broadsheet.[84] These writings are astonishing at a time when the outcome of the conflict hung in the balance; they assume ultimate victory; they address themselves to fundamental questions of Europe's destiny; their diagnosis is prophetic. Oldham writes:

> To modern Europe, Germany is the great trouble-maker and destroyer of the peace; to modern Germany Europe is a collection of sham states, clinging to discredited economic theories and pretending to all sorts of social and democratic ideals which are only a cloak for narrow and corrupt ruling groups. ... There can be no hope of an enduring peace until this recurring conflict has been brought to an end by far-reaching changes both in Germany and the rest of Europe. ... Future world peace depends on finding a solution which the four great nations of Germany, Russia, Britain and America will be willing permanently to accept and actively to uphold.[85]

We get a glimpse here of a mentality which is light years away from any cheap triumphalism in victory. Oldham saw that, after victory, the first task for the Allies would be a massive one of relief work and 'carefully planned reconstruction of German institutions' as an essential part of European reconstruction. 'The thought of revenge should have no place.' In long-term policy, realism demanded effective control of German military power but 'each individual German must have the same opportunities and the same status as that of other Europeans'. Oldham specifically links this new style of wartime perspective with the Christian faith:

> These attitudes are not peculiar to Christianity but they are attitudes proper to Christians ... [Christians know that] only a renewal of our life by divine grace can deliver us from the corrupting influence of power and give us the courage, imagination and disinterestedness that are necessary for the gigantic task of establishing a new order in the world'.[86]

This is capped by a second prophetic broadsheet from PEP which is summarized with approval in *CN-L* on 7 January 1942:

> The world is moving inevitably to a new international distribution of

power. .... It is a question of effecting a revolutionary change in our whole outlook and way of life. .... What is desired is a Europe which all its citizens have a common interest in maintaining ... and in which all of them ... will come to feel a loyalty commensurate with their loyalty to their own country.[87]

From this mid-war perspective the PEP planners envisage a clear Anglo-Saxon leadership in this great new mission and Oldham sees this both as a call and as a danger: a call to throw off the lack of clear purpose and hesitancy of British foreign policy, but a danger because 'mission can be either divinely or demonically inspired'.[88]

As the final crisis of conflict inexorably approached, *CN-L* returned again and again to the weight of British responsibility in Europe: was there the moral stamina and political maturity to make right judgements? Michael Polanyi, cited in Supplement 197, warned against succumbing to the idea that nothing is real but power, maintaining that 'Nothing will grow from moral unbelief. The bolder our plans for the future, the deeper must they be rooted in the original ideas of our civilization' (i.e. 'the obligations of the moral law').[89] Contemplating 'The Road out of Chaos' in May 1944,[90] Oldham turns to a pamphlet by Macmurray, *Through Chaos to Community*: 'The real truth is that we are ourselves part of the ruin,' Macmurray writes, 'The desolation we see around us is the reflection of ourselves in the mirror of history.'[91] To apply a naïve and superficial idealism to the situation would be useless. A fundamental revolution in social habits was needed – and here Oldham refers again to William Temple's dictum that our crisis is cultural:[92]

> The cure is not to be sought in what the Church is at present principally doing, namely, insisting on ideals and in efforts to intensify the will to pursue them, but in the quite different direction of seeking to re-establish a unity between men's ultimate beliefs and habits and their conscious aims.[93]

In January 1945 *CN-L* carried the text of Bishop Bell's speech to the Lords on the previous 19 December. Speaking on the churches and European reconstruction, he stressed that 'the culture which all European people have in common' was the only lasting foundation for reconstruction.[94]

The post-war needs of Europe, described in graphic detail in *CN-L*, ranged from hunger and physical suffering to the 'spiritual vacuum' emphasized by Barbara Ward.[95] Reinhold Niebuhr believed that Britain might play a key part in relating Christian thought to the immediate problems of rebuilding community. He based this hope on his belief that the historical tradition there of fusing Christian faith and social reform might, at that moment of desolation, have something to give to Europe and the world.[96]

When on 6 August 1945, the nuclear horrors of Hiroshima changed the whole outlook, the cry which went up from the world was a Babel of confused voices. But a steady, Christian voice was soon raised, speaking in part through *CN-L.* How do Christians contemplate the possible destruction of civilization? 'The bomb is a symbol of the forces which science is putting into human hands', wrote Oldham.[97] Once again he gives us a highly rational and penetrating analysis of the positive and negative aspects of atomic power, yet he also writes 'We are living in apocalyptic times' and he quotes Bertrand Russell, speaking in the Lords: 'Can a scientific society continue to exist or must it inevitably destroy itself?'[98] It was this vast question which a commission on the era of atomic power, set up with commendable speed by the British Council of Churches, sought to address. Oldham chaired it and the whole subject was searchingly examined in the Moot,[99] and fully discussed in *CN-L.*[100] In the midst of all the contradictory arguments, two fundamental Christian principles emerged, like twin pillars for a new world. First, in the words of Oldham,[101] 'We have to offer an unending resistance to the forces making for dehumanisation, to re-establish the primacy of the human person and the relations between persons as the ultimate end of all human activities.' Secondly, there must be a 'recovery of a sense of the transcendent. Only if man is fundamentally related to what is beyond society has he the right and power to resist the absolutism of the totalitarian state.' This alone can be the true basis of a renewed democracy, supplying the conditions for 'subjecting power to the control of reason and justice'. All this adds up to a deep change of outlook: 'the human mind must jump'. It was in the same context of the atomic crisis that Niebuhr called for a new 'synthesis between the proximate and ultimate issues of life': 'Only a faith which understands both the historical and the eternal dimensions of life can guide men in this era, in which the fear of mutual destruction must prompt us to significant achievements in building a broader and more brotherly community.'[102] Fifty years on these truths still stand.

## Notes

1. Published by Dr J. H. Oldham for the Council of the Churches on the Christian Faith and the Common Life and issued from 20 Balcombe Street, Dorset Square, London NW1.

2. But note that in *CN-L*, L338, 25 May 1949, K. Bliss records: 'The proposal to start the *CN-L* took shape in conversations between Dr. Oldham, Archbishop Lang and Archbishop Temple in the first week of the second world war'.
3. There is no pagination in the *CN-L* until the later issues. All references here will be to number, Letter or Supplement and date.
4. The complete list of collaborators is as follows:

| | |
|---|---|
| The Archbishop of York | Sir Hector Hetherington |
| The Revd M. E. Aubrey | Professor H. A. Hodges |
| Professor John Baillie | Miss Eleanora Iredale |
| The Master of Balliol | Professor Karl Mannheim |
| Canon F. R. Barry | Principal N. Micklem |
| Dr S. M. Berry | The Revd T. R. Milford |
| Henry Brooke | Sir Walter Moberly |
| The Revd Henry Carter | J. Middleton Murry |
| Lord David Cecil | Professor Reinhold Niebuhr |
| J. T. Christie | Walter Oakeshott |
| Professor F. Clarke | Dr William Paton |
| Dr J. Hutchinson Cockburn | Miss Margaret Popham |
| Canon F. A. Cockin | Canon O. C. Quick |
| Dr A. C. Craig | Miss Dorothy Sayers |
| Christopher Dawson | The Revd Gilbert Shaw |
| Sir Wyndham Deedes | The Bishop of Sheffield |
| The Revd V. A. Demant | Mrs Mary Stocks |
| Professor C. H. Dodd | Professor Norman Sykes |
| T. S. Eliot | Arnold Toynbee |
| Professor H. H. Farmer | Professor R. H. Tawney |
| Professor O. S. Franks | The Revd A. R. Vidler |
| The Revd W. D. L. Greer | President J. S. Whale |
| Kurt Hahn | The Bishop of Winchester |
| Viscount Hambledon | Sir Alfred Zimmern |

5. *CN-L*, L170, 27 Jan. 1943. In the first number Oldham also listed the main topics the *CN-L* intended to cover: 'the religious meaning of the experience through which we are passing; moral and social problems created by the war; the outlook and problems of youth; the illumination of present events by the lessons of history; constructive efforts which are helping to create a new order; the Church universal; encroachments on religious and civil liberties; motives and principles which make for a just and enduring peace'.
6. *CN-L*, L4, 22 Nov. 1939, where an enlarged list of collaborators is given, numbering 52.
7. *CN-L*, L15, 7 Feb. 1940, where a correspondent reports that it quite frequently finds its way to the village pub, where it is invariably listened to with respect.
8. *CN-L*, L26, 24 Apr. 1940: Oldham notes that the *CN-L* 'has now spread to almost all parts of the world; we have members in 38 countries' (list given). 900 copies went abroad each week.
9. *CN-L*, L247, 14 Nov. 1945.
10. *CN-L*, L341, 6 July 1949.
11. Two general surveys of the *CN-L* history and impact appeared in L234, 16 May 1945, and in the final number L341, 6 July 1949.
12. *The New Christian*, edited by Trevor Beeson and published between 1965 and 1970, perhaps comes closest to it.
13. *CN-L*, S.L1, 1 Nov. 1939.

14. *CN-L*, S11, 10 Jan. 1940.
15. *CN-L*, L12, 17 Jan. 1940.
16. *CN-L*, S15, 7 Feb. 1940.
17. *CN-L*, S16, 14 Feb. 1940, entitled 'Wrong Answers to Unanswered Problems'.
18. *CN-L*, S53, 30 Oct. 1940.
19. *CN-L*, S323, 27 Oct. 1948.
20. This was inaugurated at Amsterdam, starting on 23 Aug. 1948.
21. Barth replied in *CN-L*, S326, 8 Dec. 1948: 'A Preliminary Reply to Dr Reinhold Niebuhr'; Niebuhr returned to the issue in S332, 2 Mar. 1949 in 'An Answer to Karl Barth'.
22. *CN-L*, S325, 24 Nov. 1948. The British Council of Churches' report on 'The Era of Atomic Power', published in May 1946, was sent to all church headquarters and other organizations for consideration. See p. 42 for discussions on it.
23. *CN-L*, L96 27 Aug. 1941. Temple himself sought to fill this gap in his *Christianity and Social Order* (Penguin, 1942).
24. *CN-L*, L43, 21 Aug. 1940.
25. *CN-L*, S88, 1 July 1941, the first part of a paper in two parts on 'The Predicament of Society and the Way Out'.
26. *CN-L*, S2, 8 Nov. 1939.
27. *CN-L*, L2, 8 Nov. 1939.
28. *CN-L*, L&S14, 31 Jan. 1940: 'Educating for a Free Society'.
29. *CN-L*, S42, 21 Aug. 1940.
30. *CN-L*, S39, 24 July 1940: 'An Effective Approach to Social Change'.
31. *CN-L*, S14, 31 Jan. 1940.
32. *CN-L*, S201, 8 Feb. 1944. Lionel Curtis: at that time a fellow of All Souls, author of *Civitas Dei*, a blue print for the future.
33. *CN-L*, S18, 28 Feb. 1940. See above, pp. 26–8, for relevant discussions.
34. J. Middleton Murry, *The Price of Leadership* (SCM, 1939), pp. 132, 134.
35. *CN-L*, S274, 27 Nov. 1946.
36. *CN-L*, S280, 5 Mar. 1947.
37. *CN-L*, S284, 30 Apr. 1947.
38. *CN-L*, S198, 29 Dec. 1943. Written not long before his death, this supplement of Temple's was much in demand, much discussed and within a short time issued as a pamphlet by the SCM Press.
39. The extent to which the Buber philosophy had penetrated Christian thinking is apparent here in the fact that Temple can use its language without directly citing either Buber or Macmurray.
40. *CN-L*, S257, 3 Apr. 1946 'The Incompetence of Unaided Virtue or the Mischief of Ideals'.
41. *CN-L*, L203, 8 Mar. 1944.
42. See also *CN-L*, S24, 17 Apr. 1940.
43. *CN-L*, S92, 30 July 1941.
44. *CN-L*, L226, 24 Jan. 1945.
45. *CN-L*, S90, 16 July 1941.
46. *CN-L*, S112, 17 Dec. 1941.
47. In a pamphlet, *Challenge to the Churches* (Kegan Paul, 1941), Macmurray argues that institutions are instruments only for the purpose of serving societies: 'Democracy is, first and foremost, not a political but a social conviction' (p. 9).
48. *CN-L* S281, 19 Mar. 1947.
49. All the following quotations are from Oldham unless otherwise stated.
50. *CN-L*, L108, 19 Nov. 1941.

51. *CN-L*, L94, 13 Aug. 1941.
52. *CN-L*, L14, 31 Jan. 1940.
53. *CN-L*, L72, 12 Mar. 1941.
54. *CN-L*, L14, 31 Jan. 1940.
55. *CN-L*, S14, 31 Jan. 1940, 'Educating for a Free Society'.
56. *CN-L*, L125, 18 Mar. 1942.
57. A visitor from the USA commented in *New Era*, 24/7 (July/Aug. 1943) on the widespread interest in educational issues: 'The number of groups for whom the Ministry of Information supplies speakers is much greater, in proportion, than in the USA. The interest of the "common man" in education is exceptional. Education is the second major interest in army discussions.'
58. *CN-L*, L41, 7 Aug. 1940.
59. *CN-L*, S215, 23 Aug. 1944, 'Education and the Social Order'.
60. *CN-L*, L146, 12 Aug. 1942. Though the education of girls was not ignored, the main focus of the discussions in the *CN-L* was on young males, according to the assumptions of the time.
61. South Wales Council of Social Service, *The Young Adult in South Wales* (1941), the result of a study commissioned in three areas of the UK by the Carnegie United Kingdom Trust in 1936. Its findings were similar to those of the report published in 1938, *Men Without Work*, instigated by a committee which included William Temple, Joe Oldham and A. D. Lindsay, in the research for and writing of which Walter Oakeshott played a major role.
62. *CN-L*, L136, 3 June 1942.
63. *CN-L*, S47, 18 Sept. 1940, 'Youth, the War and the Future'.
64. *CN-L*, S265, 24 July 1946, 'The Education of Young Workers in Industry'.
65. *CN-L*, L97, 3 Sept. 1941.
66. *CN-L*, S200, 26 Jan. 1944.
67. *CN-L*, L169, 20 Jan. 1943.
68. *CN-L*, L5, 29 Nov. 1939.
69. *CN-L*, S28, 8 May 1940.
70. *CN-L*, S33, 12 June 1940: G. Fedorov, 'A Russian Voice'.
71. *CN-L*, L139, June 1942; S84, 4 June 1941; S118, 28 Jan. 1942.
72. *CN-L*, S19, 6 Mar. 1940; L8, 20 Dec. 1939.
73. *CN-L*, S10, 3 Jan. 1940.
74. *CN-L*, L86, 18 June 1941. Representatives came from Greek, Romanian, Armenian, Russian, Danish, Dutch, Finnish, French Protestant, German, Norwegian, Swedish, Swiss, Czechoslovakian, Moravian and W. African churches.
75. *CN-L*, L72, 12 Mar. 1941.
76. *CN-L*, L19, 6 Mar. 1940.
77. *CN-L*, L54, 6 Nov. 1940.
78. *CN-L*, S98, 10 Sept. 1941.
79. *CN-L*, L126, 25 Mar. 1942; L130, 22 Apr. 1942.
80. *CN-L*, L33, 12 June 1940.
81. *CN-L*, L36, 3 July 1940.
82. *CN-L*, L&S5, 29 Nov. 1939.
83. *CN-L*, S68, 12 Feb. 1941.
84. *CN-L*, L95, 20 Aug. 1941. Oldham cites besides the PEP broadsheet, E. H. Carr, *The Future of Nations* (Kegan Paul, 1941); S. King-Hall, *Total Victory* (Faber 1941); T. H. Minshell, *What to do with Germany* (Allen & Unwin, 1941).
85. *CN-L*, L95, 20 Aug. 1941.

86. Ibid.
87. *CN-L*, L115, 7 Jan. 1942.
88. Ibid.
89. *CN-L*, S197, 15 Dec. 1943. This is a summary of Polanyi's article, 'The English and the Continent', *Political Quarterly* (Oct–Dec. 1943).
90. *CN-L*, L209, 31 May 1944.
91. J. Macmurray, *Through Chaos to Community* (published by the National Peace Council, 144 Southampton Row, London WC1).
92. See above, p. 62.
93. *CN-L*, L209, 31 May 1944.
94. *CN-L*, L225, 10 Jan. 1945.
95. *CN-L*, S240, 8 Aug. 1945.
96. *CN-L*, S246, 31 Oct. 1945.
97. *CN-L*, L251, 9 Jan. 1946.
98. Ibid.
99. See above, p. 42.
100. *CN-L*, L260, 15 May 1946.
101. Ibid. Oldham wrote the summary of the Commission's report in *CN-L*.
102. *CN-L*, S246, 31 Oct. 1945: 'The Religious Level of the World Crisis'.

## Chapter 4

# Outside Ecclesiastical Organization: The Christian Frontier Council

Daniel Jenkins and Marjorie Reeves

## Origins and Development: 'Tunnelling from the Other End'*

In September 1942 the British Council of Churches – born out of the 1937 Oxford Conference – met for the first time under William Temple's chairmanship. On 7 October 1942 Sir Walter Moberly introduced to *CN-L* readers a new auxiliary Christian undertaking, 'under lay direction and concerned with Christian action in the sphere of secular life'.[1] Moberly saw it as a freer and more unofficial body than the BCC.

> When it is desired to bridge over a chasm or to tunnel under a hill it is usual to start from both ends at once. The Council of Churches, consisting mainly of Church leaders and officers, starts naturally from the side of institutional religion. ... But there is need also of a body tunnelling, as it were, from the other end, and consisting of persons who, while having a Christian outlook, are themselves mainly engaged in practical affairs.[2]

The name chosen for the new body used a second metaphor. 'The Frontier' was 'the borderland between the normal work of the church and the general life of society'.[3] Its members, on average between 20 and 30 in number, drawn from the spheres of politics, commerce and industry, the labour world, the professions and so on, were people who held positions of key responsibility in British public

* This section is by Marjorie Reeves.

life. In spite of the pressure of their many other duties, most of them gave the monthly Frontier meetings a high measure of priority. Subgroups on special aspects met separately. At the outset the Council defined its functions thus:

(i)   To create opportunities outside the sphere of organized religion for the discussion of Christian beliefs, standards and practice, and their application to current problems;

(ii)  To examine the nature of the forces working in modern society ... and to endeavour to direct them towards a more Christian order;

(iii) To understand the efforts being made by various groups to influence these forces, and to cooperate with those ... which are contributing towards Christian ends.[4]

In Moberly's description of how the Council functioned we trace, once again, the mark of Oldham's characteristic method:

Those concerned with a particular field meet, sometimes as two or three who have a meal together, sometimes for an evening as a somewhat larger party including other persons with special qualifications, but always with the object of producing results which would rouse respect through their quality.[5]

The fellowship of friends fuelled their intellectual energy, while a draft paper by one of their number usually provided an expert base for their deliberations. Moberly lists the subjects they were then tackling as those which 'seem the most immediately urgent: the needs of youth; problems of local communities; the public attitude to politics; human relations in industry; problems of business management; the planning of industry; the profit motive'.[6] What an agenda! From the first the *CN-L* editors and the members of the Frontier saw themselves as interdependent: the *CN-L* relied on the Frontier to supply expert material; the Frontier used the *CN-L* as a major channel for publicity. In March 1943 a Frontier discussion on the Beveridge Report resulted in a *CN-L* supplement by Oldham which gives a vivid impression of its reception. Oldham notes the amazing world-wide interest and how Archbishop Lang had said in the Lords that 'he could remember no occasion on which the conviction and feelings of the masses of our people were more united'.[7] But Oldham also remarks shrewdly that the government was dragging its feet. Analysis comes under three heads.[8] First, 'Are we prepared to abolish Want?', that is, to give priority to insurance against want over individual claims to wealth in excess of reasonable requirements. Here he makes the sharp point that a debt of honour was owed to those from whom at the very moment unlimited sacrifice was being demanded. Secondly, on the 'Technical Means', he takes the typical Frontier position that, though Christians as such cannot make scientific judgements, they can insist that they receive 'a disinterested answer in the light of the best expert knowledge'. Analysing, thirdly, the 'Background of Social Philosophy', he counters the fear of undermining 'sturdy independence' with the words of Lord Samuel in the Lords' debate that 'nothing hinders self-reliance more than undeserved destitution and insecurity'. The more serious issue, to Frontier members, was that Beveridge only dealt with economic factors, whereas people need 'not only to be free from want, but also to be occupied in useful and significant work, if their moral nature is to be satisfied'.[9] Christians must give the Beveridge Report 'active and discriminating support' but in the end, Oldham expresses the basic issue in the question: 'Can Christian faith in the purpose of God for human life give to men the understanding, courage and hope which will enable them to tame and master the Leviathan of modern industrial civilization and create out of it a true social order?'

In 1943 a section of the Frontier Council, described in the *CN-L* as 'all connected in one way or another with industry and all young' had presented their first findings in a supplement[10] entitled 'Responsibility and the Economic System'. Characteristically, this was devoted to a close analysis of existing conditions, putting forward at this stage no specific suggestion for reform. While recognizing frankly that people felt they were conditioned by economic forces beyond their control, it laid down the principle that for Christians the proper end of economic power was to serve the needs of the consumer, and then argued that in fact economic power was at present used irresponsibly and therefore the case for Christians to devote their attention to economic responsibility was overwhelming.

Part II of this inquiry[11] pressed home the point that, if a unit producing goods or services is not meeting a real need, 'then that part of industry had no right to exist'. The paper then focused on a detailed examination of the role of civil government in relation to the economic system. The analysis is frankly realistic but nevertheless leads to the statement of an ideal principle which certainly judges much practice then and now: 'The supreme good for the public administrator ... is *objective equity* (cf. the Book of Common Prayer, the prayer that those who are put in authority by the Crown "may truly and *indifferently* administer justice".' But whether or not public regulators act equitably, the discussion reaches a conclusion which hints at the necessity of radical change in the trading units themselves. Everything depends on whether their aims 'are substantially in line with the interests of society as a whole'; 'economic responsibility, especially responsibility to consumers, cannot be restored by ... increase in government control while leaving the structures of trading units unchanged'.

In the immediate post-war situation, political elections in the United Kingdom and on the continent highlighted the impact of left-wing politics and the urgent need to think out the Christian position in the political scene. Here the Frontier group on politics came into play with a series of three supplements published in *CN-L*. The first, 'Christians in Politics', appeared in June 1946.[12] It took the stance that the presuppositions of both 'conservatism' and 'radicalism' needed searching re-examination in order to restore 'a true dialectic based on the recognition that both are necessary to fruitful political development'. Yet the Christian perspective recognizes the relativity of party divisions. Because there is a truth which transcends them, party contest cannot be no-holds-barred and on occasion both will be called to unite against a common evil. A Christian party member must exercise a longer perspective and a critical sense. In their second supplement,[13] 'Christian Influence in Politics', the group starts from the principle that there is a Christian interest involved in trying to make democracy work, and asks how ordinary Christians can best practise this: by conference resolutions, letters to the paper, pressure groups, etc.? Perhaps, but the group argues that Christian activity in politics has to find a new form which is not yet clear.[14] The third paper[15] deals with the temptations of a politician. To achieve anything practical, it seems, a politician has to persuade his fellows that he is the right person with the right answers. A long and penetrating discussion follows which, drawing on Croce's *Politics and Morals*, leads to three concluding points: (i) Christian politicians must be aware of the corrupting power of unconscious bias; (ii) they must never be without a consciousness of the fallibility of their own judgement as sinful men; (iii) but equally they 'will not recoil from difficulty and costly decisions' while deeply aware that 'the only thing which makes it possible to act responsibly ... in a world in which the consequences of our actions are hidden from us ... is a firm belief in the ... over-ruling providence of God'.

A progress report in *CN-L* in 1945 emphasized that, as they entered the post-war era, it was vital for the joint enterprise of Frontier and *CN-L* 'to be fed by a continuous stream of information and knowledge from those in constant touch with different spheres of human activity'.[16] It was at this point that Daniel Jenkins became the secretary of the Frontier Council and Donald Mackinnon (philosophy fellow at Keble College, Oxford) was recruited as a part-time researcher, with a particular focus on a critical examination of 'the presuppositions present in Christian attitudes to secular society' and 'the ideas and forces which determine the character of modern society'.[17] Thus the energies of the Frontier in this post-war period turned, to a considerable extent, towards the challenges of industrial society. The *CN-L* letter for 22 January 1947 widened the idea of 'frontier' to embrace all Christians under pressure from secular forces:

> Outside the boundaries of the institutional Church, pressing up against the walls of every building specifically devoted to Christian purposes, lies the everyday secular world. Every Christian lives on the Frontier and must discover his obedience in his work and political purposes.[18]

'We lack guidance', said Kathleen Bliss, 'on how to meet the challenges of the workplace.' The BBC had found it difficult to arrange a series on 'My Faith and My Job' because so few Christians had a clearly held position on which they could base action at work. 'Many believe their Christian duty stops if they abstain from obvious bad habits at work.' She made the illuminating observation that 'the Church has never fully accepted an industrial society or believed that God was at work as effectively in history since the industrial revolution as he was before'. But, citing Niebuhr's view, she concluded that the Christian obedience of the layman was that of 'realizing the potential of modern society' rather than 'drawing in his skirts from certain defilements'. 'Christians must work for *koinonia* in an industrial society.'[19]

In the supplement to this number T. M. Heron, an industrialist who was a keen member of the Frontier, wrote on 'Incentives to Work', concluding that 'the task before this age is that of retaining the benefits of contract while regaining those of "status" which the industrial revolution in its exuberance threw away'.[20] These supplements were widely distributed, both through the *CN-L* membership and as separate leaflets. There was a strong concentration of concern in the post-war period about the Christian position on the frontiers of power in the areas of both economics and politics, with a constant affirmation that 'the frontier', with all its moral tensions and ambiguities, was precisely where Christians must be. (Sadly, further records on these aspects of the Frontier's thinking have not come to light.)

A group of Christian doctors, including some Roman Catholics, met together for three years, from 1945 until 1948 (during which time the National Health Service was established), to seek broad agreement on the ways in which the Christian doctrine of human nature affects the work of a doctor. Amid rapidly advancing knowledge and the development of new techniques, as well as the new role of the state in medicine, ethical problems had a renewed urgency. It was the theologian in the group, Daniel Jenkins, who prepared for publication the results of their deliberations in *The Doctor's Profession* (SCM, 1949), emphasizing throughout the crucial importance of recognizing every patient as a *person* in the sight of God, and the responsibility of the Christian doctor to bring the insights of his faith to bear on professional ethical problems. This received considerable publicity: *The Lancet* printed five long extracts which provoked a three-month-long correspondence.

The educational work of the Council developed in several directions. One Frontier group, led by Moberly, set out to consider whether or how higher education could direct students towards a theological critique of social order. Later this project was merged with a similar SCM enquiry. The final section of this chapter, 'Young People and Work', records the thinking of another group engaged with the problem of the translation from school to work.

More broadly, the general question of how 'the educated' relate to 'the masses' in a rapidly changing society was brought to a focus in a group led by Daniel Jenkins, greatly helped by a grant from the Nuffield Foundation. A long series of discussions issued in the publication in 1961 of *Equality and Excellence*. This prompted the foundation to agree readily to support a second volume, *The Educated Society*,[21] which examined some of the wider issues arising from the massive expansion of higher education already taking place in Britain. In the next section Dr Jenkins reflects on the thinking in these two books in the light of today's further expansion and its problems.

In one of the last numbers of *CN-L*[22] a final report on the Frontier Council and its ongoing work appeared. This emphasized again the importance attached to its lay composition, small size (30), ecumenical outlook and focus on concrete problems, not abstract principles. Throughout its life the Christian Frontier Council explored, through specialist groups, and through its publications, a wide range of issues. A new Christian Frontier today might well find its main contribution lay in bringing together a range of 'single-issue' concerns for examination in a broader frame of the total human experience. The future of Britain-in-Europe cries out for fresh Christian thinking set in relation to its converse, small-scale democratic initiatives within Britain itself. The enormous implications of technological expansion for mobility of people, for barrier-breaking and for standardization of behaviour patterns needs to be examined from an overall perspective of social democracy. Has there yet been any theological analysis of issues raised by the use of computers and the Internet? Why do we allow the pressures and stresses of a market-driven economy to dominate our 'quality of living', or, conversely, destroy the dignity and motivation of the work-less? Are there theological reasons for championing both parliamentary democracy and the reactivation of local initiatives (the principle of subsidiarity)? Does not the present obsession with scientific power over human life and death call for a reaffirmation of the priority of human relationships within community?

## The Educated Society*

### Equality and Excellence

Returning to *Equality and Excellence* and *The Educated Society* a generation and a half later has been an interesting and salutary experience. I can perhaps claim to have a slight measure of detachment in making any observations, whether positive or negative, because, although they no doubt bear my personal stamp, both books were primarily the fruits of frequent and sustained discussion by members of the Frontier Council. Drafts were constantly scrutinized and determined efforts were made to consult outside people directly involved in particular aspects, while many commission and committee reports were used. The special mark of our two books was that they made a conscious effort to deal with matters which were too often considered in isolation from each other and to seek points of mutual illumination even where the issues involved were controversial. The distinctiveness of this approach was particularly evident in the first book where political differences were at their sharpest. During the war and, despite the break-up of the coalition government, for several years afterwards, Britain enjoyed an unparalleled degree of social solidarity but by the late 1950s and into the 1960s political, economic, social and generational differences were becoming more pronounced. True, it was still widely felt that the communal gains of the previous 20 years – with the virtual elimination of primary poverty, the establishment of the National Health Service and a larger degree of co-operation between the various parts of the educational system – should be preserved.

* This section is by Daniel Jenkins.

The experience we had lived through had given us a greater degree of social equality than ever before in our history but, as the constraints of the war years and their aftermath were gradually removed, it became increasingly clear that part of the price paid was the prevalence of a bland and colourless uniformity. The Festival of Britain lit a flickering lively imagination in 1951 about the future but it was not sustained for long, witness the singularly uninspiring architecture in the rebuilding of this period. Equality had made progress but had it been achieved at the expense of a decline in the pursuit of excellence? Were the two incompatible, as so many of the children of privilege had always alleged? These questions prompted the study which produced our book, *Equality and Excellence*.[23]

There were two reasons why the Frontier Council was particularly apt for this enquiry. First, it was not tied to any political party and it cut across denominational and social class divisions. Secondly, as a Christian organization largely composed of lay people, we regarded ourselves as heirs to the thinking of two of the few people who had tackled the problem in the pre-war period: R. H. Tawney, author of the classic *Equality*,[24] and A. D. Lindsay, who in *The Modern Democratic State*[25] made the then challenging statement that democracy itself demands an 'express insistence', not on equality, but on quality.

The book started from the insistence that the root of the most creative awareness of our common human equality lies in the Christian acknowledgement that we are all God's children and that any special vocation which might carry particular responsibility and privilege takes place within the whole range of personal relationships. Privilege cannot be claimed as of right: 'To understand fundamental equality means recognising something ultimate in one's neighbour which he shares equally with oneself and which gives him inviolable personal standing and dignity ...'[26] This great truth is built into the fabric of creation for it is recognized by Christian and non-Christian alike. Jacques Maritain, as a Thomist, sees

> the equality in nature among men in their concrete communion ... it does not lie in an idea, it is hidden in the heart of the individual. ... If you treat a man as a man ... to that extent you make effective in yourself his closeness in nature and his equality or unity in nature with yourself.[27]

Karl Mannheim declares 'all embody the same ontological principle of humanness'.[28] Walter Lippmann emphasizes that inequality of gifts make no difference:

> There you are, sir, and there is your neighbour. ... By any and every test of intelligence, virtue, usefulness, you are demonstrably a better man than he, and yet ... these differences do not matter, for the best part of him is untouchable and incomparable and unique and universal ...[29]

One of the main theses of our book was that – contrary to many opinions – equality and excellence should not be seen as necessarily in conflict with each other:

> although there are various superficial tensions which arise between equality and excellence, it is ultimately only those who believe in and try to express fundamental equality who can create the best conditions in which the most important kinds of excellence can be achieved.[30]

Equality *demands* the pursuit of excellence for its realization and vice versa. How is this so? First because

> to hold communion with one's fellowman means that one should make it easy for him to give the best of himself by offering him the best of oneself. This does not, of course, imply that we are both to aspire to the same kind of excellence nor that we necessarily achieve similar degrees of excellence. That would be to deny the unique way in which we are equal. It does mean that we recognise our common obligations to contribute our best gifts for the ... enrichment of each other and the whole community.[31]

Secondly, excellence of a high order flourishes where there is concern for the realization of the potential in everyone. (This can be expressed as a paradox that the pursuit of excellence for the few requires pursuit of excellence for all.)

> The artistic genius, the prophetic religious leader, the scientific discoverer, the industrial innovator, is generally a single individual. ... But this individual can very rarely operate without a tradition upon which he builds and a lively community to which he can offer his work in the hope that it will ultimately find it to be valuable. The stronger the tradition and the more developed the community, the greater his achievement is likely to be.[32]

Unless the creative interaction between equality and excellence is vigorous there is a strong temptation in society to settle for mediocrity.

> Lazy egalitarianism without a strong sense of community responsibility based on fundamental equality and without standards of excellence produces a Subutopia of the mind and spirit as well as of physical setting. ... All kinds of excellence are not open to everyone but because

all are equally called to follow 'the more excellent way' of love, each individual and group must cherish their own excellence in relation to others and for the sake of the whole.[33]

Insisting that the varieties of gifts embraced not only those wealthy through finance, heritage and social position but also the intellectually, artistically and religiously 'wealthy', we claimed that any 'gift' was misused unless it was held as a trust for the sake of all. We explored the implications of this as specifically as possible in industry and the professions.

## The Educated Society

*The Educated Society*[34] was a development of some parts of *Equality and Excellence*. We had already received notice of the great expansion of formal education, especially in its higher stages, which was already taking place in the most technologically advanced countries. This raised wider social issues than those immediately obvious in the world of education itself. Peter Drucker, himself a person of Christian conviction, had announced about a generation earlier that we were entering the era of what he called 'the Educated Society'.[35] Britain had already shown awareness of this by a move surprisingly dramatic in so conservative a society, especially in its academic enclaves: the establishment of a whole cluster of new universities. These were, in fact not so much the creation of the 1960s when they actually started, but of the planning and preparation of the 1950s, an underrated period of discriminating reflection before the noisy demonstrations of the 'swinging sixties'. The fact that so many prominent academic figures, secure in their professional status, moved so readily into these entirely new institutions, using the opportunity to change curricula and redefine relations between subjects, was refreshing evidence of their vitality. On the other hand, the rapidity with which new universities were started distracted attention from the wider social implications of their development. As the solitary part-time executive officer of the Frontier Council I myself moved into the first of these new creations at Sussex. This had obvious advantages, not least in the happy chance that two leading American students of educational policy, David Riesman and Martin Trow,[36] chose to spend sabbatical years at Sussex and were actively interested in our enterprise. But the change meant that the main body of Frontier members could not be as directly involved in the second book as in the first.

Within this context of expansion the book was focused on certain fundamental issues which still receive remarkably little examination, whether within or without the academic community. It began by underlining the reasons for academic expansion and how this was creating a new relation between the academic community and the wider society. It claimed that 'the most fundamental reason for educational expansion on all fronts remains that, unless it takes place, the technically-dominated industrial society which had made it possible will become corrupt and self-destructive'.[37] Modern culture, largely based on a common technology involving rapid mobility and unparalleled ease of communication on many levels, had to be a common culture. In this situation relations between the highly educated and the rest of the community became more complex and more crucial than ever before. The issue of power was obvious:

> We all know that great power can be easily misused if our wills are evil, with far more terrifying consequences than in pre-technological ages. What is not so obvious but, in the long run, hardly less serious, is that technology and industrial organisations have built into them tendencies towards simplification, standardisation and centralization of control which need to be carefully handled if they are not to become even more destructive of the life of society than conscious evil.[38]

We asked a question rarely considered in a wide enough setting: Was the expanded academic community in itself equipped to be a school of maturity in this kind of society?

The second section of the book, 'Educational Privilege and Social Cohesion', asserted that 'Modern culture must be a common culture' and discussed *inter alia* the use of power by the educated. This was followed by sections on 'The Academic Community as a School of Maturity' and 'The Sources of Intellectual Vitality'. The principles underlying these detailed discussions can be summarized in two short extracts:

> In A. D. Lindsay's words, democracy of our kind needs an 'express insistence upon quality and distinction', and it is not a healthy democracy unless this insistence finds expression in every part of the community's life and not merely in that of a privileged minority ... those who are the custodians and exemplars of high culture must see themselves as trustees for society as a whole ... they must enter the Educated Society with a will, because – and this is a part of the core of the argument of this book – the idea of this society does not make sense unless its members believe that a substantial degree of common culture ... provides the best soil in which the fruits of excellence can grow. .... It

is from the popular culture that most exponents of high culture emerge, especially in these days of great social mobility.[39]

The common-sense, the respect for traditional patterns of living, the unpretentious functionalism, the simplicity, the staying power and the distrust of an unrooted cleverness, which good people who do not have an intellectual vocation display, are the necessary counterweights to the virtues of the academic community, and both are essential if the community is to find its right balance.[40]

The educational expansion which had prompted the book turned out to be even greater than we had envisaged. In one later development we could claim to have had some small part, for during the planning of the Open University we were in touch with Harold Wilson and others involved in its inception. On the other hand, with hindsight, we ought to have pointed up more emphatically the consequences of the general encouragement given to young people to leave their homes and follow academic education in almost self-subsistent communities of their own peers. This might fulfil a natural desire of the young but it did nothing to promote the general communal renewal for which we hoped, either in the new educational institutions themselves or in those communities which had been passed over as possible sites. Few attempts have been made to consider either the impact on old established communities of these superimposed new communities or the degree of social impoverishment suffered by those places suddenly bereft of their ablest young people. Our vision of an educated society in which 'high' culture could be rooted in 'common' culture has vanished, leaving much of the power in present-day society in the hands of what Frank Musgrove has called the 'migratory élite'.

## The need for a new Christian Frontier today?

Rereading these two books highlights how little public discussion has taken place either on the questions we raised or the great changes themselves. The only issues which have commanded attention are those in which specific interests are involved, such as relations between state and church schools, independent and state schools, ancient and modern universities and so on. One might have expected that the scale of change would precipitate a much livelier debate. Even more, one would have thought that the sudden transformation of polytechnics into universities in the mid-1990s would have created an uproar of public debate, but it appears to have taken place with hardly any public discussion. Does this not affect the whole idea of what constitutes a university and were polytechnics in particular so uncertain of their distinctive functions and, in many cases, their distinguished history, that they could accept their transformation so easily?

An important factor in this apparently uncritical attitude lies in the very experience of expansion. Institutions have been so busy growing that they have little time for reflection. Yet universities, in particular, exist partly to foster self-criticism. They should be asking themselves whether all the growth over two generations has yet produced much by way of improvement in the quality of general culture, whether in literary creation, scientific discovery, political maturity, economic efficiency or humanely civilized behaviour. It is, perhaps, too early to gauge what is happening to common culture. One positive indicator is that, in spite of prognostications that 'the era of the book is over', bookshops in Britain have never been so numerous or so prosperous. This may be a hint that, since most creative new developments tend to be unobtrusive in their early stages, more may be stirring than is yet obvious. Yet so many signs, including the degradation of the mass media, point the other way. Modern Britain might be more accurately described as the mis- or sub-educated society than the kind of society Drucker envisaged.

It could be claimed that *The Educated Society* proved uncomfortably pertinent in its analysis. The *Durham Journal* went out of its way to produce three reviews in the same number. Two were from professors of education and were merely critical and defensive, apparently resenting that people with wider interests should trespass in their field. The third however, by the editor, Professor Roger Sharrock, implied that the two other reviews had missed the point and that the book had raised issues which needed extended discussion in the academic community itself. He might have put the point more strongly if he had lived to see the transformations effected by government diktat, with little regard for processes of consultation or academic autonomy.

The Christian community itself has responded to the challenge but too narrowly. The various social responsibility departments of the denominations are active. The churches have contributed constructively in such spheres as inner-city poverty, family breakdown and social deprivation. Christian groups in schools, colleges and universities, however, have tended to narrow their range and although there are more church-appointed chaplains in higher education than ever before, too often they appear not to be tackling the relationship between theology and social order in any systematic way. Yet it is surely crucial that the next generation of the highly educated should reflect on the institutions which educated them, the pluses and minuses of a high-technology culture and their own future roles in society. What is missing is a strong lay membership of a body such as the Frontier Council, composed of independent people who bring their own expertise and experience of responsibility in the secular institutions of society to bear on the fundamental causes of fragmentation in the common life. This fracture of cultures calls for a more holistic effort, an attempt to go to the spiritual and psychological roots of our malaise. This needs the concerted thought and action of all those in public life who are acutely aware of the situation. There are already many separate signals of a desire to build a human-scale common culture. A new type of Frontier Council, gathering together Christians and humanists, lay professionals and grass-roots leaders, the experts and the wise, would cut across party divisions of all kinds. It could work by dialogue rather than by confrontation in exploring new possibilities for activating social cohesion by pursuing excellence on the basis of equality.

## Young People and Work*

The sharpest focus of tension between the community and the growing young person lies at the point of work: the demand for well-honed instruments to serve the economy on the one hand; the demand for a satisfying role in society on the other. The unattainable ideal towards which we aim must be a fruitful balance, for each contributes to the other. Today a major concern is the moral apathy which causes adolescents and young adults to opt out of any commitment to purposes beyond their immediate desires. Strangely, the echoes of a similar concern can be heard even in 1943 in the midst of 'united' war effort. An article in the *New Era*, began:

> Most people are agreed that the most challenging fact about education is that we have been bringing up a generation of young people whose characteristic mood is apathy. They are unwilling or unable to commit themselves to any belief that is a basis for action, to embrace any long-term purpose with emotional zeal.[41]

The article conceded that the war had provided short-term purpose

* This section is by Marjorie Reeves.

93

but the irony of a situation in which a community at war alone could provide adequate motivation was not lost. The bitter truth was that peacetime community purposes had been eroded to the point of collapse. Fred Clarke wrote of the 'disintegrating and inharmonious society' in which so many of the young were growing up. 'Rich purposes are born out of ordered, harmonious experience, where life is all of a piece; they gather up and bring to a focal point all the manifold meanings of life.'[42]

So where was the focal point in education at the stage of transition and how should we seek to organize the experience of the young as they reach the end of schooling? Where was the most fruitful locus in which the realization of one's own worth in society could develop? The answer given was 'at work'. It must be remembered that this was the period when the raising of the school-leaving age, first to 15 and ultimately to 16, was being furiously debated in every educational forum. Whatever the view on the point at which education in the protected environment of the school ought to give way to education in the real adult world, most of us were convinced that what happened after schooling was crucially important for the making of a person. At the same time we were aware that, for the majority of adolescents leaving school at 14 or 15, education 'on the job' could be a cruel farce in the huge industrial workplace of those days, where the only experience was that of feeding the Great Machine, hour by hour and day by day – feeding it with articles of whose origin you knew little and for whose destination you cared less, feeding it for no discernible reason except that you got a meagre pay-packet thereby.

The nation's shame in its neglect of its adolescents was a theme passionately pursued in the *CN-L* right from its first number when 'the outlook and problems of youth' appeared as one of its eight major concerns.[43] In his latest book, *New World Order*, H. G. Wells had pointed to 'frustrated young people' as a major source of world unrest.[44] Oldham commented that a surplus of young men for whom life in existing societies had ceased to have any rational meaning had fostered the growth of the Nazi movement. The phenomenon was not confined to Germany:

> these dammed up and balked energies are a force capable of disrupting every social order. The only means of averting an internal explosion is to find a satisfying life and rewarding employment for this mass of youth which for the most part is without any real aim in life.[45]

But it was not the *danger*, so much as the *waste* in this situation that Oldham brought again and again before the Christian conscience. In September 1940, presenting a supplement, 'Youth, the War and the Future',[46] he says (even while expecting invasion) 'We must find the spiritual energy to think about our future' and quotes from a recent *TES* article:

> The vision which we must all see is that of a united nation caring corporately for its adolescent population; determined to create the environment and the organisation which will enable them to make the most of their lives. The entire nation must be made to see this vision.

The problem of the 'shocking waste of youth' was in fact engaging a number of bodies, including political parties, during the war.[47] With the Nazi model as a warning, there was hot debate on the degree of compulsory training, especially in physical education, which was compatible with democratic liberties. But Christian thinking, expressed mainly through *CN-L* while taking account of such schemes as the County Badge, discerned a deeper complex of educative issues in the question of how 'going to work' could contribute to the making of a full person – or fail to do so. While the change from school to work could be 'catastrophic',[48] Oldham saw 'struggling to the birth ... a broader and richer concept of education'. The connection between education and life was vital. 'There can be no real national culture or sound educational service that has not a living relation to the major occupations by which the people live.'[49] This whole line of thought was pursued among *CN-L* supporters by a group of teachers convened by the master of Balliol, who summed up the discussions in a supplement 'Fourteen to Eighteen'.[50] While recognizing that there does come a point where 'the real world is no longer school' for many teenagers, the group issued a typical scholastic caveat to employers: 'If these boys and girls go to you, it is primarily because they will be best trained with you and we must see that you do train them.' The Christian Frontier took up this problem and initiated an ongoing project on the real education of the young worker. Visits to factories, discussions with personnel in charge of adolescent workers and analysis of training schemes at work revealed both a new upsurge of concern and ambivalence as to aims. From 1940 onwards training schemes proliferated. Statements of purpose ranged from 'to give the worker factory sense and make him machine minded' and 'to teach correct movements for a particular job' or 'to produce semi-skilled labour in a short time' to 'industry should play an active part in the broader educational development as well as the vocational training of young citizens' and 'our aim is to make them think and act for themselves, thus counteracting the sluggish habit of mind resulting from very monotonous jobs'.[51] The tension between the concept of 'industrial fodder' and 'the young citizen' approaches is clearly brought out and although the nature of the first work experience has drastically changed since then – compounded for too many by the lack of any work experience at all – the real educational imperative still clamours for solution: we must find ways of giving the next generation their first meaningful chance to realize their potential as contributors to their society.

Meaningfulness is the key concept here. But how, in the face of complexity on the one hand and fragmentation on the other, is it to be found? Some aspects of building up meaningfulness at work were analysed in a 1946 *CN-L* supplement which arose out of the Frontier project.[52] Obviously proper initiation comes first. A crucial element of personal meaning is to be able to grasp the nature of the whole in which you are becoming a participant. The underlying purposes of initiation are (1) to reduce chaos to order, (2) to give status, and (3) to keep alive interest. Secondly, proper training in the required techniques is essential for the building of confidence on which personal dignity is based. Thirdly, how much did a young worker need to know – as little as a 'hand' needed to become efficient or as much as a person demanded for understanding? Here the basic conflict between 'individual' and 'person' came out strongly. Today, many would argue that the competing individual only cares to know enough to make money and climb the career ladder. But, significantly, some organizations are now searching for a wider participatory basis. In 1946 we talked about the culture of the industry and imaginative ways of opening up a whole range of activities behind 'the job', for the young worker should be given 'not as little as he needs to know to perform an unskilled operation, but as much as he can absorb as a person about the implications of his work for society'.[53] Fourthly, one has to ask: who are the real teachers at the transition from school to work? Though good schools, of course, build up fruitful contacts with employers, it is clear that the effective role models for many teenagers are people in the 'real world'. Again and again we found that the attitude of a lad's immediate boss was crucial and we were told 'that the way the management treats the foremen and what it expects from them will largely determine the manner in which they deal with the juveniles under them'.[54]

In 1946, while the implementation of the 1944 Act was going forward with regard to schools, the imaginative plans for post-school education, particularly county colleges, were hanging fire. The gap worried many people, both in education and industry. This fuelled urgent discussions which continued into the later 1940s. Two conferences initiated by the Frontier Council in 1946 led to a broader based one in January, 1948, at which 56 delegates met, covering a cross-section of employers, education and training officers and teachers in factory schools. The moving spirit behind this initiative was the Chief Factory Inspector, Sir Wilfred Garret. Speakers included Sir Charles Bartlett from Vauxhall Motors, Mr Harold Perkins from ICI, and Mr J. V. C. Wray from the TUC. A summary of speeches and discussions was issued afterwards as *The School in the Factory* by the YMCA.[55] The conference started from the premiss that both teachers and industrialists were concerned with more than training a pair of hands:

> Behind that pair of hands is a curious motor power which consists of a mind and a spirit – the motor of a person. That motor, like any other, will work only on the right fuel and that fuel is not only the fuel of the wage packet or the fear of unemployment. It is our job to discover the right kind of fuel, and with this problem both the educationalist and the industrialist are concerned.[56]

The question of incentives took a central place in discussions. Mr Perkins suggested three motivating forces: a 'must', an 'ought' and a 'want to', while in an evaluating exercise by group members, 'interest in the job' and 'worthwhileness' came out – surprisingly – ahead of 'money' and 'security'.[57] A second significant point of discussion arose out of the relation of technical to general education in this post-school period. Mr Bartlett was clear that 'the fitting of learning to reality must be our task in industry' and the industrialists in the group felt that works schools could play a key part in keeping county colleges in touch with the workplace. On the other hand, the trade-union view expressed by Mr Wray saw continued general education as the chief purpose of the county colleges, affording 'the finest opportunity for educating for citizenship'.[58] In the event, the county college idea was never consummated and the unsolved problem of the dichotomy between 'general' and 'vocational' education in adolescence is still with us.

These discussions signalled a remarkable change of attitude in many industrialists. *CN-L* commented:

> there is growing in many places in industrial life a sense of the responsibility of firms for the welfare of their young workers, and whereas a few years ago welfare was deemed to be concerned with first aid, safety precautions, cleanliness and so on, now a wider conception has developed and many are asking what is the effect of the work itself

upon young people, and how it can be used to good ends ... a philosophy of work is essential.[59]

This Frontier initiative had a considerable impact. In May 1947 *CN-L* reported that 'every week some new request for copies of the report of these conferences [i.e. 1946 ones] is made by educational or industrial bodies', adding 'This seed is sown in places which would never have been reached by, shall we say, a pamphlet on the Christian doctrine of work.'[60] This comment underlines the Frontier's characteristic method of work.

Going to work is a vital stage in the making of a person. The new relationships, both technical and social, can be cruelly destructive or vitally enhancing. Behind this whole educative experience lies the fundamental question of the work ethic in the community at large. The 1946 supplement ended thus:

> We need the training of the imagination to see work not in terms of fat profits for shareholders and thin wages for workers, but as services rendered to the community with proper recompense. But it is a betrayal of the young to inculcate such a doctrine unless it really corresponds to the facts of industrial organisation. Can we at present honestly say to the youngsters: 'Your work is for the service of those who most need it?' This issue of the meaning and purpose of work is the fundamental problem to be attacked.[61]

That language is dated but the problem is still with us.

## Notes

1. *CN-L*, S154, 7 Oct. 1942, 'The Christian Frontier'. The whole supplement forms a clear exposition of the relationship between the Christian and the secular world which is also God's world. Much later J. H. Oldham recorded that 'the Frontier Idea' was born out of discussions between Archbishops Lang and Temple with other leading churchmen as members of the Council on the Christian Faith and the Common Life which preceded the British Council of Churches: 'Without the initiative of Archbishop Lang it would not have come into existence.' (*Frontier*, 4/3 (1960), p. 24.)
2. *CN-L*, S154.
3. Ibid. The early records of the Christian Frontier Council appear to be lost, but the Central Library of the Selly Oak Colleges (996 Bristol Rd, Birmingham B29 6LQ) holds minutes of meetings 1961–4 and some 'correspondence on industry', including minutes of the Industrial Group 1957–75.
4. *CN-L*, S154.
5. Ibid.
6. Ibid.
7. *CN-L*, S178, 24 Mar. 1943, 'Christians and the Beveridge Report'.

8. Ibid.
9. *CN-L*, S190, 8 Sept. 1943, 'Responsibility in the Economic Sphere'.
10. Ibid.
11. *CN-L*, S204, 22 Mar. 1944, 'Responsibility in the Economic Sphere – Government Regulation'.
12. *CN-L*, S263, 26 June 1946, 'Christians in Politics: I – Christian Conservatism and Christian Radicalism'.
13. *CN-L*, S270, 2 Oct. 1946, 'Christians in Politics: II – Christian Influence in Politics'.
14. See below, Part III, pp. 212–19.
15. *CN-L*, S277, 8 Jan. 1947, 'Christians in Politics: III'.
16. *CN-L*, L234, 16 May 1945.
17. Ibid.
18. *CN-L*, L278, 22 Jan. 1947, 'Incentives to Work'.
19. Ibid.
20. *CN-L*, S278, 22 Jan. 1947.
21. *Equality and Excellence* (SCM, 1961); *The Educated Society* (Faber, 1966).
22. *CN-L*, L339, 8 June 1949. From 1953 to 1958 the journal of the Christian Frontier Council was given the name *Christian Newsletter*, appearing quarterly. From 1958 to 1975 it appeared as *Frontier*, edited by John Lawrence. Lambeth Palace Library holds a complete run. The Council itself was disbanded in the early 1970s.
23. *Equality and Excellence*, ref. above, n. 21.
24. R. H. Tawney, *Equality* (Allen & Unwin, 1931).
25. A. D. Lindsay, *The Modern Democratic State* (Royal Institute of International Affairs, 1943).
26. *Equality and Excellence*, pp. 21–2.
27. Quoted, ibid., p. 20.
28. Quoted ibid., p. 21.
29. Quoted ibid.
30. Ibid., p. 37.
31. Ibid., pp. 39–40.
32. Ibid., p. 40.
33. Ibid., p. 57.
34. *The Educated Society*, ref. above, n. 21.
35. P. Drucker, *Landmarks of Tomorrow* (Heinemann, 1959), pp. 114–17.
36. D. Riesman: sociologist and social critic at Chicago and then Harvard; M. Trow, well-known educationalist at Berkeley. These two American thinkers are quoted in *Educated Society*, pp. 148 and 236 respectively.
37. *Educated Society*, p. 33.
38. Ibid., p. 34.
39. Ibid., pp. 57–8.
40. Ibid., p. 63.
41. M. Reeves, 'Reflections on the Education of the 14-to-18 year olds', *The New Era in Home and School*, 24/1 (Jan. 1943), p. 1. Already in Oct. 1939 a debate in the House of Lords focused on 'the disastrous wastage of human material resulting from neglect by the community of the physical, mental and moral education of its future citizens between the ages of fourteen and eighteen'. (See *CN-L*, L1, 1 Nov. 1939).
42. F. Clarke, 'Cultural Aspects of Vocational Education', *New Era*, 23/9 (Dec. 1942), pp. 179–84. This essay echoes the call for an integrated culture which runs right through *CN-L* and forms the underlying philosophy of the Frontier Council.

Clarke was a member of the Moot and a contributor both to *CN-L* and *CN-L* books.

43. CN-L, L0, 18 Oct. 1939.
44. H. G. Wells, *The New World Order* (Secker and Warburg, 1939), quoted *CN-L*, L11, 10 Jan. 1940, in a paragraph headed 'Frustrated Youth'.
45. *CN-L*, L11, 10 Jan. 1940.
46. *CN-L*, S47, 18 Sept. 1940.
47. *CN-L*, L&S182, is largely devoted to this debate. The letter underlines 'the Abruptness of the Change from School to Work' and calls for 'An Educative Purpose in Industry'. The supplement by Kathleen Bliss is on part-time education. See also L37, 55, 85, 86 for further discussion of this general debate in the country.
48. *CN-L*, L135, 27 May 1942 quoting 'a Director of Education'.
49. *CN-L*, L136, 3 June 1942. Again, Oldham devotes the whole letter to 'The Nation and its Youth', arguing that, out of a host of tasks in modern society, this is the one we should focus on. In a footnote he lists various recent publications and papers on this task.
50. *CN-L*, S146, 12 Aug. 1942.
51. *CN-L*, M. Reeves, 'The Education of Young Workers in Industry', S265, 24 July 1946. See also T. S. Eliot, *Notes towards the Definition of Culture* (Faber, 1948), p. 16, where this supplement is quoted.
52. Ibid.
53. Ibid.
54. Ibid.
55. *The School in the Factory*. A report of a conference held at Glyn House, Broadstairs, on 12–14 Jan. 1948, published by the YMCA.
56. Ibid., pp. 1–2.
57. Ibid., pp. 13–14.
58. Ibid., pp. 9–12.
59. *CN-L*, L267, 21 Aug. 1946.
60. *CN-L*, L285, 14 May 1947.
61. *CN-L*, S265, 24 July 1946.

*Chapter 5*

# A Ferment of Ideas on Education

W. Roy Niblett and Marjorie Reeves

## Centres of Debate*

During the war of 1939–45 what better way to keep the spirit alive through the bombings, the darkened streets, the rationing, and the dire news of the collapse of France, than boldly to throw one's desires forward? Among the committees which met while the war raged outside, were the Norwood,[1] the Fleming[2] and the McNair,[3] each with far-reaching policies to propose. And the imaginative great new Education Act itself, finally passed in 1944, was a victorious outcome of many consultations, numberless to-ings and fro-ings, in the grim three years which preceded it.

Undoubtedly the suffering which the war brought, mixed with gleams of hope, fostered a community spirit in the nation and when peace finally arrived energy welled up. Chances now could be taken; all over the country emergency colleges sprouted huts for classrooms to train more teachers rapidly; most of the English universities decided to adopt the more risky but more creative of the alternative schemes proposed by the McNair Committee to link themselves with the colleges of teacher education in their region.[4]

To a considerable extent, though, the educational thinking, planning and doing which went on had been prepared for in the previous decade. The later 1940s was a time when a number of long gestated hopes could be realized. During the 1930s I was a member of the so-called Auxiliary Movement (Aux), a network of people whose social conscience had been awakened by the SCM while they were still students. Teachers in the Aux wanted schools to convey what they saw as essential Christianity not only through the

* The first half of this chapter is by W. Roy Niblett.

religious knowledge period but through other subjects, and through what later became known as the 'hidden curriculum'. We were not concerned only, or even chiefly, with the competitive success of schools but that they should be challenging yet sensitive human societies; and in real touch with each other.[5]

The enthusiasm so readily generated in SCM circles in the 1930s for improving the quality of education in schools is well exemplified in the establishment of the Institute of Christian Education. In 1931 a highly successful conference on Christian Education at Home and Overseas held at Swanwick, with J. H. Oldham as one of its key speakers, brought together 230 men and women from many sections of the teaching profession and threw up the idea that an Institute should be created to encourage teachers of religion both in Britain and overseas. Fertilized by William Temple, then archbishop of York, the idea bore fruit and after nation-wide enquiry, and a well-attended second conference, the Institute of Christian Education (ICE) was officially founded in 1934 with a thoughtful quarterly *Religion in Education* (SCM Press) as its journal.

It was the SCM tradition itself which informed the ICE from the start. This combined a strongly Christian position with open-mindedness. The concern of the ICE was that the teaching of religious education, both in primary and secondary schools, should be disciplined by an approach to the Bible which was spiritually aware but critically informed. From the start it had an under-standing of children and adolescents who were finding faith difficult. Ecumenical in its outlook, the ICE demonstrated that there could be a unity which mattered among those who differed in their beliefs and worship. By the mid-century it showed the beginnings of a real interest in the teaching of religions other than Christianity, but not more than that: for the growth in Britain of large Muslim and Hindu communities is a phenomenon of the later part of the century. The ICE did not repudiate the culture around it but instead sought to open ways by which people with Christian convictions could relate to that culture and help to renew it.

By 1939 the ICE had nearly 2000 members, and by 1945 over 3000. In the post-war years its imaginative research committee was asking such questions as what makes an education Christian? The ICE by this time was running a busy advisory service for its members. Its overseas department too – which had existed from the Institute's earliest days – had become active in practical ways. The large and representative Government Conference on Christian Education in Africa that it initiated in 1952 led to the establishment of an overseas appointments bureau. Within four years this had recruited some 250 teachers and placed them strategically in seventeen territories.

A very different but equally far-seeing group with which I had links in the 1930s was an Education Society in Newcastle upon Tyne, all of whose 41 members, apart from myself, were on the staff of its Royal Grammar School. In how many schools then or later in the century did anything like it blossom? The group owed its existence to two remarkable young members of the school's staff. One was Michael Roberts, who taught physics but had already introduced the world to the poets Auden and Spender by choosing and editing some of their work in his *New Signatures* (1935). The other was Max Black, who taught mathematics and later on became Distinguished Professor of Philosophy at Cornell. The meetings, once a term, developed into a free exchange of ideas on education, politics, religion and society. They introduced their participants to qualities in their colleagues they simply had not known about. Every meeting tended to resolve itself into a hard-hitting debate between Black and Roberts. The pay-off included an enhanced spirit of community in the school, and livelier fifth and especially sixth forms than would otherwise have been the case. Some of Michael Roberts's books (e.g. *The Modern Mind*, 1937) and articles used material which he had introduced to the group. The intelligence and tolerance of his Christian position was never concealed. After the war he spent three highly creative years as principal of the College of St Mark and St John in Chelsea. His early death in 1947 removed from the educational scene a leading spirit, but not before he had written *The Recovery of the West* (1941)[6] which foresaw some of the problems to be caused by the increase of individualism, self-interest and loss of purpose which were to mark the later part of the century.

It is hard sometimes to know whose contributions mean most in the debates which take place in the committee rooms before the production of any worthwhile report, signed as it has been by all its members. Sir Fred Clarke, director of the University of London Institute of Education from 1937 to 1945, always had ideas that mattered and was certainly much consulted behind the scenes as well as more publicly throughout his London years. He wrote the keynote chapter to the preparatory volume on education for the Oxford Conference of 1937,[7] was a particularly active member of the Moot, a highly influential member of the McNair Committee and one of the earliest to recognize the contribution which sociology might make to educational thought. His friend Karl Mannheim was appointed the first Professor of the Sociology of Education in this country, a chair invented by Clarke for him. Clarke's *Education and Social Change*[8] and *Freedom in the Educative Society*[9] challenged conventional opinion. His Christian outlook, personal experience of education in South Africa and Canada, and acute awareness of dangers of isolationism, sowed many seeds in receptive minds. He saw how significant it was that in Britain schools had freedom to be largely autonomous and he feared what might happen if this was reduced or denied to them.

To promote these ideas he encouraged me to start in 1947 an annual conference of a new kind. We sought to collect people of some influence in education with a sympathy for Christian presuppositions who would otherwise rarely encounter one another: some leading heads of public and grammar schools, some chief education officers from LEAs, a small admixture of university professors, one or two HMIs – and when possible a few leaders from teachers' unions. These 'Foundation Conferences' were held each year from 1947 to 1961. Among speakers, besides Clarke himself, were Sir Walter Moberly, Jack Longland (chief education officer for Derbyshire) and Eric James (then high master of Manchester Grammar School). Some 45 of us met at the conference each year, there being eventually 200 or more on the list of those who wanted to be invited. Among the subjects addressed were 'Education and the Christian Conception of Discipline'; 'Personal Conviction and the Claims of Society'; 'Pressures in Teaching'; 'Technology in Education'. Reports did not appear in the press but were circulated to members. The conferences aimed to promote the belief that there was unity in what we wanted education to do, whatever our job or status in the system.

Discussions at the Foundation Conferences lay behind a series of short books under the title 'Educational Issues of Today', including *The Public Schools Today, The Training of Teachers, Growing Up in a Modern Society*, and *The Neutrality of the School*. As I wrote in the Editor's Note which prefaced each volume:

It is the conviction of the contributors to this series, first, that education is a far more complex and deep-reaching affair than instruction; second, that what is taught and how we teach it necessarily reflect the beliefs we hold and our assumptions about life and what it is for; third, that the direction in which civilisation develops as the century goes on must in great measure depend upon the integrity, quality, and creativeness with which the individual is enabled to live in an increasingly planned society; and, lastly, that Christianity has insights to offer for which there is no substitute.[10]

Looking back, one can see some of the deficiencies of the conferences and the books. They belonged to their period. No Roman Catholic contributed to either; sexual issues and problems were hardly mentioned; little awareness was shown of religions other than Christianity; far too little use was made of statistics and hard evidence. But the aim of both was to energize their clientele, and introduce lively ideas about the scope and potential of education. We hoped too that they would suggest that a network, a community, of keen and kindred spirits already existed.

## The Age of Planning

By 1950 it was becoming clear that the age of planning had come to stay, bringing with it unforetellable developments in the control the planners might exercise over our lives. The success which greeted the putting of the 1944 Education Act into effect demonstrated the power which education could have as an instrument of social control. The concept of secondary education for all which the Act incorporated (abandoning the words 'elementary school'), and the promise that the minimum leaving age would be raised to 15 from 1947, marked a degree of orderly planning in our educational system which was new. Significantly, the minister in charge of the system was henceforward to be known as the country's Minister of Education instead of the President of a non-existent Board.

Might it not soon prove more and more a temptation for the planners to approach education from the outside – seeing and treating schools and colleges no longer as organisms but as organizations? The British tradition in the past had quietly made teachers, parents and school governors responsible for many choices in the education of children, and universities had had almost complete freedom to live independent lives of their own. In the second half of the century the powers of control over education which passed into the hands of the central government, with its access to financial sanctions, became far greater than ever before. In time not only the shaping of the system but the content of what was taught was going to be influenced by the planners, whether they were Ministers of the Crown, civil servants, officers of an LEA or members of a committee given a remit for considering this part or that of the educational enterprise.

In the late 1940s and early 1950s there was increasing concern among thoughtful people that the coming into being of a planned society might threaten the very idea of a liberal education. No doubt a considerable degree of planning was essential if our educational system was to be as efficient at producing skilled workers as that which other advanced countries were developing. But what sort of civilization was all the planning for? Might it not be easy to sacrifice much of the freedom and potential of human beings for a technologically based prosperity and a utilitarian concept of progress which brought with it a quite inadequate fulfilment of human hope?

Such books as Michael Polanyi's *Personal Knowledge* (1958) can be seen as manifestations of and creative responses to such questions.[11] So too can *The Cambridge Journal*. Started in 1951 by Michael Oakeshott, it put up a strong defence of the traditional liberal university, seeing it as a place in which the different disciplines, even if not conversing enough with one another, were at least united by a common and liberated spirit of enquiry within institutions which could still count upon their own autonomy.

## University Institutes of Education

Many of those concerned about the quality of the education saw the key to something better in a more adequately planned but at the same time more liberally educated teaching force. Just here was one of the most hopeful recipes for preserving humanity and freedom in our country. The Report of the McNair Committee (1944), recognized the potential of universities as centres of genuine, and liberal, thought and called on them to be more aware of their opportunities for raising the standards of teaching in the nation's schools. Most teachers were still trained in colleges belonging to the local authorities or the churches, too isolated from the rest of the higher education system. The developments envisaged would mean a far closer association of the colleges with the universities through newly created Institutes of Education. This, it was hoped, might in time bring with it a wider acceptance by universities of their responsibilities to society. For, as Harry Judge has said, 'how teachers are educated and where and by whom reflects beliefs about what teachers are for and why society employs them'.[12]

The enthusiasm which, in the decade following 1945, went into the creation and running of most of these new University Institutes of Education, was remarkable. What was involved was an attempt, on the one hand, to improve the standing of teaching as a profession – a long haul in view of the low regard in which it was held as compared with, say, medicine or law – but also, on the other hand, to modify the university's concept of itself. The Scheme A type of Institute – which eventually all the universities save Cambridge adopted – required a university to accept, gradually and over the years, that the newly named Colleges of Education in its area should become almost parts of it, with the implication that universities should begin to see that if poor standards in the schools threatened the social future they ought not to stand aside and wash their hands. Much later in the century there was to be a largely successful attempt to involve universities in a closer connection with business, with management, even with manufacturing industry. In recent years, relationships between the universities and society have become far closer than they were in the 1950s. They draw their skirts about them now less than they did. In a number of ways the Institutes of Education enterprise was a pioneer part of this general movement.

To begin with, however, much missionary effort was required. When in 1947 I joined the University of Leeds as its Professor of Education there was strong opposition from a large majority of Senate (including the then vice-chancellor) to the very idea of introducing a Scheme A Institute. Their attitude was largely that described by Sir Walter Moberly:

> Till lately at least the bulk of academic opinion has had no real belief in teacher-training and has been half-ashamed of the University's part in it. It has been like a shopkeeper who feels that convention compels him to put in his window some types of article which he would never think of using himself, or of recommending to his personal friends ...

Sir Walter added that it was widely believed that 'as a field of study "Education" resembled Mrs. Harris'; no such subject existed.[13]
It took faith in the cause and a good deal of encouragement from the people I had known in SCM, Auxiliary Movement and Foundation Conference circles to help me to convert the Leeds Senate and so get its Scheme A Institute started.[14]

Once the Institute at Leeds was off the ground all sorts of possibilities were opened up to it, though without the robust support of the incoming vice-chancellor (Sir Charles Morris) we certainly should not have got very far. With an earmarked grant from the University Grants Committee (UGC), we could begin developing more organic relationships with all nine Colleges of Education in the region and to start a number of new facilities for Yorkshire teachers. These included a variety of courses to provide higher qualifications for those willing to work for them. We insisted at first on a period of full-time study as a requirement and, such was the temper of the time, were able to secure that this was salaried. We also found it possible to build up a library open to teachers of the area as well as students from the colleges, with postal or personal borrowing. A bulletin was published each term, which was more than a list of events, and a research journal; a centre was opened for the children of teachers attending lectures or courses. Every year we used one of the cathedrals in our area (York, Ripon, Bradford, Wakefield), or one of the largest Free Churches, for an annual Institute service open to all its students and staff. In fact in every other year it took place in York Minster where over 2000 gathered, with numerous members of staff from the colleges and some from the University itself, including the vice-chancellor who normally read a lesson. Nor was there difficulty in securing some notable person each year to give an address.

Today, near the end of the century, though the Institute no longer exists, some of the colleges which gradually became more closely knit into it are themselves constituent colleges of the University in which students can read for a variety of its degrees. Their principals are professors of the University and members of its Senate.

The University of Leeds Institute would not have borne much fruit if it had not become as intimate a part of the University as we could make it, drawing lecturers to its courses from many departments of the University, and especially the Medical School. Its Senior Research Fellows, who stayed for two or three years, in several cases might well have held their fellowships elsewhere in the University. Several went on to be lecturers or professors in other universities and our first Institute Librarian eventually became Bodley's Librarian at Oxford.[15] Like the Auxiliary Movement, the Education Society at Newcastle Grammar School and the Foundation Conferences, the Institute of Education at Leeds was much more than merely an organization. Institutes throughout the country intensely disliked the name by which they were officially called by the government: Area Training Organizations – or ATO's for short.

## The Rise of Managerialism

It is a somewhat arbitrary matter to decide when what we are calling 'the present' began to emerge at a greater pace from 'the past'; but there was certainly a feeling in the late 1960s and early 1970s that a more rapid transition than usual in the national outlook was in process. This was due in part to the spread of managerialism, the detailed and resolute application of planning, now with the powerful help of the computer, affecting numerous sectors of the nation's life. The more complex and dependent upon technology society becomes, the more indispensable managerial skills become. Those in charge of education found themselves increasingly in need of the knowledge and the qualities which went into the making of a good manager.

With the growing dominance of a detached analytical frame of mind the contribution which the humanities – and religion too – could make to the education of the great majority of the young seemed to many increasingly open to question. To meet this situation I invited a number of key men and women to join a think group or working party. During the late 1960s and early 1970s four such groups came into being under my chairmanship.[16] The remit of each was, in an age when managerialism and utilitarian ideals were becoming widespread, to give thought in wider terms than was customary to the purposes of higher education and the policies which should inform its development. One of the four was on the Humanities in Higher Education and another on the Function and Education of the Expert. A third considered with more concentration the actual policies which its members thought should govern the future provision of education in the universities and what were still the polytechnics, the separateness of whose categorization they deplored.

Each working party had a dozen to sixteen members. All were concerned about the signs of a change from a more organic to a more inorganic concept of what education was about and with the increasing dominance of a detached, uninvolved temper in the management both of education and of society itself. How could the humanity of human beings be nourished, even preserved, in the kind of society towards which, consciously or unconsciously, the nation seemed to be heading? What, if anything, could universities do about it? Should they be content to develop into places where research of high quality was carried out and courses provided for undergraduates which offered rigorous training in specialisms – but with few of the long-term and fundamental questions discussed or even asked? This question is still an urgent one at the end of the century.

Study of the humanities including philosophy, literature, history and theology, might, we thought, in future be in danger of becoming anachronistic, or of being marginalized in a civilization which had lost faith in larger purposes than the short-term and whose confidence in itself was becoming increasingly dependent upon material progress. Whereas earlier in the century the central government had had little desire to control the content of the curriculum at any stage in the educational process, now there was increasing temptation for it to do so, and one not reduced by the tenure of Margaret Thatcher as Minister of State for Education and Science between 1970 and 1974.

The working parties, to whose thinking members contributed more than 70 papers, were worried at the lack of evidence of consideration anywhere in Britain to the *kind* of society for which we were educating the young. Education was becoming more and more instrumental in character. Few personal beliefs seemed to be expected. Granted that, if the nation needed many more experts trained in applied fields, expansion and modification of the education system must be undertaken, with the state forced to assume greater direct planning powers than it had had hitherto; would the state and its civil servants have a concept of the future which had depth of vision? If the only significant aim of education was to equip professionals to run a managerial, electronic and consumer orientated society, what reason was there to think that such a society would take us in the long run where we really wanted to be? Society, left to itself, would set limits neither to technology nor to growth, except those which shortages of raw materials or skills arbitrarily compelled.

One of the terms of reference of the Working Party on the Education of the Expert was to consider how experts could be given a wider sense of social responsibility. 'It remains a matter of astonishment', said Professor Tony Dyson of Manchester in a paper he wrote for it, 'that the world's increased potential for productivity appears to benefit so few. It also engages so few.' How could experts be educated so that more of them had a concern not merely with technical achievement but social benefit? And how could the public be educated to interpret social benefit in more than economic and material terms? 'Quality of life,' a term which first became popular in the early 1970s, was often interpreted as if prosperity was all.

By the mid-1970s it was clear that threats caused by pollution, by the escalation of the world's population, by the possibility that genetic engineering involving human beings was going to be practicable, needed to be taken seriously. These all imposed not merely technical dilemmas but dilemmas for the conscience, nationally and internationally. There was little evidence in the 1970s that universities or polytechnics were paying them much attention. The sectional, departmentally self-interested, approach most common where there was interest at all seemed ludicrously inadequate to meet the challenge. For to us it did not seem enough for the intelligent to be taught the techniques of architecture, engineering science, animal farming, computer theory, musical counterpoint, managerial science, without training of the introspective imagination and a discipline of foresight and insight to understand the far-spreading consequences of their knowledge. What is called 'decision making' is often only the final step in a process which will have involved listening to the evidence according to some tradition of selecting what is really evidence, internalizing it (which may involve feeling its power), and evaluating its worth as objectively as possible.

While the content of higher education must be closely related to students' professional needs, too narrow a concept of what is relevant to those will certainly prevent the production of the kinds of professional most needed. Students need to consider the consequences of the rapid growth of opportunities for control over other people which the advancement of human knowledge and powers of communication are bringing about. The question of the concept, or norm, of the man or woman upon whom those controls are to be exercised will not go away. We have clues to the norm and how it is to be sustained in, for example, the expression of mind and desire in literature, music and art; in the concepts of human potentiality which have been seen and clarified in philosophic and religious exploration; in some of the medical and psychological discoveries of the past 200 years. But to follow these clues requires a developed sensitivity and imagination, some sense of history, and a capacity to judge human nature informed by experience gained interrelatedly from life itself, books and the media. It requires that students shall not be specialists only but be able to estimate the relative importance of the factors, moral and spiritual as well as physical, which contribute to the real evidence. Only in this way will they be able to counter the threat inherent in pressing further and further ahead with small concern for the direction in which we are going.

Granted that there is a distinction between knowledge which is, as it were, external – concerned with facts, measurement and the apparent behaviour of things – and that which is more subjective, including feeling and evaluating, both kinds are indispensable to a properly human and properly humane life. The kind of personal and moral commitment which is the mark of civilized people is not an irrationality. How do we help students to recognize any authority other than factual knowledge or knowledge which is the product of logical reasoning? There is of course something absolute, something implacable, about each of those, but to acknowledge no other source of authority as our guide is to be left with an existence which has far too little direction. Much that is essential to all-round learning involves experiences which detached or technical study neatly avoids: personal suffering, personal happiness, the actual experience of cruelty, of good and evil, commitment, the mysterious, the tangle of human motives. To focus on educating people to be experts in a world that no longer has much meaning to it is a kind of madness and needs to be recognized as the madness it is. The direction in which education has been going in the last two decades, under financial pressures more and more severe, and governmental directives more and more compelling, may produce for us thousands and thousands of graduates able to solve technical problems disinterestedly. But they may well regard larger questions which cannot be made into technical ones as if they were quite marginal.[17]

## Belief and Human Necessity

Michael Roberts, mentioned earlier in this chapter, maintained that, though he appreciated the intellectual difficulties of believing in any religion, a belief in something like Christianity is for the West a social necessity. 'A community', he said, 'needs a nucleus of people who are convinced of the value and significance of life, of the radical imperfection of man and of the ultimate possibility of forgiveness and redemption.'[18] Certainly today we cannot convince our neighbours that Christianity is true, or in what sense if any it is true, by telling them that it is a social necessity. Nor did Roberts in his time think that we could. To view religion as good for producing certain types of character or even as benefiting society is to view it coldly and detachedly. From the inside, religion – like appetite or sex – *involves* the believer. Believing is a kind of belonging. It may also entail belonging to a church, to a whole group of other believers, to a community which unites the believers to others anywhere in the world who hold the same faith. True religious belonging involves beliefs and an orientation that are profoundly personal. If the believers are Christian, they will recognize that it is to God that through His grace they personally belong. An act of Christian worship is an act of humbly recognizing this belonging once more, of recognizing this relationship as undeserved, giving to the worshippers a status in the world, and the universe too, which otherwise would simply not be theirs.

The cure for the superficiality and escapism so pervasive in our society at the end of the century may thus lie in a rediscovery of belief. But how likely a recipe is it for the majority? It is certainly one which many will scorn as a self-deceiving, culpable, fancy. The alternative however – though they will fight to deny it – does seem to be nihilism. And I speak soberly.

## Growing Up in a Total Environment*

The school world of the 1930s, as I remember it in London, did not concern itself much with structures, but far more with experiences. The debate on reconstructing the public system of education still lay ahead in the preparation for the 1944 Act. But the social revolution which brought that Act to the boil was already simmering away. The Great War had cruelly exposed the 'cannon-fodder' estimate of the masses educated in the old elementary schools and by the 1930s those of us who worked in what were still the old-style elementary schools and teacher training colleges had imbibed, albeit often unconsciously, a radical new philosophy of 'persons'.[19] Education in state schools was not about shaping and sharpening individuals for the service of the economy; it was about the proper nurture of every 'person' growing up in this country. It was to be measured in terms of experiences and relationships deemed necessary for the full development of a person as well as by tests for proficiency in skills. It was about values. What experiences, we asked, do these children need in order to find a meaningful role in the increasingly complex world in which they had to live? Christians and humanists worked together in forming a new educational approach. They found much common ground in the developing study of child psychology which was greatly stimulated by the Tavistock Clinic. The new social philosophy taking shape emphasized the need for the young to find themselves through enriching relationships, in families, in groups, in local communities and at work. The acquisition of skills was only part of this agenda, a consequence of the process rather than a prime objective, for motivation is born out of experience and skills without motivation are of little use.

'Experience' in this context is a catch-all word. It embraces work and play, limitation and creativity, discipline and freedom, love and hate. In short, educational experience goes on continuously throughout the day. It is at once physical, emotional, intellectual and spiritual. Holding all these aspects together is the response of the whole person, admitting and giving house-room to the 'other' which knocks at the door. The message came over through the various organizations, discussion groups, journals of the period. The

---

\*    The rest of this chapter is by Marjorie Reeves.

Home and School Council ran a journal and organized Parent-Teacher Groups. The Nursery School Association campaigned actively to put the urgent need for universal nursery schools before the public. As far back as the 1918 Education Act LEAs had been empowered to provide for the under 5s but little had been achieved. In a wartime report of 1943 this was still a longed-for *desideratum*:

> We believe that recognition of the nursery school stage would offer more than some extra amenities under a different name. It is another 'way of life' – a way of life that would give teachers fresh opportunities, a new freedom to realise the ideals for which they have striven so steadily.[20]

The New Education Fellowship operated as an international society from it headquarters in Tavistock Square. In 1936/7 the *New Era*, its monthly magazine, ran a series of numbers on the 'free personality' and 'education and the free society'. Here R. H. Tawney declared: 'that education is ... the impact of the total social environment on the whole personality', while – wrestling with the spurious attractiveness of the totalitarian patterns of controlled education – he envisaged a truer path to freedom as a delicate balance between accepting limitation and finding a place of one's own.[21] In February 1941 the *New Era* sent out a wartime challenge to its international membership:

> Education will be a vital instrument in restoring freedom and civilization. We intend to play our part in creating an education equal to this task. The N.E.F. is now out of action in most European countries. Britain almost alone links Europe with the Fellowship's large membership in other countries. The English section invite you to join in its work of preparing the future.[22]

It was challenges such as this which drove British educationists to conferences even while the bombs were falling. In June 1940, for instance, the *New Era* announced its conference on 'Youth of Today and Tomorrow', while in the same number advertising conferences of the Nursery School Association, the Association for Education in Citizenship, and others.[23] In 1940/1 it ran a series on 'Now and Tomorrow'. H. O. Stead's contributions started from the perceptions of students themselves:

> They realize that in the modern world the ability to use a technique perfectly without a knowledge of the end for which it is used is the basis of a Totalitarian philosophy ... they desire rather to be the conscious instruments of a purpose recognized by themselves as good. They hear

much loose and sentimental talk about the individuality of the child, free discipline, and modern methods, but they have yet to find the co-ordinated activity expressive of the ideal. ... State education in this country which originated in the demand for a literate people, is now passing to the stage when its object is to produce a cultured people. ... But without a philosophy and without a sense of values, there can be no culture.[24]

In a number on 'Administrative Problems' Stead again opened the debate in words which are a text for today:

Every system of education is an institution of the society which establishes it, and can only express the principles on which that society is based. ... It is important that this should be realized for there is a tendency to believe that improvement in methods or changes in the curriculum can themselves produce vital changes in education ... some improvement can be produced ... but it should not be confused with that more radical change which only a change in the bases of society can effect in the education system which is set up to perpetuate its ideals.[25]

He goes on to argue that the war was being fought for the sake of values which were not yet clearly articulated and that the time was ripe for far-reaching changes in the framework of society. He puts forward two basic principles upon which the post-war world must be constructed: (1) There must be for every individual a background of security against which he can live his life. (2) There must be a field for 'adventure' and for 'creative activity', for this activity is the adventure we call life.[26]

These were the principles underlying the endeavour to design a living curriculum in schools. There was little faith in hammering at skills without motivation and putting together lifeless packets of facts which children 'ought to know'. We saw that 'belonging' and 'creative exploration' could be the two motors driving the will to learn. Under the first came, on the one hand, learning the skills which made you competent and confident to make your way in the community and, on the other, local knowledge of the society to which you belonged. Under 'creative activities' came the exploration of the wider world, fuelled by natural curiosity. It was the realization that, once the motor got started, children learned eagerly that framed the project method. Creative activity followed naturally, for 'personal knowledge'[27] bursts to be communicated, whether in words or movement, drama or the visual arts. So the practice of skills interacted continuously with the urge to explore. This was not 'child-centred education' but 'world-centred', nor were projects a trendy fashion. There was certainly no conscious political ideology; projects arose naturally out of the perceived needs of children within the context of a society which was rethinking its valuation of 'the person'.

The hard thinking which Oldham called for in *CN-L* was already by 1940 finding its embodiment in a series of small *CN-L* books.[28] In his preface to No. 3, *Education and Social Change*, Fred Clarke wrote on New Year's Day 1940,

> that England, no more than any other country, could withdraw from the impact of the great forces which, long gathering head, have now deployed in strength upon mankind. ... Honest and sustained intellectual effort ... is a vital part of home defence.[29]

His main thesis was that English education had for too long been based on implicit assumptions about our society which now must be, in the face of great challenges, re-examined explicitly: the educational problems under debate are 'sociological rather than pedagogical ... This book, therefore, is properly addressed to the ordinary citizen rather than to the professionals and is centred in national policy rather than classroom techniques.'[30] He concludes with two significant problems for today: first, 'Transcending the cultural-vocational distinction'[31] and secondly, 'The nature of social cohesion'. Here he asks 'Why should society cohere?' and gives his own deep-thrusting answer: 'For the making of souls'.[32] But the *how* is more problematic to him than the *why*.

> We shall not secure unity by an education which sets itself assiduously to 'teach the laws of social cohesion' in a set scheme of social studies. ... Perhaps the answer is that there can be no answer in set terms, so deep do the forces lie. But if we may venture a tentative answer ... we would say 'By faith and love'.[33]

The Christian Auxiliary Movement formed yet another fellowship which carried out its activities in groups and conferences right through the war. It defined its pledge of membership thus: '[the members] commit themselves to God and to one another in a common effort to bring a new social order which seeks to express the will of God and in which the true development of every personality can be realised'.[34] Education was at the heart of the wartime debates in 'Aux' meetings and on 4 September 1945, the BBC broadcast in its series 'What can we learn from the war?' a talk entitled 'Being Responsible' which embodied the Aux's thinking:

> We have learnt that to live is to commit ourselves to a purpose which makes belief a basis for action; we have discovered that doing things in groups fulfils the individual person, for we who were sterile in isolation

have found our significance in meeting and acting with other persons; we must therefore intend so to re-create a local environment that the next generation can find their true place in societies voluntary and involuntary.[35]

From October 1945 the *TES* carried a series on 'The Content of Education' which started from the same theme: 'Persons Growing Up within Societies'. Defining content in terms of experiences rather than subjects, it offered the following summary: 'The experience of a "given" law, order and pattern; the experience of freedom to adventure; the experience of understanding the whole of which one is a part; the experience of the transcendental element in life.[36]

## Propaganda, Commitment and Religious Education

The challenge of totalitarian propaganda, both from right and left, brought sharply to the centre of the educational debate the question of indoctrination. In 1939 the SCM and Auxiliary Movement put out a study outline which contrasted the idea of a 'Liberal Education' with the rise of 'Authoritarian Education'.[37] The quintessence of the liberal ideal had been seen in the Germany of the Weimar Republic, described by the German refugee scholar, Adolf Löwe, in a passage quoted above.[38] Löwe claimed that in the pre-Hitler educational system what mattered supremely was 'the harmonious unfolding of the innate qualities of the individual'. But, he said, the liberal idea collapsed because it gave 'neither an interpretation of life nor a directive for action'. Thus by 1938 liberal ideas in education were discredited. 'On all sides the cry is now for security rather than freedom.' The new psychological thinking, emphasizing the need for stable relations, confirmed the move away from individualism. But the extreme swing from freedom to security came, of course, in the totalitarian regimes. The 1939 study outline quotes passages from Nazi documents on education, such as: 'The State is an organism ... the school must also be an organism' (Schneider); 'Education addresses itself rather to will and emotion than to intellect' (Holfelder).[39] Significantly, authoritarian education in Soviet Russia is delineated in terms more acceptable to a democratic society. Nonetheless, 'Soviet education is set against a definite social pattern – that of the classless community – and experience through education is carefully selected and interpreted to induce the right emotional attitudes. ... Ethical standards are taught in terms of sin against the community.'

Confronted with two such models of enforced community education, where should a so-called democratic country take its stand? Liberalism 'operated in a fear of propaganda'. Bertrand Russell observed that 'Propaganda that attaches emotions ... to belief or disbelief ... is an obstacle to the scientific spirit and to civilisation',[40] while others noted that the possibilities of propaganda had been immeasurably extended since education became universal. Yet Macmurray's emphasis on the need for emotional commitment,[41] reinforced by the psychological perception of belongness as vital to a child's development, sets us on a slippery slope. Where did 'true education' of the emotions end and illegitimate manipulation by propaganda begin? In one of our discussions, seeking to describe the kind of social context in which the young could 'find themselves' through commitment to 'good' causes, I got the riposte: 'Do you realize that with a few adjustments what you are saying could be said of any totalitarian regime?' It was, indeed, difficult either to define a 'good cause' or to draw a line between manipulation by propaganda and education for personal commitment; one could only take a stand on the ambiguous ground of 'intention'. Was the intention of the teacher to secure a hold on loyalty from which there was no escape or to give an experience which led to freedom of choice?

The dilemma was inescapable. In 1942, the 'Aux' published a supplement to *Community* entitled 'Educating for Agnosticism?',[42] which contrasted 'a life of agnosticism' with 'a life of faith'. The former was defined as the life of a person who will not or cannot venture on commitment to any vision or long-term purpose and the latter as

> one in which a person embraces some purpose which embodies a vision of truth, maybe only half-felt and half-understood at first, but in which he/she gambles on the truth of it and responds to the challenge with an outgoing of emotion and determination of will.

The tragedy of the former lay in becoming enslaved by every passing desire. The paper then argued that we were failing the young because, led astray by the individualistic perspective on education, we had, in fact, been educating for agnosticism. Standing between the extremes of individualistic theory and totalitarian reaction, we had to hold the tension, as a democratic society in general and as an educating church in particular. For it was in the Christian doctrine of the person alone that the tension could be resolved, through the understanding that the nurture of the young within secure relationships could lead, not to conformity, but to the commitment 'whose service is perfect freedom'.

It was in this context that discussions on the meaning of Christian education took place. A *CN-L* supplement of January 1944 started from a distinction between 'religious instruction' and religious education'.[43] Of course formal teaching was important and this came to the fore in the negotiations in which the requirements of school worship and religious education teaching were beaten out in the stages leading to the 1944 Act. But many of us felt that 'tabloid doses of intellectual teaching administered to the mind at stated intervals' were of little use by themselves. The education of the mind was crucial – the sharp end of a more diffused experience – but our thinking led to the conclusion that 'Christian education' must embrace the assumptions that interpenetrated the whole educational process. This was powerfully reinforced by the experience of evacuating schools. Several *CN-L* supplements analysed the new insights given.[44] As against the evacuated teacher who said: 'I refuse to believe that I am responsible for these children's souls', there was abundant evidence that teachers found real satisfaction in a role which was enlarged into a new way of life. We listed fundamental educational experiences with a religious basis, that were broadly acceptable to humanists too: comprehending the natural world as a 'given' universe; learning the need for order in human societies; accepting work as a significant responsibility; finding the supreme quality of loving and being loved; finding the meaning of solitariness.[45] All these were rooted in a theology of God the Creator.

A large part of these educational discussions were summed up in a *CN-L* book published in 1942: *What is Christian Education? A Piece of Group Thinking.*[46] Part I laid out 'Basic Assumptions of Christian Education' under headings on values, the meaning of vocation, education for leadership, education and propaganda, school and family. Part II examined some educational techniques in the light of these assumptions. There was no separate chapter on religious instruction. In a perceptive foreword Dorothy Sayers picked out for approval the group's conclusion on the tricky question of educating for leadership: 'the individual must be trained both to lead and follow freely; for the dangerous conception of a "general capacity for leadership", the report substitutes the duty and capacity to *assume responsibility in a specific direction*'.[47] Summing up our agonizing attempts to draw the line between propaganda and Christian influence, the group arrived finally at four points:

(i) true influence depends fundamentally on the integrity of intention in the teacher or society exercising it: the intention must be not to draw others into the orbit of your own personality, not to make replicas of yourself or loyal conformists to an existing social order, but so to enrich the life of the individual that he will grow up more truly himself ...

(ii) The experience of the less mature must be controlled by the more mature ... but the Christian has an obligation to be as honest as he can in the use of emotional forces.

(iii) There must come a stage of understanding in adolescence when the child is made aware of the influences which have been playing upon him [*sic*]. ... Influence must never be exercised for the sake of power, but only with the intention of bringing the immature to a full degree of conscious understanding and responsible choice ...

(iv) The Christian in exercising influence must accept that right of refusal ... imposed by the 'otherness' of another person's ... autonomy.[48]

It was easier to state these principles than to see how they could be safeguarded in shaping a school curriculum. We saw that

ALL curricula are the result of a process of selection ... there can be no such thing as an unbiased curriculum ... the Christian knows that the sinful lust for power in each of us [means that] we shall be always wanting to mould children in our own likeness.[49]

We saw this principle working both in what the community decrees for its schools and what individual teachers emphasize. We said:

this choice of what a child shall know and feel is a serious and awful responsibility. Thank heaven we cannot wholly determine it, owing to the God-given defence of aloofness by which a child withdraws himself from our planned path and pursues a line of his own.[50]

It is the recognition of this inner integrity of each of God's children which is the ultimate safeguard against indoctrination. We may fairly insist on the learning of skills that equip individuals for a competent role in society; we may with less reason forcibly feed with chunks of knowledge which we deem the next generation 'ought to know'; but unless the young appropriate and make their own the riches of knowledge offered our effort is of little use.

# Notes

1. *Curricula and Examinations in Secondary Schools* (HMSO, 1943).
2. *The Public Schools and the General Educational System* (HMSO, 1944).
3. *Teachers and Youth Leaders* (HMSO, 1944).
4. For a summary of these schemes and of Scheme C, see W. R. Niblett, D. Humphreys and J. Fairhurst, *The University Connection* (NFER, 1975), pp. 103–4, 127–9.
5. The Auxiliary Movement dated back as far as 1912. Some surviving records are in the Central Library, Selly Oak Colleges, 996 Bristol Rd, Birmingham, B29 6LQ.
6. Seminal works by M. Roberts: *New Signatures* (Faber, 1935): *The Modern Mind* (Faber, 1937); *The Recovery of the West* (Faber, 1941).
7. *Church, Community and State in Relation to Education*, with an introduction by J. H. Oldham (Allen & Unwin, 1938). On this conference, see above, pp. 8–9.
8. *Christian News-Letter* books (Sheldon Press, 1990).
9. F. Clarke, *Freedom in the Educative Society*, in the Education Issues of Today series (Univ. of London Press, 1948).
10. The series was published by the Univ. of London Press, starting in the 1940s.
11. M. Polanyi, *Personal Knowledge: Towards a Post-Critical Theology* (RKP and Univ. of Chicago Press, 1958).
12. H. Judge, *The University and the Teachers* (Triangle, 1994), p. 13.
13. W. Moberly, *The Crisis in the University* (SCM Press, 1949), pp. 250–1. See also *Letters of C. S. Lewis*, ed. W. H. Lewis (Geoffrey Bles, London, 1966), p. 44, letter dated September 1918.
14. For Scheme A, see *The University Connection* (n. 4 above); for my speech to the Leeds Society, see ibid., pp. 165–6.
15. E. R. S. Fifoot.
16. Their members included Asa Briggs, Alan Bullock, David Edge, Sinclair Goodlad, Barbara Hardy, Lionel Knights, Richard Peters, A. T. S. Prickett, Stephen Spender, Campbell Stewart.
17. For some books which address these larger issues, see W. R. Niblett, *Universities between Two Worlds* (Univ. of London Press, 1974); M. Reeves, *The Crisis in Higher Education* (SRHE and Open Univ. Press, 1988); Niblett, 'An Absence of Outrage: Cultural Change and Values in British Higher Education 1930–90; *Higher Education Policy*, 3/1 (1990).
18. Roberts, *Recovery of the West*, p. 767.
19. This was the period of Macmurray's influential broadcast series, see above, p. 11.
20. *The First Stage in Education: A Report by the Nursery School Association of Great Britain* (publ. by Hamilton House, Mabledon Place, London, 1943), p. 6.
21. R. H. Tawney, 'Education and the Economic Order', *The New Era in Home and School*, 17/10 (Dec. 1936), pp. 293–6.
22. Ibid., 22/2 (Feb. 1941) advertisement for new members, p. 154.
23. Ibid., 21/6 (June 1940), p. 154.
24. H. G. Stead, 'Now and Tomorrow I: Training Colleges', *New Era*, 21/8 (Sept./Oct. 1940), pp. 189–91. See also in the same number, M. Reeves, 'Vocation and the Training Colleges', pp. 194–8.
25. Stead, 'Now and Tomorrow V: Administrative Problems', *New Era*, 22/2 (Feb. 1941), pp. 25–6.
26. Ibid., p. 27.
27. The title of M. Polanyi's prophetic book, published later in 1958, see above, p. 106.

28. See the first list of these in *CN-L*, L19, 6 Mar. 1940.
29. F. Clarke, *Education and Social Order: An English Interpretation* (Sheldon Press, 1940), pp. v–vi.
30. Ibid., p. 5.
31. Ibid., p. 60.
32. Ibid., pp. 66–7.
33. Ibid., p. 69.
34. Printed in its newsletter, *Community*, and in other circulated material. See n. 5 above.
35. M. Reeves, 'Being Responsible', BBC Home Service series 'What can we learn from the War?', 4 Sept. 1945.
36. M. Reeves, no 1 in the series 'The Content of Education', *TES* (27 Oct. 1945). The series was introduced thus: 'It is proposed to cover ... the entire field of education from the home and the nursery school to the university and the community centre ... it is hoped that they may form useful and helpful bases for discussion in educational societies, conferences and training courses'. The theme of 'persons in relationships', as contrasted with the atomistic concept of 'the individual' continued to be debated, e.g. in Dec. 1947 when the BBC broadcast four talks on 'Persons and Individuals'.
37. This 31-page outline, entitled 'Education', is a type-written document prepared by Iris Forrester and M. Reeves and issued by the SCM from Annandale, London. Including book references and questions, it gives an illuminating picture of what teachers were thinking about on the eve of war.
38. See above, p. 43.
39. See study outline. Schneider: *Die deutsche Schule in deutschen Staat*, tr. and quoted in *Friends of Europe* pamphlet, no. 11; Holfelder quotation, unidentified.
40. Quotation not identified in the outline.
41. The outline cites Macmurray's *Reason and Emotion*.
42. *'Educating for Agnosticism?' An address given at the annual conference of the Christian Auxiliary Movement in August, 1942, by Marjorie Reeves* (publ. by the CAM, Moel Llys, Kirby Muxloe, Leics.). See below, pp. 127–8 for Moberly's discussion of this dilemma.
43. M. Reeves, 'Religious Education', *CN-L*, S200, 26 Jan. 1944.
44. *CN-L*, S3, 15 Nov. 1939; L6, 6 Dec. 1939.
45. *CN-L*, S200, 26 Jan. 1944.
46. J. Drewett and M. Reeves, *What is Christian Education? CN-L* books (Sheldon Press, 1942).
47. Ibid., p. ix.
48. Ibid., pp. 22–4.
49. Ibid., pp. 39–41.
50. Ibid., p. 40.

*Chapter 6*

# A Forum for Students: Cumberland Lodge, 1947–1960

Harry Judge

## The House in Windsor Great Park

Early in August 1947 readers of the court page of *The Times* discovered that:

> The King has granted Cumberland Lodge, Windsor Great Park, as a residence for St. Katharine's Foundation.
>
> This grant has been accepted with deep gratitude on behalf of the council of St. Katharine's Foundation by the Earl of Halifax (Chairman), Dr. Tissington Tatlow (deputy chairman), and Miss Amy Buller.[1]

The earl of Halifax, a former Foreign Secretary, had twice served as President of the Board of Education, and was prominent in public life as the most distinguished lay representative of the high Anglican tradition. Tissington Tatlow had been secretary of the Student Christian Movement from its early days in 1903 until 1929. Amy Buller, whom Tissington Tatlow had recruited as a member of the SCM staff, was the effective founder and honorary warden of what was shortly to be rebaptized as St Catharine's, Cumberland Lodge. A little over a year later, Sir Walter Moberly – then about to relinquish the chairmanship of the University Grants Committee – became its first principal and in 1949 published the influential *Crisis in the University*.[2] The purposes of this new foundation, closely related to many of the initiatives recorded in this volume and faithfully reflecting the eloquent arguments of Moberly's book, were given formal shape a few months after the granting of the house. They were:

> To encourage the investigation and discussion of the nature of Man and Society; the exposition of the Christian interpretation of Life in relation

to the various secular alternatives; and to stimulate research on these and similar matters and on the interrelationship of the various academic disciplines (including Christian Theology) and their relevance to practical affairs: and to this end –

a)  To provide a College or Colleges based on the Christian faith and philosophy of life, where Courses of Teaching and Study, Reading Parties and Conferences may be held;

b)  To serve the needs of students, particularly in London University and the Modern Universities, and to encourage an interchange of thought between British students and students from overseas and, in particular, from the British Commonwealth and Empire.[3]

Moberly himself brought to the new enterprise a spirit and a style that were quintessentially Anglican, public school, Oxford, idealistic and episcopal.[4] Both his grandfathers (the one succeeding the other at Salisbury) had been bishops of the same characteristically English see. His father, R. C. Moberly, had been Regius Professor of Moral and Pastoral Theology at Oxford. After an academic career at Aberdeen, Oxford, Birmingham and Exeter Walter Moberly became in 1926 vice-chancellor at Manchester University, presiding there for nine years until his appointment as chairman of the University Grants Committee. He had been knighted in 1934.

William Temple was already bishop of Manchester when Moberly arrived in the North, and the two became close friends and allies. Walter Moberly played a central part in the 1937 Oxford Conference on 'Church, Community and State'. His membership of the Moot and chairmanship of the Christian Frontier Council completed the familiar mosaic of friendships and alliances which in the 1930s and 1940s distinguished the efforts of powerful Christians to influence both national policies and the currents of contemporary thought.

## A Powerful Critique of Universities

In *The Crisis in the University* Moberly concedes that, even if the force of his arguments is accepted, much 'further thinking and experimenting needs to be done' (p. 106). It is clear that to him Cumberland Lodge came to represent just such an experiment, albeit on a necessarily small scale. He cites Temple's argument that the crisis 'of our time is not moral but cultural' (p. 16), and so locates his diagnosis of the ills of the contemporary university in the context of what would later come to be described as the contradictions of a post-Christian society. Moberly emphasizes that his book is a summation of work undertaken by a commission under the auspices of the SCM and the Christian Frontier Council. This was crystallized in twelve pamphlets published by the SCM, of which one (on halls of residence) was of direct relevance to the efforts to found St Catharine's.[5] The 1946 Cambridge meeting of dons described above concluded that 'owing to a confusion of purpose which they share with the modern world, universities are crippled in performing their most important function' (*Crisis*, p. 9). This is the dominant theme of the whole book, and it encapsulates the problem which Cumberland Lodge was founded to address.

It is a theme which is elegantly deployed against the background of the history of universities in the West – American and German as well as British – and which is deeply coloured by Moberly's own rich experience (modestly stated) of national developments in the 1930s. Earlier and readily identified models had by the end of the Second World War been irreversibly superseded, and in their place sprawled 'the chaotic university'. The Christian-Hellenic ideal, convincingly represented by Jowett as much as by Newman, had been anchored in a powerful intellectual tradition and buttressed by ideals and practices of community and of residence. This idealized tradition exercised a strong magnetic pull on Moberly's mind but, leaving aside a few richly flavoured nostalgic excursions into a loved Oxford of bells and Latin and gowns, he accepted that the certainties of the vanished world of his grandfathers could not be resurrected. The liberal doctrine of the university had also in its time exercised its own appeal, with defining emphases on freedom of enquiry, on the interminable openness of all questions, on the priority of issues of fundamental and pure scholarship over conceptions (ridiculed by Abraham Flexner) of the university as a 'service station', on the freedom of the student to choose his own electives from a wide range of optional studies, on the virtues of principled neutrality in the face of controversial issues of politics and religion. But the moral collapse of the German universities and the inherent limitations of such a model made it no longer a credible or fully satisfying alternative (*Crisis*, pp. 39, 41, 42, 43, 54). The third and most recent model is well described as a powerful blend of the technological and the democratic. A strong emphasis on the applicable, the useful and the profitable coalesces with a widening of access to the university beyond the traditional élites to produce a powerful and appealing mixture, 'which is at once activist and optimistic'. The new students have neither the leisure nor the motivation to become gentlemen. Yet this third model of what the university should be is inherently shallow and ultimately unsatisfying (pp. 41, 45, 48, 49).

The questions which most matter to modern man are not being asked by or in a university shy of the contentious, the speculative and the fundamental. This abstinence of course represents a reaction against earlier dogmatisms and simplifications: 'But a praiseworthy reticence in the expression of one's innermost convictions is one thing; to have no such convictions to express is another' (p. 51). Some forms of neutrality are inherently false, as the experience of Hitler's Germany demonstrated only too well. False neutrality represents 'masked partisanship', and most dangerously in matters of religion.

> If in your organisation, your curriculum, and your communal customs and ways of life, you leave God out, you teach with tremendous force that, for most people and at most times, He does not count. ... It is a fallacy to suppose that by omitting a subject you teach nothing about it (pp. 54–6).

Radical thinkers like J. D. Bernal (for whom Moberly shows considerable if grudging respect) are impressive because they do address a wide range of fundamental questions about the purposes of life, but they are able (for the moment) to do so precisely and only because of the underlying assumptions they share with an establishment they appear to attack. It is essential to understand that 'the unformulated working philosophy of life of these thinkers is much richer than their own statements would convey and is not exclusively derived from natural science or by use of its methods' (p. 84). They share, without acknowledging or being aware of it, what Moberly later (in a phrase packed with meaning) calls 'the religion of the Englishman' (p. 301). Yet these unstated assumptions can, in an age of crisis, no longer be taken for granted. Universities must now assist their members to develop a 'philosophy of life', a phrase which became almost a mantra in the early days of Cumberland Lodge and on the lips of its founder. But if for Christians there is no way back to the earlier certainties, what should they do to move forward from the uneasy truces of the present? For

> while we are ourselves assured that the whole truth is to be found in Christ, we have to recognise that it is not in the possession of Christians, either individually or collectively. It never has been, and at no historical time is it likely to be (p. 104).

As Moberly moves from diagnosis to prescription it becomes clear (and not least to him) that aims can be defined with a clarity which slips away when more specific solutions need to be derived from them. This may well have been why he found, initially at least, the prospect of working on specific solutions in one country house dedicated to those very aims more congenial than pursuing efforts to develop coherent solutions either at the national level (through for example the UGC) or within a whole university (such as Manchester).[6] Moberly's chapter entitled 'Aim and Basis' reads today more like a series of reflections on coherent approaches to the deep problems he has identified than criteria by which efforts at institutional reforms might be evaluated. More to the point, each of these reflections was consistently applied to the emerging style and programme of Cumberland Lodge itself.

The first principal of St Catharine's Cumberland Lodge takes it as axiomatic that as serious academics Christians cannot be concerned with proselytizing, or restoring a lost hegemony. Their concern must rather be with 'deepening the Christian colouring' of many aspects of the life of the university (p. 141). This means that they must themselves attend, and encourage others in their own ways to attend, to 'the deep and difficult issues of the day' (p. 146). Among the most urgent tasks therefore is the development of a philosophy of life, wherever possible based upon common values. Communications must be reopened so that men of different convictions may learn from those who differ most profoundly from them. He cites as expressing a true university spirit Henry Sidgwick's remark after visiting the Anglo-Catholic warden of Keble College: 'We agree in two characteristics which are quite independent of formal creeds – a belief that we *can* learn, and a determination that we *will* learn, from people of the most opposite opinions' (p. 125). Amy Buller frequently recalled Moberly's dedication to and mastery of 'the art of disagreeing without being disagreeable'. The right to speak freely from a depth of conviction belongs as much to C. S. Lewis as to J. B. S. Haldane (*Crisis*, p. 111). This, rather than the stilted avoidance of all contentious issues, is what Moberly means by 'positive neutrality'. In all this, importance is attached to university people 'living together', as was exemplified in the conferences of International Student Service, where groups of students came together 'for frank discussion of the most controversial and explosive questions' (p. 107). Quoting directly from an unusual source – a UGC report – its former chairman concedes that

> ... it is no part of the duty of a university to inculcate any particular philosophy of life. But it is its duty to assist its students to form their own philosophies of life, so that they may not go out into the world maimed and useless. It should stimulate and train them, not of course necessarily to think alike, but at least to think, and to think strenuously

about the great issues of right and wrong, of liberty and government, on which both for the individual and for the community, a balanced judgement is essential to a rational life (p. 108).

The identity of the draughtsman of this UGC report is not in doubt. Nor is the distance between the style and intention of such an official document and those of its successors at the end of the same century.

The university needs to have a 'master-plan. . . . Some universities are, in effect, little more than a congeries of Faculties, going their several ways; they resemble England in the days of the Heptarchy. Their chief men have discordant philosophies of life or none' (*Crisis*, p. 148). Moberly is, of course, less clear about how precisely the coexistence of discordant philosophies of life (that phrase again) is now to be avoided. But he is clear that autonomy is a necessary precondition for the restoration of purpose and direction to each university as well as to the system as a whole. The imposition of a master-plan by the state would, he of course implies, be a disaster. At the same time, the relationship of universities to public policy and financing must in current circumstances be of a positive and constructive character. Since the universities are now heavily dependent on public funding, mediated through the safe hands of the UGC, they cannot behave irresponsibly (p. 227). But the state should intervene in the internal affairs of a university only as a 'last resort' (p. 229). The first words of Moberly's book (p. 7) are an approving quotation from Thomas Arnold: 'No one ought to meddle with the universities who does not know them well and love them well.' The relationship between government and university is described in glowing terms that, read at the end of the century, must provoke a wry smile or a resentful groan. That relationship is not adversarial for only in the literal sense are there two sides of the table and the distribution of public funds is sensibly achieved through a friendly conversation among like-minded people. Vice-chancellors and civil servants share the same assumptions, the same background, and their minds as well as their careers are presented as being interchangeable. 'Statesmen and higher civil servants have generally themselves been graduates, warmly sharing in that "scrupulous respect and fond and fervid affection" for the universities which Gladstone ascribed to the whole community' (p. 236).

It is the business of the university to induct all its students into a broad culture, neither confined as in the past to an élite nor limited to practical or vocational ends. For Moberly this imperative requires, not a return to the undoubted virtues of the classical tradition, but rather an openness to the 'vital intellectual currents' of the contemporary world, and especially those represented by the physical sciences. In terms which anticipate C. P. Snow's notorious attack upon the vices of *The Two Cultures* (1959), Moberly castigates the inadequacies of the arts man who not only knows no science, but further presumes to boast of his ignorance. In the decent obscurity of a footnote Moberly scornfully quotes a sentence from a letter of commendation: 'By the careful editing of a text he has qualified himself for senior academic office' (p. 183). A reader in the autumnal years of the century is left in no doubt of what this typical chairman of the UGC would have made of the Research Selectivity Exercise or the competitive rating of universities and departments.

Induction into the broad culture may be assisted by the encouragement of more courses which seek to cross disciplinary frontiers. Equally powerful would be wider professional courses, in which individuals are educated as well as trained. Education of high quality is much advanced by the corporate living of students, and it is on this theme (fundamental to the ideals and life of Cumberland Lodge) that Moberly is more than once tempted into lyricism. For students at Oxford and Cambridge, undergraduate years were

> a time of happiness and mental expansion which glows in the memory; a time when stimulating friendships were formed, when some contact was made with one or two great men who excited reverence, when the blood ran fast and the mind exulted in a new awareness of its powers. ... The beauty and dignity of their surroundings, the studious cloisters, the high embowed roof, the storied windows, richly dight, the pealing organ, impart an element of splendour to the quality of the common life and enhance the student's sense that he has become a citizen of no mean city (p. 202).

But the storied windows, richly dight, were simply not there for the students at what had recently been labelled the Redbrick universities, whose life Moberly knew so well from his Manchester years.[7] Few of these students had been at boarding public schools, many of them continued to live at home, others lived in uninspiring lodgings; the university was a place of work to which they went from 9.30 a.m. until 4.30 p.m. and was deserted at the weekends; students and staff rarely met in informal circumstances. All this is summarized as 'inspirational poverty' (p. 206). Halls of residence have the potential to provide a powerful antidote to such drabness, provided that they are well designed, well run, and have imaginative wardens. The good warden

> ... must be able to get on terms with, and to inspire, students without overpowering them. ... He, or she, must be neither a 'dryasdust' nor a 'governess'. ... He must care passionately for the things of the mind. If possible he should have a high academic qualification, and it is extremely desirable that he should have outside contacts which may help him to open windows and to correct the natural tendency of any small community to contraction of interests. A Hall in which there is frequent coming and going of visitors from the great world and from the civic community can contribute notably to the real education of its students (p. 220).

This was the kind of Warden Amy Buller obviously wanted to be as she moved from her SCM work in London to Liverpool University in 1931, at a time when Sir Walter Moberly was still at nearby Manchester and two years before Hitler came to power in Germany.

## Amy Buller and *Darkness over Germany*

The early life of Amy Buller had nothing in common with that of Walter Moberly. Born in 1891 in London into a Baptist family she was brought up in South Africa, returning to Britain in 1911 and immediately setting herself to learn German. Her experience as a student was equally distant from that of the man with whom she was to cooperate in establishing Cumberland Lodge. In London she worked as a governess while studying part-time at Birkbeck College, an institution as remote in style and purpose from an Oxford college as it is possible to imagine. During her Birkbeck years, which concluded successfully in 1917, she became an Anglo-Catholic. Tissington Tatlow recruited her to the SCM staff as organizing secretary in Manchester in 1921 – the year in which William Temple became bishop there. Her international interests were sharpened by attending a meeting on the continent in 1922, and in the same year she moved back to London.

It was in these years that she worked at bringing together students from many different backgrounds in residential SCM conferences, of which the best known were later held at Swanwick in Derbyshire.[8]

> Study Swanwick set out to raise in students' minds those fundamental questions about the world in which they lived, the faith which they had

inherited, and even the subjects which they were studying, which (by and large) the Universities were failing to ask or to stimulate (James, p. 10).

These were also the central themes of Moberly's book, growing from the same 1930s culture, and there is good reason to suppose that Amy Buller was already thinking or dreaming of 'a permanent Swanwick' (James, p. 10). She organized retreats, calling upon the support of such friends as Edward Keble Talbot. 'EKT', the son of that warden of Keble with whom Sidgwick had agreeably disagreed, was for many years the Superior of the Anglo-Catholic community of monks at Mirfield. He was perhaps the strongest influence on Amy Buller's life, and introduced her to the Halifaxes.

In 1931 her appointment as warden of a well-established hall of residence for women students in Liverpool was 'smoothed' by Walter Moberly, still at nearby Manchester (James, p. 18). William Temple (now archbishop of York), A. D. Lindsay, W. R. Matthews (the dean of St Paul's) and many other lively visitors sharpened the intellectual stimulus and encouraged that engagement in issues of fundamental moral importance which Moberly himself was later to celebrate as marking the best of the halls of residence. Amy Buller soon won the support of Francis Scott, the chairman of the Provincial Insurance Company, whose home near Windermere was within easy reach of Liverpool and which became a centre for many of her students, friends and allies. Among these were Father Talbot as well as Edward Woods, bishop of Lichfield and a chaplain and counsellor to the royal family. The many threads – of ideas, people, influential connections, royal interest, Christian groups, financial backing – were being slowly drawn together.

William Temple and Lindsay encouraged her to strengthen her connections in Germany, where she watched with fascination and horror the disintegration of a society which, wracked by unemployment and anarchy, was falling under the spell of the false but persuasive Nazi ideology. She feared that intelligent and well-intentioned, but increasingly isolated, men would lose all contact with the traditions of a liberal and Christian West. She led two visits in 1935 and 1936 and, although diplomatic tensions led to the cancellation of a third visit, a group of Nazis did visit Oxford in July 1938 (James, p. 29). Amy Buller's eagerness to engage in serious discourse with Nazi leaders and thinkers on fundamental issues (of the meaning of life, the power of religion) naturally made her suspect in certain quarters. Walter James reports that J. H. Oldham and Amy Buller saw little of one another in the 1930s since he distrusted her views on Germany while she regarded his position on

South Africa as 'too liberal'. She certainly resented her exclusion by officialdom from making a contribution to German reconstruction after the war (James, pp. 27, 141).

Amy Buller decided to publish her reflections on these German discussions in a book that was widely noted at the time, *Darkness over Germany*.[9] By her own account it emerged from discussions with students on fire-watching duty in the Liverpool hall of residence during the winter of 1940–1: the spirit of Dunkirk and the new dynamism generated by the opposition to Nazi Germany had dissipated the apathy of the 1930s and she and her students were thrown together by adversity into an intense form of residential life. People young and old began at last to discuss the big issues which really mattered to human destiny. The text was written during 1942 and appeared in the following year with a characteristic foreword by A. D. Lindsay: 'If we are going to have the least chance of bringing young Germans back to sanity after Germany is beaten we had better understand what made them insane' (p. v). Amy Buller perceived Nazism as 'a jumble of good and bad ideas' and, without accepting his conclusions, was sympathetic to the tortured argument of an SS man in a beautifully cut uniform:

> How can you in your country just criticize and say we are anti-Christian? It may be some silly things are said by some leaders in the Party, but tell me, is it not religious to believe that there is a purpose for everyone in this life? For myself, I am again religious, for I now believe that I was created for something and that there is a design and meaning in life, whereas for five years I could see none, not only for myself but for my generation, and for my country (p. 109).

For Amy Buller what matters is 'a keen purpose in life' (p. 13). This insistence echoes similar discussions already recorded on how the young could be rescued from a pervading purposelessness without becoming enslaved by propaganda.[10]

Above all, if the dangers of a vacuum (to be filled by any dangerous nonsense) are to be avoided, constructive and open dialogue must be maintained, and that conversation (as within the fire-watching teams) must engage fundamental issues. It was precisely because Germany's own academics and teachers had failed in this critical duty that the disaster had occurred.

> I sometimes think that Hitler would never have made the progress he has if German teachers in schools and universities as well as in the Church had not so often been purely academic and remote from life and in particular from the life of the young. ... Perhaps I should say that the

real tragedy lies in a betrayal of a whole generation of youth looking for leadership and eager to serve (p. 111).

How could one anxious to serve, and indeed to lead, help the young of her own country to achieve a valid 'comprehensive philosophy of life', with which to combat false gods and false promises (p. 122)? In Britain, as in Germany, it was self-evident that this could not simply be left to 'the purely academic' who dominated so much of the university world. Could 'a permanent Swanwick' help, and what form could it take?

## The Threads are Drawn Together

*Darkness over Germany* provided the impetus towards the brave enterprise at Cumberland Lodge. Amy Buller herself was, by the time she had finished the book, restless and in search of new challenges. Francis Scott came, as so often, to her aid and guaranteed her salary for a period of years so that early in 1943 she could move back to London and the centre of affairs. The house into which she moved was leased to E. A. Bennet, a Jungian psychiatrist (and Anglican priest), who was away on war service. That house within Regent's Park was part of St Katharine's Precinct, which had a curious history derived from a medieval hospital of that name which was demolished in 1825 in order to facilitate the building of St Katharine's Dock. Although that foundation, displaced from the slums of the East End to the more salubrious Regent's Park, had by 1914 more or less ceased to function, it did have a legal existence, a Christian character, property, trustees and Mary the Queen Mother as patron. Amy Buller's plan, as it now began to take shape, was to graft her 'dream' (as she liked to call it) onto this redundant and displaced medieval foundation. With Temple now archbishop of Canterbury, and other powerful friends poised to help, protracted negotiations began.

The first meeting of potential backers, attended by Sir Walter Moberly, was held in July 1944. Meanwhile Edward Woods, bishop of Lichfield drew the attention of Queen Elizabeth to *Darkness over Germany*. This led to a request from the Queen to meet Amy Buller, in March 1944. The interview was a fruitful one.[11] In July 1946 Halifax the chairman, Tissington Tatlow his deputy, and the rest of the council received a document from Amy Buller claiming that

There is an urgent need for the re-assertion of a basic Christian philosophy in international as well as national affairs, and in the realm of individual relationships.

Whether we are concerned with the atom bomb or food for Europe, with the work of the Security Council or the plans for the health and homes of ordinary people and above all with the education and care of youth, profound moral and spiritual issues are at stake. Men acutely aware of the chaos are driven to seek the solution in political or economic creed or in the scientific method as the way out of all our ills, often without any awareness of the fact that these presuppose a view of man which may be false. ...

We believe that a college based on the Christian faith and Christian philosophy of life, where students could reside for a part of their vacation or at week-ends, would make a real contribution to the problem. If an experiment near London, in which is the largest of modern universities, succeeded in attracting London and other students, it would indicate a line which in one form or another might be developed in relation to a number of modern universities (James, pp. 74–7).

The Queen gave her support to an appeal. On the death of Lord Fitzalan, the last viceroy of Ireland, Cumberland Lodge – the grace and favour house which he had occupied in Windsor Great Park – fell vacant, and the King observed: 'That's the place for Miss Buller's College' (James, p. 91).[12] On 5 August 1947, the official announcement appeared in *The Times*. The Queen Mother was concerned at the possible confusion caused by two foundations with royal connections having the same name, and in 1948 the Cumberland Lodge St Katharine's was rebaptized St Catharine's, to distinguish it from the existing medieval foundation (James, p. 95).

## A Philosophy of Life

St Catharine's, Cumberland Lodge, was at last in place. In 1949 Sir Walter Moberly assumed his responsibilities and Roger Young (later Sir Roger Young and a distinguished headmaster) became the first resident tutor. The earliest study groups arrived in the Easter vacation, and included A. D. Lindsay, Mary Glover and Martin Jarrett-Kerr from Mirfield. The central principles which had crystallized over the past fifteen years, within the SCM and the Christian Frontier Council, and which underpinned the writings of Moberly and Buller, were now clearly articulated. Three such principles interlocked to constitute the rationale of Cumberland Lodge in its early days. First, of course, was the insistence on the Christian background (as distinct from a formally Christian mission) and an associated emphasis upon the importance of asking the fundamental questions, and so assisting each participant in every event to establish and refine a personal 'philosophy of life'. False neutrality was to be avoided, as was the pretence that traditional liberalism or scientific humanism did not themselves represent a world-view, which (like the Christian interpretation of life) should be openly and politely challenged. Although the Christian faith had indeed lost its universal power, it was the urgent duty of every believer to inject a Christian colouring into contemporary debates. A neutrality which reflected only an emptiness of any conviction was pernicious, as the German experience had showed. The reality was that when a man ceased to believe in something, he did not thereby come to believe in nothing; on the contrary, he was more likely to believe in anything.

This first principle impacted upon the second, namely that wholeness and integrity needed to be restored to higher studies. Specialization and fragmentation had enclosed scholars and teachers in conceptually unrelated worlds, between which communication had broken down. Cumberland Lodge should, in its own way, strive to re-establish a holistic debate and oblige philosophers, psychologists, doctors, historians, economists, physicists to talk to one another and to organize that discourse around such overarching themes as 'Responsibility'. Conversation of this kind, raising the perennial questions of the meaning of life and the determination of human conduct, could best take place in a newly appropriate version of the residential life of the ancient universities. Students in the modern, shapeless, neutral, bare, urban, fragmented universities lacked any experience of the common life, of learning from one another by being together in the style eulogized and immortalized by Newman. From this hard truth the third principle followed: students and teachers alike could begin to learn from one another in the communal life of a great country house, the style of which would be elegant rather than luxurious.

St Catharine's, Cumberland Lodge, was and is a distinctive place. In the early years the rambling house was furnished with sparse elegance. The style was that of country houses of a vanishing age, its sense of theatricality heightened by an aura of imperial myths and the nearness of Royal Lodge, whose private chapel could be attended by St Catharine's visitors. The existence of a small chapel in the house itself was never publicly mentioned lest there should be any hint of proselytizing: it was a necessary if symbolic part of 'the Christian colouring'. Amy Buller, who remained as honorary warden until 1964, battled to establish a distinctive style in a society which valued casual informality. Visitors were expected to behave as guests. There was no bar, although guests – provided that their return across the Great Park was discreet – were expected if not encouraged to pay relatively brief visits to the nearest inn. The warden and her senior colleagues invited, in the supposed manner of Oxford dons, a judiciously chosen cross-section of guests to sherry (South African, of course) before dinner, at which a small high table was reserved for a handful of guests – not all of whom welcomed this distinction. Walking and talking in the Park were encouraged during the generous hours of leisure. Late evening tea (curiously reminiscent of fire-watching rituals) was served at precisely 10.00 p.m. and preceded by the clanging of a bell. After that ritual, students who 'tired the sun with talking and sent him down the sky' would be smiled upon, although an unobtrusive night porter and weary tutor were always on hand to mark the distinction between the kind of conversation favoured by Newman and the frivolities of a student Saturday evening.

Within this context, groups of students from the London colleges came to the Lodge for virtually every weekend of the academic year. Boarding a train at Waterloo on Friday afternoon they were met at Egham station by an assortment of vehicles, welcomed by a tutor or resident secretary at the main entrance to the Lodge, and escorted to rooms, most of which were in effect small dormitories. The first working session followed after dinner, usually preceded by a brief introduction to St Catharine's and some gentle advice about the habits of the house. The content of the programme was determined by a joint effort of the relevant university department and St Catharine's staff. The perspectives of the foundation were built into the planning of the weekend, by visits to London by the resident tutors as well as by discussions at Cumberland Lodge itself. St Catharine's would, for example, often suggest a guest speaker who would be willing to spend the weekend with the visiting group, and introduce one of the sessions. Nearly all the groups that visited the Lodge welcomed this variety, even though the main purpose of the weekend was to build a stronger sense of community among senior as well as junior members of such groups. Discussions continued on Saturday morning, as well as before and after dinner on Saturday and Sunday. No discussions were ever scheduled for the afternoons – another echo of the habits of a since-vanished Oxford? – and the group departed immediately after breakfast on Monday. Immediately after that, the staff met in order to discuss the failures and successes of the weekend, to take careful notes of those who would obviously welcome invitations to take part in other aspects of the life of the place, and to outline future plans.

These details of domestic style were an important part of establishing a network of connections, many of which survived for decades. The history freshers from University College London, at the outset of their undergraduate years, enjoyed meeting in these structured yet congenial circumstances such scholars as Alfred Cobban (whose championship of the Enlightenment made him the most amiable yet determined of sceptics) and Joel Hurstfield. Such people were not shy of asking the larger questions about the nature of history, or its relationship to such disciplines as sociology, or the nature of religious prejudice, or the purposes of a university. LSE, and especially its international relations department, quickly established a similar relationship. King's and Queen Mary Colleges came early and often. The London Institute of Education, encouraged by such friends of the foundation as Sir Fred Clarke and Roy Niblett, found the context and principles of St Catharine's especially congenial. These powerful connections survive today, and visits from the constituent parts of London University still constitute about half of the work of Cumberland Lodge.

The London connections also provided an important element in the development of the even more central initiatives represented by what were for many years called 'reading parties'. Many of the participants in these meetings, which generally lasted for a week, had identified themselves during the regular London visits. Others were attracted by discreet advertisement and personal introductions. The dense network of personal connections which facilitated the establishment of St Catharine's furnished many of the names of those invited to stimulate the discussions in the reading parties. Senior guests often stayed for the whole week, establishing a strong sense of community and continuity of discussion, and brief visits just to 'give a talk' were not encouraged. The nurturing of such connections owed a great deal to informal as well as formal advisers – among many others, R. H. C. Davis, the distinguished medieval historian who taught at London and Oxford before accepting a chair at Birmingham, W. G. S. Adams, the ubiquitous adviser to Lloyd George and warden of All Souls who became the visitor, and John Mabbott, firmly established at St John's Oxford, of which he was later to become president and who was for many years the adviser on studies. Reading lists were prepared for all those attending these meetings, and the recommended books made available at Cumberland Lodge.

Alongside the meeting on responsibility, cherished by Moberly, there grew up a strong tradition of an annual reading party on an arts and science theme: this was above all, of course, an effort to draw into discussion scholars and students from widely divergent disciplines. A 1952 meeting was led by Christopher Longuet-Higgins (himself as polymath), the art historian Ernst Gombrich, and Alasdair McIntyre (whose first major book, on *Marxism and Christianity*, was to appear two years later). All of them returned time and again. A decade later, provoked by but not overly respectful of Teilhard de Chardin's book, a meeting on 'The Phenomenon of Man', was stimulated by Francis Crick (who argued against the building of any more college chapels), Michael Polanyi and Sir Hermann Bondi, who first came to Cumberland Lodge through King's College London and was later to become chief scientific adviser to the Ministry of Defence. In the late 1950s and early 1960s a sequence of reading parties – the first of them on the Elizabethan age – was planned around a particular historical period, and attracted scholars and students alike from the fields of literature, philosophy, religion, medicine, history and science. The youthful and then unknown Roy Strong manifested the unusual talents that were later to attract so much public attention. The ambition, preserved for many years, was to host three or four such meetings annually. Alongside them were shorter meetings, usually for a weekend, devoted to researchers in a variety of fields.

All this activity was deployed against a background of the continuing life of the house. At that time, almost all members of staff were resident: above all the warden, but also the deputy warden, the principal when that office was filled, the director of studies, the two tutors (recruited for short-term contracts from enthusiastic participants in previous weekends), three secretaries. Others came to stay for shorter but not insignificant times. Marjorie Reeves, who first visited the house in 1949, regularly arrived with a group of her own undergraduates from Oxford. Graduates were encouraged to stay in the house for periods of private study, while others came to write. Of particular importance to the community was the small group of Rhodes Scholars, mostly from South Africa, who lived in the house, taking part in its varied activities and receiving extensive tutorial guidance, for the six months or so before going up to Oxford or Cambridge. The international emphasis was consistent, and never more visibly so than at the Christmas party which replicated on a grand scale all the traditions of the English festival and which was enjoyed by students from the Commonwealth and more widely. On these occasions the chaplain was the scholarly and convivial monk Martin Jarret-Kerr, first introduced to Cumberland Lodge by Father Talbot himself.

The evolution, in rapidly changing circumstances, of the life of Cumberland Lodge would be the subject for another chapter, or another book. The themes which Moberly and Buller addressed, although now cast in different forms, are at least as relevant at the end of the twentieth century as they were in the 1930s. Indeed, the contemporary incapacity to ask any fundamental questions about the purposes of higher education, or to take seriously the implications of a Christian (or any other) view of the world, is perhaps even more alarming now than then. As for Cumberland Lodge itself, at the celebration in the Royal Chapel of its fiftieth birthday in the presence of the Queen and of Princess Margaret (who is now its visitor) the bishop of Oxford – himself a former dean of King's College London and now a trustee of St Catharine's – could quote from the founding documents and derive from them the efforts which still continue in the Great Park.

## Notes

1. *The Times* (5 Aug. 1947).
2. Sir Walter Moberly, *The Crisis in the University* (SCM Press, 1949). All references in the text are to this edition.
3. This quotation is drawn from the invaluable early history of St Catharine's written by Walter James, and published in mimeographed form in 1979. Walter James, a distinguished journalist and editor, was principal of the establishment from 1974 until 1982. The following pages are heavily indebted to this document, supplemented by the personal knowledge of the author of this chapter, who was director of studies at Cumberland Lodge from 1959 until 1962. Page references to 'James' are to the 1979 text.
4. For Moberly in the Moot, see above, pp. 37–9.
5. See below, pp. 148–50
6. It is surprising, given the ideals which linked the work of the two men and their common background, that Moberly makes no reference to the pioneering work of A. D. Lindsay at Keele. See Drusilla Scott, *A. D. Lindsay* (Blackwell, 1971).
7. Bruce Truscott *Redbrick University* (Faber, 1943).
8. For the ideas behind 'Study Swanwick' and its operation, see below, pp. 144–5.
9. E. Amy Buller, *Darkness over Germany* (Longmans, 1943).
10. See above, pp. 117–21.
11. In the tangled negotiations which followed, well summarized by Walter James, the 'project' was modified and adapted. At first there was an emphasis on 'psychological training', whatever that might have meant in practice. The hesitations between an Anglican or overtly interdenominational character continued for as long as an association with St Katharine's seemed possible. When those hopes faded, the energetic search for a house generated compromises and confusions: the Cecils withdrew their tentative offer of Hatfield when it became

clear that the new foundation would not be specifically Anglican. But by the end of 1945 the purpose stabilized in terms of the needs of young people as perceived both by Sir Walter and by Amy Buller.

12. On the earlier history of the house, and some interesting details on its transfer to St Catharine's, see Helen Hudson, *Cumberland Lodge: A House through History* (Phillimore, 1989).

*Chapter 7*

# The Student Christian Movement and the Critique of Universities

Ronald H. Preston

## Blind Guides in a Changing World

The 1930s was a traumatic decade. The early years saw the mass unemployment which followed the Wall Street crash of 1929. It was this that decided me not to read history honours but to turn to economics (naïvely, as a 19-year-old), because I wanted to understand why the Western world was in such a mess. There were six million unemployed in Germany when in 1933 the Nazi Party got the most votes (but still a minority) in the last free election. In the UK it was only rearmament which made a dent on the unemployment figures in the late 1930s. When I arrived as a curate in Sheffield in September 1940 I found many boys and girls of 10 or so who had never known their father in work, many of them skilled men. The fear of graduate unemployment dominated the horizon of undergraduates. (Graduates in economics were thought to be in a better position to get a job than those in science or arts.)

The middle and later years of the decade were dominated also by the militarism of fascism and Nazism and by the Stalinist show trials in the USSR, which were a profound shock to the many who had regarded it by contrast as a beacon of light. The Spanish Civil War pointed to a coming international war. The League of Nations was inept. The country was deeply divided socially and politically.

The universities were curiously untouched as institutions; the term 'ivory tower' seemed appropriate. The London School of Economics was an exception. In my fresher year I found myself entertaining Hunger Marchers from Jarrow. (It was shortly after there had been riots in Sheffield and Glasgow because the Assistance Allowance for children had been reduced from 3s. to 2s. a week.) In general, however, universities kept themselves apart from these ominous signs of the times, content to say, if asked, that they stood for freedom of speech and the pursuit of truth wherever it might lead, without examining any more closely the bounds within which this ideology could operate, let alone its adequacy. This ideology, of which the German universities were thought to be the outstanding example and on which many British universities modelled themselves, collapsed like a pack of cards when faced by the Nazi challenge. British universities made some response to this by adopting Jewish scholars hounded out of their academic posts, but did not see the necessity to examine the roots of their own academic communities more closely.

The Christian churches shared in the malaise of the 1930s. They had accommodated themselves to the liberal-democratic culture of the 'Western' world after the 1914–18 war and they wrung their hands over the deteriorating situation, but had no serious analysis of why events were going so wrong, and offered no remedy except to urge every individual and nation to behave better. The UK as a whole shared a Protestant culture,[1] much eroded, it is true, by the acids of modernity, but still an identifiable force. It was a 'culture Protestantism' which had baptized too easily the evolutionary and progressive view of human development in history which had been fostered by the spread of 'Western' culture and religion in the nineteenth century, often called the 'Protestant century'. In particular it did not understand the depths of depravity of which humans are capable, was bewildered by fascism and Nazism and took a long time to credit the latter's excesses. It did not understand the role of power in human life, in economic and political life, nationally and internationally, its necessity and the need for safeguards against its abuse. (The pacifist movement which was fairly strong in Anglo-Saxon churches was no help, indeed a diversion, on this point.) The principal of my theological college is a good example of what I mean. He was fond of referring, as an ultimate criterion in evaluating an issue, to 'the rational, moral and spiritual consciousness of mankind', as if there was a straightforward standard against which any truth claims, religious included, could be judged. (This could be interpreted as implying a natural-law theology, but that was not intended, nor how it was heard.)

Christians formed by this or similar outlooks, took the theory of the League of Nations at its face value and could not understand why it did not work. It required a strenuous emotional and intellectual effort to see through this ideology, to look at the realities of power politics in international politics and in the economic order. In particular a deeper Christian faith was needed if the menace of

Hitler's Nazism was to be faced before it was too late. The deep divisions in the country after the Munich Agreement reflected the difference between those who had suffered a change of vision and now saw the Nazi evil more clearly and those who remained 'appeasers', moved by fear of communism and the inevitable loss of life which war would bring. The former, the 'realists', were conscious of the inevitable ambiguities in political decisions and, when the war they expected came, joined in as 'Sceptical Crusaders' (to quote Arthur Koestler's term for them), acting vicariously on behalf of all those threatened or oppressed by Nazism, with no illusions that the negative task of removing the Nazi threat would lead to a utopia.

It was the embryonic ecumenical movement which led to this deeper understanding. Both its Life and Work and Faith and Order sides came to a focus in the Oxford Conference of 1937 described[2] above and the Edinburgh Conference a month later. The war of 1939–45 intervened, and the World Council of Churches was not launched until 1948, but the essential decisions had been made by 1939 and its leaders held together across the divide of war. Young Christians were brought into this incipient movement from the beginning, and were in later years to provide many leaders internationally. They came from the World Student Christian Federation (WSCF) founded in 1895. In the UK this was represented by the Student Christian Movement of Great Britain and Ireland. At this time it was a considerable force in the British universities. It was deeply ecumenical. Conservative evangelicals had, and have, their own movement, and Roman Catholics until after Vatican II (1962–5) were forbidden to have anything to do with the ecumenical movement. Although firmly church-rooted, the SCM was deeply dissatisfied with the divisions between churches, but so far it had taken the university structures and ethos for granted. Now it began to query them.

A beginning had been made in 1937 with the publication of a book *None Other Gods* by W. A. Visser't Hooft, General Secretary of the WSCF (later to become the first General Secretary of the World Council of Churches), in which, influenced by theological currents discussed below, he charged Christian intellectuals in the universities and the graduates produced by them with what might be called intellectual schizophrenia: with one part of their minds they thought about their faith and took part in prayer and worship but with another part they carried on their degree or research studies, and their professional activities after graduation, within academic disciplines which were based on explicit or unavowed assumptions drawn from modern culture and antithetic to Christian faith.

Visser't Hooft called for a more self-conscious sense of vocation on the part of Christian intellectuals. However, only a few had read his book by the outbreak of war.

The year it broke out saw the publication of *Blind Guides: A Student Looks at the University*, by David Paton. This came from the British SCM. Paton had been on the staff of the SCM as Inter-Collegiate Secretary in Birmingham, 1936–9. He cast a critical eye over the triviality, superficiality and sentimentality of student life, culturally and intellectually, compared with the grand claims universities were apt to make for themselves, and the rather feeble version of the Christian faith exemplified by the religious societies (including the SCM), seen against the darkening political situation of the decade and continuing mass unemployment. In the year of the 'phoney war', 1939–40, university life went on much as usual and Paton's book had little time to make much impression before everything became disrupted. It was 1943 before the issues raised by him could be taken up.

Meanwhile the SCM had made a practical protest against undue reliance on listening to lectures and regurgitating them in exams, by inventing 'Study Swanwicks'. The summer conferences at Swanwick in Derbyshire were the apex of the SCM year. Previously there had been two five-day general conferences, with a brief officers' conference in between. In 1938 the SCM substituted a ten-day study conference for one of the general conferences and the officers' conference. There was only one talk in each day. Apart from daily worship and Bible study, there was a series of themes, one of which was chosen by each conference member. Each had a syllabus and there were four hours reading time each day prior to a daily seminar in fairly small groups. By ingenious efforts a library of 2000 to 3000 books was got together to resource the study hours. This was repeated in 1939, and was considered so successful that as soon as the SCM could return to Swanwick in 1947 it was resumed.

Behind the books of Visser't Hooft and Paton lay theological changes which were having profound effects within ecumenical circles. Totalitarianism inspired a new stress on the church, which had been somewhat downplayed in favour of a concentration on building the Kingdom of God (naïvely conceived). It also produced an anti-liberal reaction in the sense of being strongly opposed to the kind of 'culture Christianity' I have already mentioned. This needed a more careful handling than it always received, for 'liberal' is a protean word and, as we shall see, some senses of it had to be reaffirmed. However, there was a considerable period when 'liberal' was a dirty word in SCM circles. Young intellectuals are likely to exercise their critical wits against the pundits who immediately precede them, or are established figures at the time. And there was certainly much to criticize in 'culture Christianity'.

On the continent the dialectical theology of the early Karl Barth was powerful, especially in its attack on natural theology. At this time it was little read in England, more in Scotland. Little had been translated. Indirectly its influence was powerful, chiefly as the intellectual inspiration of the small Confessing Church within the German Lutheran Church (the EKD) which opposed Nazism when it interfered with the internal life of the congregation (but not, alas, in its anti-Jewish policies). The leaders of the British SCM were closely in touch with this through the German branch of the WSCF.

Then there was 'biblical theology', influential in the 1930s and remaining so until its collapse in the early 1960s. The SCM ran a large number of study groups in its branches and half of them were Bible study groups. The biblical theology movement reacted against the immense variations in the various books of the Bible, which the critical studies of the previous hundred years had revealed. By contrast it endeavoured to bring out unifying threads, not only in its central witness to the coming of Christ, his mission and message, and the church which was the result of it, but in other more incidental but nevertheless important themes. So there were books on the biblical doctrine of work, or the state, to take two examples. The effect was greatly to increase respect for the Bible and its weight and authority. Somewhat independent of this a book which had great influence was C. H. Dodd's *Parables of the Kingdom*,[3] which cut through a lot of moralizing on the basis of the parables, to bring out the stark challenge they made – and still do – as a central feature of Jesus' mission transcending their cultural setting in a remarkable way.

Lastly there was the influence of Reinhold Niebuhr. Unknown in the UK at the beginning of the 1930s, by the end of it he was giving the Gifford Lectures in Edinburgh. His first book of great importance, *Moral Man and Immoral Society*, although published in the USA in 1932 and in a London imprint in 1933, was not available in an English edition until 1962.[4] However, his *An Interpretation of Christian Ethics* was quickly published in the UK in 1935, and his *Sermonic Essays Beyond Tragedy* in 1937. Many books were to come later. During the war he was an enormous spiritual support both to the embattled churches and to political leaders in the UK. To many of the senior and student leaders of the SCM he reinforced the Christian confidence which had come from the biblical and theological renewal by showing how the basic understanding of human life and destiny in the Christian faith led to a more acute diagnosis of the political and economic issues than any other, and could guide us through the details and ambiguities of political and economic choice, however dark and intricate the situation. These influences (and some others less central that I have not mentioned) led to a sober sense of Christian self-confidence. It did seem that the Christian faith could teach one to outthink those who produced diagnoses on a secular basis. It was with such a background that the SCM had the courage to undertake a critique of the university structures and assumptions within which its work was set. That had to wait until 1943.

## The SCM Commission on the Universities

Although the war limited SCM activities, it remained a powerful influence. In 1943 I became study secretary and editor of the *Student Movement* with a circulation of 14,000 to 17,000. In December 1943 the general council of the SCM passed a motion, proposed by Colin Forrester-Paton,[5] to set up a senior University Commission to consider the fundamental presuppositions of university education and their implications for the working of the SCM in the post-war university. In his speech Forrester-Paton said that the SCM had tended to be external to the university; it had failed to have a mission to the university as such, or to declare God's purpose for the university. What was the relation between the search for truth and technical training? What was the relation between the truth and the truth Christians believe in? How far was the alleged neutrality of the university on basic matters of faith or philosophy in fact an a-Christian or anti-Christian one? The burden of such an enquiry had to rest on senior members, and the SCM needed their help in understanding its own role.[6]

In September 1944 and 1945 the Commission met for long weekends at St Deiniol's Library, Hawarden, by courtesy of the warden and librarian, Alex Vidler, with written contacts in between. I was the secretary.[7] Its conclusions were published very cheaply in twelve pamphlets by the SCM Press in September 1946. The decision to publish them separately and not in a book was taken in order to persuade students to buy them or some of them, though they would have been more influential among senior members as a book.

From September 1946 onwards there was active planning for a conference of 2000 students in Westminster Central Hall in January 1948. The University Pamphlets were a central feature of the planning. Meanwhile the Christian Frontier Council had independently been studying the university question under the chairmanship of Sir Walter Moberly.[8] A joint conference of the SCM Commission and the Frontier Council was held at Westminster College, Cambridge, in September 1946 with the University Pamphlets as the agenda. The upshot was that Sir Walter was asked to write up the work of both enquiries in his own way in a major book. This he did. *The Crisis in the University*, a book of about 120,000 words, was published by the SCM Press in 1949. This marked the end of the SCM University Commission, and is here dealt with in Chapter 6.[9]

As far as the SCM itself is concerned, the Westminster Conference marked the end of the first stage of its university enquiry. Each member of the conference was enrolled in a group on one of four themes. One of these was 'Christian Obedience in the University'. The groups met once a day for seven days following a syllabus circulated in advance. Each theme was allotted one major speech to the whole conference. Daily worship and Bible study made up the rest of the programme.

So much for the basic details of the University Commission and its immediate follow-up. What of the content? By coincidence the same year that it was set up, 1943, a seminal book *The University and the Modern World* was published in the USA (and two years later in the UK by the SCM Press). The author, Arnold Nash, had been a member of the SCM staff in Sheffield and London before the war, and was on the staff of the Canadian SCM when he wrote it. His theme was part of a discussion which was breaking out in many countries in the WSCF[10] and his book became influential. The British SCM was considered to be taking the lead.

Nash attacked the alleged scholarly neutrality of the university in all questions of value and maintained that in fact it promoted a view of life which he called 'liberal rationalism'. It was rarely explicitly avowed but was pervasively implicit. He identified four elements in it:

1. That reason is presuppositionless, its model being scientific and mathematical thinking, the objectivity of which is the touchstone against which all branches of learning are to be tested.
2. Confidence in this method leads to the assumption that human beings are essentially good natured, and that human life can be perfected and human problems solved in accordance with this objective scientific method.
3. Truth is to be pursued for its own sake (a certain inconsistency here with 2).

4.   Pursuing any line of enquiry is justifiable wherever it takes you.

Nash maintained that it was these assumptions which had been blown to pieces by Nazi and Marxist attacks, before which the 'liberal' universities had crumbled. The fate of the German universities, greatly admired as at the forefront of 'Western' culture, was particularly ominous. 'Western' intellectuals had given in to a synthetic intellectual barbarism. If the hollowness of their values had been exposed, could a remedy be found on a Christian basis? Nash called for a fellowship of lay theologians, whatever their academic discipline, who would regard it as part of their vocation as scholars to relate their various specialized disciplines within an overall Christian understanding of human beings, their nature and destiny under God. In this way the role of a university within the 'divine economy' for human well-being could be established.

## The University Pamphlets and the Westminster Conference

Surveying the University Pamphlets, I start with John Baillie's *The Mind of the Modern University* in which he maintained that the university as the most exalted institution of learning should actively pursue the highest knowledge, with no upper limit to its intellectual activity. Teaching should be carried on at the growing point of knowledge with dons and students engaged in it together. What was to be the principle of selection? Some unified critical outlook was needed. Judgement could not be suspended on everything. Hidden presuppositions needed to be made clear. One of these was often that reliable knowledge could only be obtained by the methods of the natural sciences. Another was the assumption of inevitable progress in human affairs.

H. A. Hodges wrote two pamphlets. In *Objectivity and Impartiality* he urged that intellectual freedom and impartiality (objectivity) in the university be strongly affirmed, and the complexities involved in this made clear. This would enable us better to cope with the realization that total impartiality is impossible, and that value judgements cannot be expelled. Christian dogmatism was as objectionable as 'liberal rationalism'. In *The Christian in the Modern University* he characterizes the virtues of the good scholar as charity, patience, honesty, toleration and openness. The aim should be not to bury liberalism but to save it from itself by giving it a spiritual stamina. Christians should stand for a Christian liberalism, claiming no privileges for Christianity and demanding that there be no bias against it. We should beware of forms of Christianity which have a hypnotic self-confidence.

Dorothy Emmet, *The Foundations of a Free University*, stressed the role of the university in passing on the cultural heritage of the community, and adding to it by original work. For this trained minds with a sense of responsibility were necessary. Impartiality by itself was useless; the necessary presuppositions for this enterprise needed to be made clear (and they were not peculiarly Christian ones). They included the need for fairness, accuracy, the ability to recognize nonsense, toleration (not indifference), and moral courage. It must be affirmed that the things of the mind were worth pursuing and that the social responsibility of the university was to be the intellectual conscience of the community. This must be so no matter how vocational and technical university courses may be.

The title of A. R. Vidler's *Christianity's Need for a Free University* speaks for itself. Daniel Jenkins's *The Place of A Faculty of Theology in the University To-Day* expresses Christian confidence in holding its own in the university, suggesting that we were at the beginning of what might turn out to be a great Christian renaissance, referring to Barth, Berdyaev, Brunner, Maritain and Reinhold Niebuhr. Balancing this emphasis is the insistence of W. G. Symons, *Work and Vocation*, on the relative autonomy of the 'secular', independent of religious control but – in a Christian perspective – under God. There is no reason why Jenkins's theological renaissance should not allow for this.

Running through the pamphlets of Colin Forrester-Paton, David Paton, Paul White and the collective report on halls of residence is the conviction that dons and graduate and undergraduate students are together engaged in a common task, and that fruitful contact between them is to be encouraged. An 'us' versus 'them' attitude, which was very characteristic of the National Union of Students at the time and later, was to be avoided. Still less appropriate was the idea that students are consumers engaging dons in a kind of contract. Lastly there is the pamphlet by L. A. Reid, *Vocational and Humane Education in the University*, which criticizes studies in both sciences and humanities, as currently carried on, for not producing a humane education.

The upshot of the pamphlets is tolerably clear. They are not an attack on specialism as such, or on technical and vocational courses.[11] They are concerned with the kind of communities within which all these are carried on, and the research which lies behind them. Still less do they claim a privileged place for Christians.

Christian control of university institutions is not ruled out if it abides by the fundamental assumptions required by a 'liberal' university. The pamphlets are a plea for what Donald Mackinnon at the Cambridge Conference in 1946 called 'The re-creation of the liberal university at a much deeper level of self-consciousness'. This requires a strong sense of vocation and a new perspective on universities by Christian students and dons; an abhorrence of shoddy work; an ability to relate academic work to a life of prayer and worship; and a sense of social responsibility both in the university itself and in the graduates it sends into the community in the great variety of professional occupations without which a modern society would collapse.[12]

The pamphlets shunned the idea that universities should be indifferent to changing public pressures. It is a question of how these priorities are addressed, compatible with the role of the universities as the intellectual conscience of society. (The roles of the church and the university are very similar and they should have a natural affinity with one another.) Above all, with the awful collapse of the German universities in mind, the question is raised: what must the university community stand for to maintain its integrity; what must it be prepared to suffer and, if necessary, die for? Christians will add 'under God'. Others will doubtless have different faiths or philosophical bases for their convictions, but all must ask themselves this question.

The Westminster Conference syllabus clearly followed the pamphlets in its orientation. The first section summarized current dissatisfaction with the universities. The second summarized their historical development, ending with Nash's 'liberal rationalism' critique. The third took up the fragmentation of university life, leaving a dangerous opening for an 'ivory tower' attitude on the one hand or that of the totalitarian fanatic on the other. The fourth was concerned with the pursuit of truth in the sciences and the humanities. The fifth dealt with the Christian student as seeker and collaborator, including a powerful quotation from von Hügel's *The Mystical Element in Religion* (which had also been quoted by Dorothy Emmet):

> The intellectual virtues – candour, moral courage, intellectual humility, scrupulous honesty, chivalrous firmness, endless docility to facts, disinterested collaboration, unquenchable hopefulness, love of bracing labour and strengthening solitude – these and many other cognate qualities bear upon them the impress of God and his Christ.[13]

The sixth study reached the hub of the matter with the title 'The

Integral Student and the Integral University'. The primary task of the Integral Christian student, after prayer and worship, was to use the brain which brought him or her to the university, not making a criticism of its defects an excuse for sloth. As for an Integral University, it was one

> in which there is not a spurious neutrality covering an implicit faith (liberal rationalism) but in which the real assumptions and philosophies present among the senior members are openly stated, where real discussions on the fundamental issues of life are encouraged, and where the need for Christian commitment and the impossibility of the 'spectator attitude' become evident.[14]

It adds

> Such a university would have fundamental beliefs but those beliefs are such as would arise out of the intellectual task itself and would not be peculiarly Christian, though they would certainly be consonant with a Christian view of the world, and be much closer to it than, say, the Marxist view.

That is to say, a 'Christian test' for university teaching was not wanted; experience of this in the past and the present indicated that it would be bad both for the university and for Christianity. 'Christians want a fair field not special privileges.'

The last study concentrated on the SCM member in the present-day university. He or she was to become a lay theologian in the sense of seeing the bearing of Christian faith on the entire life of the university, as a community with an intellectual task in the universal economy of God. This included resisting evil, injustice, infringements of liberty, not trying to prop up what was decrepit, but seeking to infuse it with new life.

One fruit of the SCM's critique of the university, Study Swanwick, had preceded the University Commission. There were one or two immediate upshots afterwards. One was the innovation of Freshers' Introductory Conferences to the university. The first was inspired by William S. Morris in Newcastle and Durham in 1947. Morris was then Inter-Collegiate Secretary in the area. In the next year five other universities took it up, and it rapidly and properly ceased to have any connection with the SCM which had initiated the idea.

Sir Walter Moberly's book was published in April 1949. In January of that year over 100 dons met at Swanwick with page proofs of the book as their agenda. An impetus developed which led to a considerable number of groups in different universities meeting to consider the challenge made by Moberly. These were co-ordinated very informally by a small Dons' Advisory Group, which for a short period had some staff time provided by the SCM and the Christian Frontier Council jointly. Subsequently it became the University Teachers' Group (UTG) and has now become part of the Higher Education Foundation. Chapter 8 describes a central project of the UTG.

Then there was *Student Prayer*, published by the SCM Press in July 1950, though in active preparation from 1947. I collected a group of students and dons to work on it and together with T. R. Milford, then chancellor of Lincoln Cathedral, produced the final edition. The SCM had had *A Book of Prayers for Students*, originally published in 1915 and revised several times. But it was increasingly out of date in terms of the intellectual, cultural and political situation of the 1930s and 1940s. In particular it had practically no reference to the intellectual vocation of the student or that of the university's task within the social order as a community of learning, senior and junior members together. So, in addition to providing basic guidance on prayer and worship, and including a treasury of basic prayers, *Student Prayer* attempted to suggest by examples ways in which different academic disciplines could be related to both the total intellectual enterprise of the university, and to the many aspects of discipleship within the community of Christian faith. It was a pioneering effort which badly needed to be built on and developed. As far as I know, this has not been done. The SCM's creative work continued through the 1950s but in the 1960s diminished until it was caught up in student unrest.[15]

## Universities Today: Consensus or Chaos?

How does the work of the University Commission look after half a century? Others writing in this book look at this and other Christian initiatives at the time. I conclude with some very brief reflections. Clearly the cultural situation has greatly changed. It is much more varied. And science is now seen to have a much more sophisticated basis than was then thought. However, that has not necessarily led to a more sympathetic attitude towards religion. Some academics still have attitudes which have affinities with liberal rationalist assumptions. More serious is the post-modernist outlook which is so impressed by the cultural relativities of all human knowledge and its effects on language (so that language uses us rather than we use it) that a quest for objectivity becomes vain. We each work within our own framework and there is no commonality between them. This outlook has proved a temptation to some theologians, who rejoice that Christianity operates within its own faith language structure where it is impervious to any attack from outside. It can only witness (or preach) to others; and it would hope in doing so to outlive them in quality of life, but it cannot engage in meaningful dialogue with them. At the same time other Christians are taking an opposite view, that humanity will only hold together and not destroy itself in sectarian strife, if there is some accord between those of differing faiths and philosophies; and that cannot happen unless such adherents meet and engage with one another in the search for some common ground. The first attitude is the product of the same Christian self-assurance which underlay much of the Christian critique of the universities in the 1930s and the 1940s. It was more justified then than now. Behind the University Commission had been a concept of 'Christendom' involving a still valid assumption of a Christian hegemony in intellect and culture, although the growth of a post-Christian situation was not ignored. Now globalization in economic life has brought all the great religions of the world into much closer contact.

The University Commission had also focused on a small élite. Only 3 per cent of young men and women of the age group entered the university then, and of them only a minority obtained first and upper second class honours. Now we are in the era of mass higher education. One-third of the age group is in college and the Dearing Commission wants to see that expanded to 40 per cent in the next decade. I cannot think, however, that the convictions expressed by, for example, Dorothy Emmet herself, and her quotation from von Hügel, can be applied only to, and only appreciated by, the high-fliers in honours degrees. Many of the assumptions behind the University Commission are culturally outdated, but the content of what it arrived at is not. According to their ability, every Christian is called upon to use his/her brains to face honestly the ambiguities which faith and life present. Intellectual activity is one of God's gifts to human beings. It requires the virtues articulated by Emmet and von Hügel if it is to flourish. So does the social order if it is to flourish. The recreated intellectual liberalism, for which the University Commission strove, is right for today, though the setting in which it argued for it was very different.

It is disturbing to contemplate how many Christian thinkers in this century have embarked on blanket condemnations of liberalism, forgetting how much they owe to a liberal society and liberal institutions which, however imperfect, gave them the space to do it.

Each decade produces a fresh crop. It is also distressing how many of them join in emphasizing the differences between competing intellectual positions and the impossibility of mutual communication. We should be clarifying basic intellectual values and the moral values closely associated with them, and seeking allies wherever they can be found. Christians may well think they have the strongest grounds for holding to them, but others may equally well – and we must hope will – hold to them on different, but sometimes partly overlapping grounds.

Today the university world is in a ferment. Since the 1980s outsiders have been looking at us as they might a business or a government office, and scrutinizing our efficiency by criteria they might apply to a car-assembly plant. Universities are big business and are coming to resemble transnational firms. Vice-chancellors might well be called chief executives. Students are becoming customers who make a contract with their suppliers.

In 1996 Harvard University Press published a book by Bill Readings *The University in Ruins*, which argues that the rows between traditionalists, multiculturalists and post-modernists (and others) are unresolved; there can be no consensus on what constitutes 'truth' so that we must create a 'university of dissensus'. This is a recipe for social disaster. Some commitment to the virtues for which the University Commission argued is urgent. Little, if anything, is said on this in universities at the moment, or by those who frame or try to influence government policy. The concentration is on the contribution of universities to economic survival in a competitive global economy. It is time fundamental matters were specifically addressed.

## Notes

1. I leave aside the Roman Catholic Church here. Its story was not, I think, fundamentally different.
2. For these conferences, see above, p. 8.
3. For Dodd's seminal books, see above, p. 4.
4. For Niebuhr see above pp. 14–16. Scribner, NY, published the London imprint, 1933.
5. At the time on the SCM staff as Edinburgh Secretary 1943–6. Prior to the war he was a leading member of an exceptionally strong SCM branch at Oxford which presented an acute critique of the university to a number of dons.
6. I follow closely ch. 4, 'A New Self-Consciousness about the University', in Davis McCaughey *Christian Obedience in the University* (SCM Press, 1958). This fuller account is an indispensable guide to the varied activities of the SCM in the period 1930–50. He succeeded me as Study Secretary in 1948.

7. The members of the University Commission (apart from four members of SCM staff) were two University vice-chancellors, Emrys Evans (Bangor), and Hector Hetherington (Glasgow), and the following dons, Dorothy Emmet (philosopher, Manchester), John Baillie (theology, Edinburgh), H. A. Hodges (philosopher, Reading), W. R. Niblett (English, Leeds), L. A. Reid (philosopher, Newcastle), Karl Mannheim (sociologist, London), Marjorie Reeves (historian, Oxford), Paul White (physics and mathematics, Reading), and D. Whitteridge (physiology, Oxford); also A. R. Vidler, theologian and warden of St Deiniol's Library, Hawarden.

8. See above, pp. 124–5.

9. See above, pp. 124–30.

10. See John Coleman, *The Task of the Christian in the University*, first circulated in mimeograph by the WSCF in 1947 and subsequently publ. by the Association Press, NY, 1947. Coleman, a young Canadian mathematician, was on the WSCF staff 1946–9.

11. Four years later the Hazen Foundation of New Haven, Conn. published a series of studies *Religious Perspectives of College Teaching*. They included the physical sciences (Hugh S. Taylor), music (Joseph S. Daltry), political science (John H. Hallowell), anthropology (Dorothy D. Lee), biology (Edward McGrady), English literature (Hoxie N. Fairchild), experimental psychology (Robert B. MacLeod), philosophy (Thomas M. Green), classics (Alfred R. Bellinger), sociology and social psychology (Talcott Parsons), the preparation of teachers (Robert Ulrich), history (E. Harris Harrison), economics (Kenneth Boulding). Mathematics is one omission. They were subsequently published in a book (Ronald Press, NY, 1952), with an introductory chapter by George F. Thomas.

12. In this perspective the position of Oxford and Cambridge is no different from that of other universities.

13. Friedrich v. Hügel, *The Mystical Element in Religion as studied in St Catharine of Genoa and her Friends* (Dent, 1908), 1, p. 179.

14. See above, p. 126, for Moberly's concern with this issue.

15. I published an article 'The Collapse of the SCM', *Theology*, 89/732 (1987), and a fuller version is deposited at the headquarters of SCM in Birmingham. I do not yet think I have got to the bottom of it. There were special features in the British situation, but the same thing happened all over the 'western' world. One feature was that the Constitution assumed that everyone would behave in a 'gentlemanly' fashion. It was never envisaged that a group (religious or religio-political) would organize to capture the organization, so it was wide open to a minority group to do so. This happened in the student ferment of the 1960s. It wrecked the SCM. But why has it not recovered? It produces an excellent termly journal *Movement*, but it has practically no constituency. Meanwhile the SCM records, which are invaluable for a church historian of this century, are safely housed and indexed in a special room in the Central Library of the Selly Oak Colleges, Birmingham.

# Chapter 8

# Making All Things New: The University Teachers' Group Project, 1966–70

W. Salters Sterling

## People who Defined the 1960s

Anyone wishing to reflect on the 1960s in Britain, even in an area as focused as the activities of the University Teachers' Group, must first of all remind themselves of the character of that period. We speak in the 1990s of defining moments. A generation earlier the definition came from people. John XXIII in Rome, John F. Kennedy in Washington and Nikita Khrushchev in Moscow dominated the scene. They were liberated and liberating people defying the constraints of their office. Pope John, at the end of a long life, incarnated the wisdom of unfettered friendship and beneficence. John Kennedy, one might almost say at the beginning of life, expressed the potency of youth and optimism. Nikita Khrushchev, somewhere in the middle of life, enshrined some sense of the possibility of change. In concert they created the sense of a new lyric of living and how significant that was both for those who, encumbered with the memories of war and survival, yet yearned for peace, and for those who, being young, had no desire whatsoever to perpetuate the politics of destructive power. Across the generations they most evidently grouped as the Campaign for Nuclear Disarmament, which, having rooted some years earlier, flourished at this time.

In Europe the importance of personage also predominated in Adenauer and de Gaulle in particular. Both wrestled with the emerging reality of the vision of Monet, a Europe so structured and interrelated as to exclude the possibility of war. Both achieved the constitutional and social order necessary to facilitate the Herculean task of reconstruction. Neither was quite able to embrace the vigour and enthusiasm of the generation next-but-one to their own.

In Britain, Harold Macmillan wore with avuncular elegance a mantle woven of the warp of committed leadership in time of war and the woof of appreciation of the fundamental importance of the welfare state. He was, *par excellence*, the principled pragmatist, seeking to discern winds of change, but when they failed to materialize in South Africa, willing that it should be manifestly obvious that it was the issue of apartheid that would secure the exclusion of that country from the Commonwealth of Nations. Midway in the decade, Harold Wilson was the new man for a new job. A university man of professional standing without aristocratic connections and with a background in the industrial north of England rather than the shires, Wilson epitomized a nation ready for change. He had the reputation of being competent in economics, a faculty highly prized by a people uncomfortably becoming the losers in the world wealth race. He seemed able to give expression to a style of equality of opportunity that fitted well with those who had first benefited from the educational advantages introduced under the Butler Education Acts, and that could reinspire the social concerns of a cradle-to-grave caring construct after half a generation's practical experience of such.

Straddling the premiership of both men was Michael Ramsay, archbishop of Canterbury. In appearance the anthropomorphic archetype of God, in intellect an Oxbridge Colossus, in spirituality disclosing the simplicity of sainthood, in character quintessentially gracious and benign, as a preacher proclaiming, as a pastor caring, as a priest sharing, as a teacher discerning. It is probably true that Michael Ramsay most completely personified the spirit of these years in Britain, certainly in church circles. Not that he can be immediately associated with the music of the Beatles or the Rolling Stones or at all with the transient fashion of Carnaby Street or the drug culture of Hampstead Heath. These are, however, but the froth surfacing on a brew that was a potent mixture of intellectual enquiry, political reappraisal, theological investigation, economic development, educational advancement and social renewal, and here Michael Ramsay was very much at home. So was the University Teachers' Group.

## Two Key Publications in 1963

This was the setting for the University Teachers' Group in the 1960s. From its inception in 1949 it had always sought to understand educational issues from a unified perspective combining professional as well as theological understandings. Maintaining this unified focus had become increasingly difficult. When Moberly wrote *The Crisis in the University* it did not appear too peculiar to presume a largish measure of agreement about the values which should pervade the academic enterprise. Within some ten years such a presumption had begun to appear positively ridiculous. Yet consider the quite extraordinary consequences of the publication of *Honest to God* by Bishop John A. T. Robinson[1] in 1963. That book created a moment in which it seemed almost as ordinary and commonplace to think and speak theologically as it had been in Scotland at the time of the Reformation. Its sales were a publishing-house spectacular, in English and many other translations. Everyone seemed to have a copy and to have read it, and not just in university and higher education circles. Analysis attributed this to the fact that it was a bishop of the established church being delightfully indiscreet. That may indeed have been a significant reason, but much more fundamentally it introduced ordinary people to the writing and thinking of Dietrich Bonhoeffer and Paul Tillich among others, and both of these men seemed to create vibrations of three-dimensional sense in an immense range of people from the highly intelligent and well educated to persons of modest ability and limited experience. I witnessed its transforming effect in the richly endowed common rooms of Oxford and Cambridge and in the impoverished constraining slums of Dublin and Belfast. The sense of liberated empowerment which Bonhoeffer's vision of 'Man Come of Age' created, in partnership with Tillich's portrayal of the depth and ground of Being, disclosed the commonness of all our shared humanities. At one and the same time, individual uniqueness and human solidarity were revealed as hard realities with an immediacy and tangibleness in stark contrast to a world in which the exercise of power seemed increasingly remote from ordinary people and the certainty of ultimate oblivion too close to the bone for comfort. For a time there were many opportunities for people who were concerned with values in the context of human existence to get a sympathetic hearing. The University Teachers' Group decided to strike while the iron was hot, by initiating a programme of sustained study which would examine the major issues facing higher education in Britain 20 years on from Moberly.

In 1963 the Robbins Committee Report[2] was also published. It offered a succinct definition of higher education as involving the development of the powers of the mind, the development of skills useful in the general division of labour in society, the search for new knowledge, the transmission of common standards of citizenship and culture. The report proposed a considerable increase in the numbers to benefit from higher education and a flexible set of interrelationship arrangements between institutions providing higher education. Underlying it were two quite simple understandings: that higher education was an essential prerequisite for economic and social development, and that higher education was a good and necessary thing in itself, and therefore that an increasing percentage of national resources should be devoted to its development. The philosophy of the report essentially abandoned any élitist sense of higher education, while recognizing that not all institutions of higher education would achieve the same measure of excellence.

Responses to the report were vigorous and immediate. Within two weeks of its publication, the University Grants Committee had received 45 applications from local communities to be considered in the siting of the six new universities proposed in the Report. In the same period the government itself had received requests from 30 Colleges of Education and Technical Colleges that they should be considered for university status. Higher education became the flavour of the fortnight. The government itself recognized the enormous national and social need for higher education. On the other hand, the university sector dismissed the need for any significant increase in the number of universities, using the argument that an expansion in the university population might well lead to a lowering of academic standards. Indeed, the slogan 'more would mean worse' was coined by those who opposed expansion. The availability of resources quickly came to be a central issue. A companion issue was one of power. The Robbins Committee did not prescribe a binary system for higher education, yet it was clear to those in a position to discern the mind of the Department of Education and Science that such a system was to be the outcome of the post-Robbins developments, if only because the Robbins Report failed to provide any coherent relationship proposals for a sector which comprised more than 600 institutions of very diverse sizes and ranges of activity. Indeed, Robbins could be said to have perpetuated and reinforced a very hierarchical model of inter-institutional relationship in which the universities presided in the splendid isolation of their autonomy at the apex. Institutional autonomy was not to be available to non-university institutions. As the guarantor of standards in the non-university sector, the Council for National Academic Awards had to emphasize academic values, thus inhibiting curriculum development.

## The University Teachers' Group Project

This outline shape of things to come was already apparent when the University Teachers' Group study investigation was inaugurated.[3] Indeed it was the capacity of the UTG to articulate very precisely the fundamental questions facing the development of higher education that prompted the trustees of the Joseph Rowntree Memorial Trust to fund the study project for three years. The precision with which the questions could be put arose from the conferences and seminars which had been held annually in the years preceding 1965, several of them leading to major publications such as *18 +, Unity and Diversity in Higher Education*, edited by Marjorie Reeves.[4] But university staff on their own were not sufficiently representative of the higher education endeavour. There was need for the university core to be enlarged by staff from the Colleges of Education, the Colleges of Advanced Technology and the Colleges of Technology. It was the fact that the membership of the University Teachers' Group already included people from these institutions which made it possible for the UTG to envisage a holistic review of higher education. The Rowntree trustees, in agreeing to fund the project, pointed out one deficiency – there were no student members of the UTG, and yet students were a crucial ingredient in the higher education mix. How prophetic was their comment and how wise was the UTG to agree to incorporate both undergraduate and graduate students from university and non-university institutions in the exercise! Even from the distance of a generation, it is still possible to re-experience the differences that the presence of students as active participants in the enterprise meant. Discussions were constantly being earthed in reality as a result of student questions and comments. They generated a sense of the urgency and the importance of certain issues. They provided alternative ways of thinking about priorities. Their collaboration authenticated the worth of the project. Without them the project would have been a lame duck in and beyond 1968, the year in which the world-wide movement of student protest escalated to a new intensity of institutional and government confrontation. As it was, their involvement meant that the spectrum of opinion and experience incorporated in the project stretched from senior university vice-chancellors of whom Sir Derman Christopherson would be representative to undergraduate students such as Ray Smith, part-time further education student. This was a unique coming together, certainly in Britain, and almost certainly in Europe and possibly North America, in those years of tension and disruption in third-level educational institutions.

# A Crucial Issue: The Nature of Knowledge

The justification for the project came from this inter-institutional, inter-generational, inter-occupational participation which it invited and facilitated. But no sooner had it been established than it met with the serious criticism that the project was not being conducted in a manner in keeping with the professional practices and methods followed in such subjects as sociology. This criticism raised a fundamental point, for it stemmed from an understanding of knowledge and knowing in which the authority of knowledge derived from the perceived professional correctness of the method used to determine it. Such an understanding of the authority of knowledge was explicitly or implicitly held by many within the academic community, not least by members of the University Teachers' Group itself. It was not, however, an understanding of knowledge which the leadership of the project could concede as absolute, either for the project itself or for the general activity of learning and knowing at whatever level or in whatever sphere. The project was deliberately planned as a dialogue about those hidden values in higher education which elude statistical measurement.

> We are pursuing an exercise in self-criticism and examination as a group of persons professionally interested in the present condition and the future of Higher Education and the Institutions functioning in this area. We are interested in the purpose of Higher Education ... whatever we produce, it will not be a 'Robbins Report' or a professional blueprint for Higher Education, as over against some other form of professional blueprint for Higher Education. It will be rather a statement of a kind that says – Here are the danger lines of advance and here are the constructive lines of advance as we see it.[5]

In a broader sense, the criticism was seen to be of crucial significance, representing the very restricted epistomology now becoming dominant in academic thinking, planning and practice, an epistemology that offered change at the heart of the *raison d'être* of higher education. Roy Niblett reflected on the matter thus:

> There is a very widespread assumption in our time that *real* knowledge is finite, verifiable knowledge: about facts and about things that are safely dead. The means to such knowledge are observation, the more careful the better, and logical deduction. What is supposed to be a scientific attitude, one of detached examination, is almost the only educated attitude that is thought to be respectable and right for a person in which to indulge. To imagine that one can get anything that can really

be called *knowledge* about people or animals by insight, or sympathy, or intuitive understanding, is ruled out. At best such knowledge is thought of as undependable, at worst as self-deception. Knowledge is flat, two dimensional, as it were. People themselves, animals themselves, are essentially *things*. There are no great men or women: greatness is always puncturable and reducible – Byron behaved the way he did because of his gammy leg; Dostoevsky compensated for his social misbehaviour by writing novels about criminal types, saintly types and so on. Religion, the Arts: these are forms of fancy or mysticism. Unselfishness, forgiveness: these are not of importance or even reality. Virtue indeed is no more permanently significant than vice. ... This concept of the nature of real and true knowledge is very pervasive in Western Civilisation. It is manifest at one level in the certainty in the minds of boys and girls at any typical East End secondary modern school that the only subjects to be really attended to are those connected with facts and the main chance: science and technics and the 'facts of life' – these are O.K.; history, literature and religion are out. It is manifest at a very different level in the avoidance by contemporary philosophers of any mention of love as a capacity of man, or of forgiveness. Sin does not exist. External behaviour is concentrated on rather than insight. The idea that virtue itself is a form of knowledge – three dimensional knowledge – is discounted. Morality is essentially a matter of decision and choice: vision does not enter into it. Sincerity and will: these are among the few really approved qualities of modern man. Sympathy, imaginative understanding, spirituality: these are treated as unimportant or forms of self-deception. ... Now this modern theory of knowledge strikes me as quite desperately inadequate – offering little scope to the spirit and practically none to religion. University and higher education are, of course, confined to teaching knowledge in the thin sense I have been describing. It is not their business to educate three dimensionally.[6]

The University Teachers' Group could not endorse such a diminished understanding of knowledge and knowing and certainly those men of goodwill whom I mentioned at the start of this chapter were role models for a three-, if not a four-dimensional model of the map of knowledge and the learning process. How fundamentally inadequate had university and higher education become? Had the great medieval tradition of humanistic learning been sold for some latter-day mess of mechanistic pottage? It was agreed that the issues surrounding 'knowing' needed to be pursued vigorously. Not that the analytical procedures and processes should be diminished in their role, rather that they should be complemented by making provision for the human capacities of appreciation, sympathy and educational experience. We reminded ourselves that the Greek root of the word *analyse* means to dismember to the smallest parts and that the process loses much of its meaning if reassembly is neglected or cannot be achieved.[7] When that occurs, so much for the inspiration that creates masterpieces in poetry, prose, music, art, drama! So much for the multi-layered nuances of language itself! So much for the leap of imagination that maps new horizons and creates new methods in science! So much for the entrepreneurial endeavour in engineering and commerce that explores the novel and manufactures the new!

If this issue of 'knowing' was the key question of the project almost from its outset, other issues of importance can be summarized as follows –

- the much larger number of persons involved at every level of higher education with a consequent new interdependence between higher education institutions and society
- the need to treat all institutions of higher education as a whole, considering the university as a major element in the constellation of institutions
- the predominance of 'applied knowledge' over pure knowledge, i.e. knowledge as instrument over knowledge as search for the truth
- the abandonment of the traditional intellectual ideals of the university by many teachers and students
- a new self-awareness among students leading to a breakdown of personal relationships between the senior and junior members in all institutions of higher education, with a resultant questioning of the traditional structures of authority
- the questions of responsibility raised by an education designed to educate people to promote change in society and therefore to exercise power.

Many of these issues are of a kind which is going to be with us always. They do not lend themselves to absolute answers. It was to the receiving of a kind of absolute and immediate answer that most of the student leaders of the protest movement immediately before and after 1968 looked. We managed to embrace some of these leaders, like Charles Wright of Birmingham, in the work of our project. Their presence caused an initial tremor of fear, or should we say frisson of chilling excitement, among our vice-chancellorial colleagues. The rocking of the fragile barque of LSE or Essex or wherever was for some a distressing experience. Universities and colleges could not survive prolonged disturbances. The project developed its own language to make sense to both groups. The same grace is needed in each generation to find the appropriate answers to the same questions which any generation faces, and unless history is truly meaningless a generation can learn from the previous ones.

## Knowledge = Power

In 1964 Marjorie Reeves wrote: 'There is a powerful new fuel which is already providing tremendous fresh motive force in education: it is the realisation that knowledge = power.'[8] This force was basically political, in that education was viewed primarily as training for the use of power in society. It was an equation now fully grasped by governments and societies the world over. Institutions of higher education were (and are) universally seen as potential power-houses from which nations expect to draw the knowledge and expertise they regard as 'useful'. In numerous statements – in the press, on the radio, by vice-chancellors, by taxpayers, by businessmen – the point is more and more clearly made that 'usefulness' may legitimately be defined by demands external to the institutions and that he who pays the piper calls the tune. The obverse of this is the vital part played in the development of young people to maturity by the acquisition of instrumental knowledge, accompanied by the realization that power brings responsibility.

This clear enunciation of the relationship between knowledge and power made a great deal of sense then. It is even more pertinent now, for in the intervening years the potency of knowledge has come to be recognized even more clearly as wealth-creating. While some of this knowledge is generated outside the formal structures of higher education, much of it is created within them. The most immediate and striking example of this is the 'Celtic Tiger' economy of Ireland, built almost exclusively on the quality products of Irish institutions of higher education, together with their partnership approach with industry to research and development activity.

Yet juxtaposed to this equation we placed another: knowledge = enjoyment. 'Enjoyment' was here used as an umbrella term to cover both the exhilaration of a search for truth and the personal enrichment of which Roy Niblett wrote so eloquently. It is the response of the personality to all that is exciting, stimulating, beautiful and aweful in the expanding fields of knowledge open to exploration. Were these two equations incompatible or complementary? What kind of educational experiences were needed to hold them in tension? On the one hand, education must acknowledge the dangers of power for persons and for societies. It must include training in the methods of applying critical scrutiny to its manifestations and of assessing their implicit values, examining the ends for which the community deploys the means of power. That examination involves the relation between generations, for human beings grow to maturity partly by striking their roots into the past. At the stage of higher education this transmission of values must be made explicit and open to critical examination, so that every generation has the opportunity to create its own understanding of human life in depth and wrestle with the issues surrounding the nature and destiny of humankind. It was here that we made an almost unperceived transition to the second equation: 'It is enjoyment that sparks us oft and keeps us alive. ... Experiences of spontaneous delight – in colour and sound and shape, in exciting ideas ... in great visions grandly expressed ... feed back into the energy which has to be applied usefully.'[9] We must feed the imagination and the spirit on the works of God in nature and in humanity in such a way as to open up the ultimate questions, and such enquiry must inform each of the very diverse disciplines which constitute higher education – not just be some kind of liberal arts overlay on them. Education for power and education for enjoyment must be seen as obverse and reverse of one coin and stamped upon this is a divine superscription.

## Learners and Learning

For some of us, the first step to be taken on the road to true humanity in education was to set aside, if not abandon, the designation 'higher education' in favour of the description 'higher learning'. This move opened up many horizons for growth. Education conveyed, and often still does, a sense of being done to or being done by. There is a prescribed programme of activity which the teacher effects. Education can too easily be about filling buckets from the muck-heap of knowledge and emptying them in the divisive process of examinations. Learning should be about sharing rather than receiving, making rather than being made, finding out rather than being told; examining is about endorsing and reinforcing learning rather than categorizing and pigeon-holing individuals. Learning is a partnership between older and younger; it endorses community and personal experience. The dynamic replaces the static. Flexibility and experimentation become key criteria in the way educational institutions are organized for learning.

Within this 'learning' ethos is another human feature, to do with human explicitness. Sir Eric Ashby in 1969[10] identified the academic profession as a very young profession, as against its long and earlier history of what might be described as an amateur occupation. That change to professional status seemed to promote levels of personal detachment in staff of all kinds in higher education, a trend to which the race to publish and be promoted also contributed. Intra-disciplinary competitiveness reinforced attitudes of secrecy about knowledge and first-in-the-field success evoked postures of *prima-donna* primacy. Nothing of this has much to do with healthy learning. So a human and humane experience of higher learning becomes concerned with how the achievement of outstanding distinction could be combined with commitment to community engagement in each institution. The pressure is all against being oneself, and yet at the end of the day the student acclaim is still for those who have made some kind of effort to share the process of learning and care for those who want to be part of that process. Being oneself is not something which comes easily to many professional people. Masks are worn in public for all kinds of reasons. They provide protection in moments of confrontation with the truth, as when a student starts to ask questions of immediate relevance. They disguise identity in moments when to be personal would be too costly. Masks do have their uses, but one of them is certainly not to prevent comradeship between the learned learner and the learning learner in the pursuit of knowledge. It was difficult to convince higher education staff of the need for human explicitness in the turbulent times of the era of student protest. Uncivilized behaviour threatened the *stabilitas* of individual academics and shook the foundations of many quite venerable institutions even in Britain. A way of life wrought on the anvil of scholarship appeared to be disappearing overnight. Dons of a Marxist persuasion delighted in the disruption of the decadent, as they saw it. Dons of an Erasmean hue sought to preserve some semblance of pastoral patronage towards the young. Most college staff were mystified in the maelstrom of institutional upheaval.

The call to human explicitness was the response of the University Teachers' Group to this danger. To be openly human was a challenge to those in authority not to rely solely on the status of office, or the manipulation of information, as they sought to manage their corporations. To be openly human was a challenge to the leadership of the revolting students not to use brute force of numbers, practice of demonization or ideological cant, as they sought to be heard and to secure a voice in the affairs of their communities. To be openly human was a challenge to those caught in the middle, both staff and students, not to be mesmerized or conned by either party but to require of both intellectual clarity, reasoned argument and respect for persons as they sought to go about their daily business as learners.

An invitation to openness of being was an invitation to a new theatre of discourse. The extent to which the rulers and the ruled actually shared common ideals constantly amazed project members. No vice-chancellor or college principal that I came to know wanted to be a party to injustice inside or outside his or her own institution. Few, if any, were really attracted to institutional paternalism in the treatment of students. Their students almost unanimously showed a horror of social and economic injustice at personal, national and international levels, and perceived corruption as endemic to the exercise of power, in politics, commerce and academic institutional organizations. If those in authority behaved as potentates and those in servitude as proletariat, the outcome was confrontational pandemonium and personal paranoia. Where those in authority acted as servants of a common endeavour and those in a position of powerlessness acted as agents of communication, then the outcome was creative engagement and common enrichment. And such did happen without and within the study project.

It was as if a parable was being played out. The search for openness of being, for human explicitness, made good common sense. Higher learning in its essence has never been about the exercise of power *per se*. Clerks in the service of church and state – the products of the great medieval universities trained for the chanceries of pope and bishop, prince and baron – had as their first duty the service of God. Academic life *sui generis* had as its vision the pursuit of truth. The service of God and the pursuit of truth are both activities calculated sooner or later to endow the most mighty with some measure of humility. When either or both are absent, the propensity of persons to become aridly arrogant propels even the best of academics, politicians and ecclesiastics into orbiting the space of territorial imperative and institutional domination, where the exercise of individual authority becomes authoritarian.

## The Nature of Authority

The word authority is beginning to assume a central importance here. It is time to explore some of the dimensions of its meaning as they came to the attention of the project. Historically the authority of the university, expressed in its autonomy, had been frequently the subject of external challenge from the very agencies of church and state which it had sought to serve. The modern challenge from students started in the United States when the civil rights movements engaged the imagination, energy and convictions of a whole generation of students inspired by the compelling vision of Martin Luther King. The issues rapidly became comprehensive in their criticism of how institutions of higher education were organized, managed, governed, including what they taught and how they both taught and examined it. Eventually the movement spread to Europe and Britain, but even before the Year of the Young Rebels, as Stephen Spender designated 1968, the UTG project had already begun to examine in depth the multi-faceted challenge to authority as it affected institutions of higher education.

Charles Wright demonstrated student concerns in respect of authority from his standpoint as president of the Students' Union in the University of Birmingham, in a paper given at the UTG conference in Bristol, July 1968. He highlighted the separation of higher education from almost all of society except 'the old big business men'. This produced a hierarchic form of personal relationship within the institution derived from a hierarchic view of intellectual activity which militated against community. Further, he identified higher education as very much a middle-class pursuit even if many students were un-class-conscious. He noted

> I think there is a very real problem particularly for working-class students and the few students which there are from Secondary Modern Schools, whom I know, who find themselves completely unenamoured of the academic tradition and are generally part of the dropout culture of sitting around the union listening to records and disassociating themselves from the whole thing.[11]

This middle-classness leads to paternalism, to an expectation of deference. The moral authority of the institution now derives from a concern with its good name rather than its role *in loco parentis*.

> You cannot get drunk in the street. ... One way to expose how ridiculous this is, is to contrast the nature of a student's life in a Hall of Residence with that of someone of, say twenty or twenty-one, who left school at fifteen. The latter is possibly married, raising a family, even trying to get a mortgage on a house. If one contrasts these two styles of life, and one further notices that the student is the educated person, then one realises how ridiculous this form of authority is.

Wright further identifies control by the few, the divisiveness of academic specialization, the increasing impersonality, the mechanical pursuit of good order as contributing to the climate in which the student is challenged to confront the authority of institutions of higher education. All this leads to a basic irrationality at the heart of authority in higher education in that such authority is not rationally planned or defended.

> Because 'authority' exists very largely from habit there are 'ways of doing things' and if you do not do things this way, you are accused of being irresponsible, or of being an agitator, or of being apathetic, or of 'not behaving in a manner conducive towards the function of an academic community'. One is accused of doing something which is so incredibly vaguely formulated that it is more an irrational gesture, than a rational justification. I note particularly the use of the word 'responsible' by Vice-Chancellors, which I think has become so debased as to be used completely irresponsibly. And the use of the word 'rational' has also become so debased that it is used completely irrationally. When students really push it, the last justification is that you must put up with things as they are; that things *will* change. But they must change slowly and this is, in fact, not an explanation of what will happen, but a justification of the *status quo*.

So there it was. Higher education in its isolation was out of touch, was middle class, was hierarchic, with control in the hands of the aged few, its activities increasingly divisive, its operations unresponsive and sclerotic. How could institutions of which this is a description appeal to any kind of authority? There were few, if any, within the membership of the UTG prepared to defend the *status quo* or even challenge as caricature the picture which Charles Wright presented. Most wanted to achieve change without disposing of the baby with the bathwater. Charles Vereker of Durham, challenged us to be radical – to go back to our roots by examining the *auctoritas*, the *magisterium*, and the *stabilitas* of the European university tradition.[12]

*Auctoritas* leads either to authority backed up by force of arms or authority which functions on a moral basis without anything that one would normally call a sanction.

> What I want to suggest to you is that right from the beginning of what we call academic activity (and we can go back, I suppose, at least to Socrates), it is this latter kind of 'authority' which places of learning have stood for. They are in some sense dedicated to discovering what is called truth.

In the beginning, Vereker claimed, once the assertion of the truth had been made, it could not be altered. Now that has changed and the established truth is open to critical reappraisal. The sense of absolute authority has to be modified by the authority of critical reappraisal. Together this double tradition constitutes the excitement of European civilization. The question is, how can it be incarnated in a contemporary institution of higher education?

Vereker regretted several analogical parallels which were then beginning to have currency and are still around today. Institutions of higher education are not shops selling more or less nourishing items from which one can make a choice. They are often purveyors of dusty answers, the significance of which may only be discerned properly after 20 or 30 years. Again, they are not analogous to industrial plants. What are their products? Degrees? Degree holders? Nor are they suitably analysed in political terms as some kind of state with member citizens. If institutions of higher education are not analogous to shops, or factories, or states, what are they and what form of authority is appropriate to them? Vereker argued:

> We have somehow got to have an institution in which the authority attaches to the awareness that what is going on is seriously worthwhile, that the people who are doing it can be seen to be doing something which is fascinating, and which should be accorded respect, and that the kind of relationships we have within it make this plain all the time.[13]

To illustrate this he reached for the apprenticeship model, laying the onus on the masters and doctors to teach the 'tricks of the mystery'.[14] The conditions in which such learning will thrive are those of *stabilitas* but the *stabilitas* of the great cathedral, of the quiet scholar and of the saint are not appropriate. In our time what is required is the slightly inebriated ice-skater, having enormous fun as the processes of change happen, as knowledge is transformed, as juniors begin to teach seniors, and as voluntary academic poverty takes the place of a scramble for money, power and status.

Vereker's vision was one that was taken seriously in the project. We accepted that, in higher education, authority is that moral force which compels respect and assent without the use of anything one would normally call a sanction. So what then is the moral force which compels consent without sanction? Does it inhere in the body of knowledge which is inherited within a given discipline? Yet our methods of developing, expanding, marketing knowledge are methods based on analysis and criticism which assume that everything which is given can be called into question. Could it be that the methods of knowing are the moral force? Not entirely, since the methods of knowing are themselves the subject of constant review and adaptation. Again is it possible that the knower is the source of moral authority – so-and-so is an 'authority' in such-and-such? This position is no more satisfactory than the previous two. While recognizing expertise and competence as the possession of a particular individual in a particular field of study, the history of the development of knowledge precludes any attempt to accredit the 'knower' with absolute moral authority. The knowledge of the knower is the subject of rigorous scrutiny. Could it be that academic authority resides in some kind of amalgam of knowledge, the method of knowing and the knower? We returned to the Vereker *stabilitas* of the ice-skater (slightly inebriated). At the end of the day, we settled for an alchemy of authority involving personal integrity, openness to change, and social awareness, joining the knower, the knowledge and the method of knowing as ingredients in the mixture. The quantities of each we left for experimentation by each institution in its particular situation. Not, you may say, a tangible outcome. But then authority is not a particularly tangible characteristic in persons or in institutions.

## The Role of Teachers

The project produced an almost unanimous view that the teachers in institutions of higher education are the key ingredient. We understood the role of the teacher as defined by two questions: 'What is needed for the making of a real person at the student level?' and 'What are the necessary ingredients in this process which the older generation must contribute as teachers (or more advanced learners)?' To the first question, Marjorie Reeves provided two answers – the achievement of personal autonomy and the achievement of personal significance.

> The first represents the personality in its aspect of aloneness, the second in its aspect of togetherness. By the growth of personal autonomy I mean the process by which a developing person learns to test and assess the experiences that crowd in upon him or her, selecting, forming judgements, determining long-term objectives. It is a process of drawing a circle around oneself and realising consciously: 'Inside this circle – this is I myself'. The second represents the personality found in and through relationships.[15]

Here personal significance is discovered in the roles that can be played in smaller and larger units of society and the contribution that this makes to community living. We should concentrate therefore on nourishing an expanding power of exploration coupled with reflection, a growing sense of function coupled with responsibility. Reflection is the process of making this experience one's own within the circle of autonomy. Sense of function here means the perception of the varied ways in which one's knowledge and skills, one's understanding and one's very enjoyment, can be given to the community. So what must the older generation contribute to the fostering of these experiences? Teachers must communicate their own sense of meaningfulness and enjoyment in the fields of knowledge in which they teach. It is useless to be learned if with learning one conveys a sense of its triviality or irrelevance or dead dullness. In addition they must put their experience in their respective fields at the service of students who do not know the full riches they might be exploring. Sloth or inertia, in sticking to old syllabuses and courses when expanding horizons of knowledge offer new possibilities, constitutes a denial to the student at precisely the point at which the older generation might have something to give. Further, teachers must constantly stimulate the process of analysing and reflecting on all that is learned and experienced. This goad – challenging assumptions, exposing muddled thinking, pushing reflections deeper, encouraging personal judgements – is constantly needed.

The complementary roles of the teachers relating to function are that they do not live their academic lives in ivory towers, but in full relationships with the full community; that they constantly press home to students the full extent of their reliance on the community; that they should experiment with syllabuses which are oriented towards community issues; that individual teachers will discuss specific functions with particular students. This agenda of roles for the senior members of institutions of higher education was accepted and endorsed as a visionary remoulding of the ideals of inherited values with the demands of the contemporary challenges. The question still remained: could individual teachers be expected to be paragons of such good practice? That question brought into focus a further concern about the nature of academic community.

Were existing academic institutions really nothing but agents of oppression, aligned to establishment interests to such a degree that only their complete overthrow could satisfy radical Marxist students?[16] Charles Wright had given us a more temperate but still deeply critical view. The UTG listened attentively to him and to some of his more extreme contemporaries but rejected such an analysis. The fundamental importance of autonomy to the well-being of the individuals and institutions involved in higher learning led us to the clear recognition that enslavement to or by an ideology is no less damaging than similar enslavement to or by governments, churches, major corporations or wealthy benefactors.

Nevertheless, to reject such an analysis did not mean that some form of radical review of institutions of higher education as 'communities' was unnecessary. Oxford and Cambridge as models of university good practice had long occupied centre stage in the grand narrative of Anglo-Saxon universities. Their formula of small self-governing institutions providing all the essentials of living, and many of the non-essentials, was regarded as providing the near ideal for academe. Community in these terms was closely knit, highly ordered, life-lasting, career-promoting, all-providing and reputation-sustaining, at least for those who conformed to the conventions. Smallness of numbers and scale was a prerequisite for community life of this all-embracing intimacy. In terms of rediscovering what knowledge and knowing are, what the proper form of authority is and what the role of the teacher ought to be, it had much to commend it.[17] Three important considerations made it an impractical model. These were early recognized in the project. The movement towards mass education, though hesitant in the 1960s in Britain, was regarded as irresistible. The costs associated with providing small units for larger numbers were recognized as prohibitive. The ivory-tower element of the closed society was regarded as less than desirable.

But did the rejection of the Oxbridge model mean jettisoning the concern with community? The answer was an emphatic no. Were it otherwise, it would have meant a dismissive rejection of all that the great Scottish tradition of university education, as expressed in St Andrews, Edinburgh, Glasgow and Aberdeen, stood for, not to speak of the worthy traditions and achievements of universities like Bristol, Birmingham, Manchester, and the Greater London colleges. Given the historical experience represented in this roll call of distinguished institutions, it was immediately obvious that any search for a blueprint of community would be from the beginning a utopian exercise. What was the alternative? Given the complexity of the task, the answer could be no more complete than a series of axioms, each of which emerged at different times and which were never compiled into a comprehensive and coherent collection. They are nevertheless worth contemplating.

- In some way institutions of higher learning must promote caring as both a corporate and an individual feature of their existence.

- Decision-making in institutions of higher learning must be by processes which encourage maximum participation by staff.
- Participation by students in the decision-making processes is also to be encouraged except in those areas where to do so might appear to jeopardize the quality of the academic process or the academic award.
- Large institutions should organize their physical environment, their academic arrangements and their cultural activities in such a way as to encourage and promote the emergence of small-scale community life.
- Paternalistic practices and relationships in the organization of student unions, halls of residences and student cultural activities should be abandoned in favour of either student-led arrangements or partnerships of equal standing for both junior and senior members.
- In the conduct of examination and assessment procedures the objective of learning should be as important as the objectives of judgement and classification which are inherently divisive.
- In organizing courses, structures of learning are as important as 'customer choice', but maps of knowledge do not have fixed boundaries; some measure of discourse across them is highly desirable.
- In matters of social mores the process of consent should replace the requirement of conformity.
- There is a responsibility on the senior members of the enterprise to be publicly explicit about the traditions, practices and procedures of the intellectual life, very particularly those which are shared across all areas of knowledge, such as the anathema of plagiarism and the fraudulence of falsifying results or evidence.
- The need for good communication is paramount for two reasons – because it is a fundamental element in the building of trust, and because without it there is a real danger of institutionalized hypocrisy developing in institutions whose *raison d'être* is, among other things, the provision and handling of information.

These themes of knowing and learning, human explicitness, authority, the role of the teacher and the nature and characteristics of the academic institutional community were the dominant concerns of the project. There were many others too numerous to be included in this appraisal. The tangible results of the project were six broadsheets,[18] published for the UTG by the SCM Press, and a book by its chairman, Sir Derman Christopherson. But its business was unfinished. In 1970/1, a further project was floated with the title 'Towards an Ethic of University Existence', which never materialized through lack of funding. The cultural climate was changing and the probing of fundamental values at the frontier between the spiritual and material worlds no longer seemed so important.

Perhaps the abiding value of the project lay in its quality of extraordinary openness to ideas and persons – a quality often equated with a dangerously spineless lack of conviction. Not so in the UTG project. Charles Wright identified its core quality as being that of a profoundly held Christian understanding of personhood encountered in the way both listening and speaking occurred. Not everyone would or could have consciously acknowledged a lordship of Christ in their thinking and doing. Nor was such acknowledgement necessary. Rather was the truth articulated by Albert Schweitzer in the *Quest of the Historical Jesus* powerfully reaffirmed in our company:

> He comes to us as one unknown, without a Name, as of old, by the lakeside, He came to those men who knew Him not. He speaks to us the same word: 'Follow thou me!' and sets us to the tasks which he has to fulfill for our time. He commands. And to those who obey Him, whether they be wise or simple, He will reveal Himself in the toils, the conflicts, the sufferings which they shall pass through in His fellowship, and, as an ineffable mystery they shall learn in their own experience, Who He is.[19]

If not for all, certainly for some, that happened, and the colleges and universities of Britain and Ireland were the better of it.

### Notes

1. J. A. T. Robinson, *Honest to God* (SCM Press, 1963).
2. *Higher Education* (HMSO, 1963).
3. For the origin of the UTG in the more cautiously designated Dons Advisory Group, see above, ch. 7, p. 152.
4. The change of name (DAG to UTG) in 1960 signalled a realization that academic issues could not be separated from moral and spiritual ones. The conferences in the following years struck out more boldly, tackling in 1961 the proliferation of new universities (see W. R. Niblett (ed.), *The Expanding University* (Faber, 1962)); in 1962 the widening concept of higher education (see M. Reeves (ed.), *18 +, Unity and Diversity in Higher Education*); and student motivation in 1964 – a prophetic conference foreshadowing W. S. Sterling (ed.), *Reflections on Student Protest* (SCM Press, 1968).
5. Quoted from the Project Papers. This collection of project meeting minutes, conference reports, commissioned papers, secretary's reports is at present in the possession of W. S. Sterling and will ultimately be deposited in the Central Library, Selly Oak Colleges, Birmingham.

6.  Project Papers.
7.  This issue of the use and abuse of the analytical method surfaced at several UTG conferences, e.g. 1972, with the general title 'Either–Or: Tensions in the University', in a session on 'Academic Techniques: "We Murder to Dissect"'.
8.  M. Reeves, *Education for Power or Education for Enjoyment*, Winifred Mercier Memorial Lecture (Whitelands College, 1964).
9.  Ibid., p. 14.
10. Eric Ashby, *The Academic Profession*, British Academy Lecture (1969).
11. Project Papers.
12. Charles H. Vereker, Professor of Political Theory and Institutions, University of Durham, 1966–73.
13. Project Papers.
14. The apprenticeship model has since been used with great effect by Alasdair McIntyre in *After Virtue: A Study in Moral Theory* (Duckworth, 1981).
15. Project Papers.
16. At a WSCF conference at Turku 1969, a student orator proclaimed loudly: 'Universities are the lead-dogs of capitalism.'
17. See above, ch. 6, *passim*.
18. N. Spurway, *Authority in H.E.*; C. Vereker, *Learning and Thinking*; K. Wilkes, *Community and Identity in H.E.*; R. Chester, *Towards a Satisfactory Way of Academic Life*; B. Fletcher, *The Freedom and the Autonomy of the Universities*; W.S. Sterling, ed., *Reflections on Student Protest*.
19. Albert Schweitzer, *The Quest for the Historical Jesus: A Critical Study of its Progress from Reimarus to Wrede*; translated from the German (Tübingen, 1906) by W. Montgomery (London, 1910).

# Part III

*Chapter 9*

# Then and Now

David L. Edwards

Almost all human lives make very little difference to the way the world is; that is certainly true of my own existence since birth in 1929. But one feels the world through one's own life and it has so happened that I have experienced for myself, in a small way, some of the major changes which have altered the connections between Britain as a society and Christianity as an ingredient in it, over almost 70 years.

I have felt the end of empire. I grew up in Egypt, then a colony more or less, where my father was an inspector of schools. One memory is of people throwing their sun helmets into the Mediterranean as the liners left Port Said and the Canal on their voyage 'home' from India. I thought of the empire as being British territory from Southampton to Sydney, and also as being an instrument for good somewhat vaguely linked with the hand of God; and when I began to think seriously about Christianity's relevance (years later) I found nothing strange in the widespread pride in the powerful defence sustained by Britain as a world power against the evils of Hitler and Stalin. But I have lived to see the empire gone, the 'Christian values' fought for in the Second World War replaced by 'pluralism' if not by a thorough secularization, and a more naked Britain shivering on the brink of real membership of the European Union, with an extremely reluctant but growing awareness of the need to learn lessons as well as languages from fellow Europeans. Again and again the Union Jack has been lowered.

Because of a scholarship open to sons of 'colonial civil servants', and later because of a grant from the welfare state, I was given a good education and found myself in 1952 a fellow of All Souls College, Oxford, reputed to be one of the most élitist establishments in Britain and to a considerable extent living up to its reputation. So

I entered a world of privilege: quite a small world full of superior brains but one where the assumption of a right to give 'leadership' of one sort or another was softened by a sense of duty to do so honourably, courteously and if need be at some self-sacrifice. I also belonged temporarily to that world when I was a canon of Westminster Abbey and the Speaker's chaplain in the House of Commons. And I inhaled the same air of *noblesse oblige* when I was on the staff of the Christian Frontier Council, a group of laity in 'responsible' positions which stimulated or sponsored much of the thinking discussed in earlier chapters of this book. But I have lived to see that what may be called 'posh goodness' is out of fashion, for many reasons about which readers do not need to be told. What is relevant to this book is that Christian thinkers are now obliged, if they are to reach their contemporaries, to remember all the time that Britain is a democracy, with ideas implanted less by the leadership of 'the great and the good' and more by the music, the images and the soundbites of the media. The public is no longer deferential. Would Archbishop William Temple get much of a hearing now? Would T. S. Eliot?

I went to the King's School, Canterbury, and although most of my contemporaries were not at all churchy the influence of Canterbury Cathedral, and of what it represented, strengthened the immature conviction already in me that I was called to be a priest of the Church of England. I have had many happy experiences of that church – of course, because I was on the staff of St Martin-in-the-Fields, observing all its religious and social work, and later on the dean of the cathedral which is the central symbol of Norfolk, and I have ended up in retirement in Winchester. I have written a number of books about Anglican and wider church history and between 1976 and 1989 I wrote almost all the editorial leaders in the *Church Times* in addition to longer commentaries on ecclesiastical affairs. So I have enjoyed what was the situation of many of the people whose thinking has been presented in previous chapters: a solid base in church life. But from the early 1960s downwards I have lived to see not only a large statistical decline in my own church but also a similar or even more alarming decline in most other churches. And the dream that the Church of England, Methodism and the United Reformed Church might unite was shattered. The optimism which surrounded the Second Vatican Council can scarcely be remembered.

In greyer days the energy of the British churches has gone mainly into the hard work of survival, into internal debates about what message might be heard by the unchurched millions, and about the spiritual or emotional 'new life' which the churches can offer despite their divisions and contractions – perhaps more strongly just because they are now self-conscious minorities. It is not the case that the churches have become entirely introverted (I served as the chairman of Christian Aid and know from that experience that many churchgoers have wide-ranging consciences), but the old assurance of central significance and moral leadership in society has gone. While I was the editor of a theological publishing house (the SCM Press) we brought out a small paperback, Bishop John Robinson's *Honest to God*, which became the hotly denounced and hotly defended summary of deep self-questioning within the churches. The excitements of that period, the 1960s, have died down but the mood has continued to be very different from the general acceptance of traditional dogmas in most of British history (with, of course, battles over which dogmas were the more correct). To be honest, the churches have been in no position to exert much influence in politics or in any other aspect of British life.

Three years after publishing *Honest to God* I moved to an environment which opened my eyes more fully to the diversity in the religious situation. I was then the dean of King's College chapel in Cambridge, a masterpiece of architecture and church music surrounded by a university which, for all its own heritage of gracefulness, was not untouched by the turbulence of the youth culture and the student protests. Coming from a background in the Student Christian Movement, I felt sympathetic with the passion of many of the young to greet and enter a new world of personal liberation and social justice; yet I was responsible for the maintenance of a dignified beauty which also had its value. The tensions helped me to understand why the SCM moved away from historic churches and in the process ceased to be a large-scale organization. I was involved in the work of the British and World Councils of Churches, bodies with a radical cutting edge partly because many of their leaders had been trained by the SCM, but I lived to see the BCC disbanded (in favour of a less active council including more churches) and the WCC much reduced in influence (at least in Britain). What survived more vigorously was a more conservative kind of religion, evangelical or catholic or aesthetic, which answered timeless personal needs. The kind of Christianity which the 'liberal' SCM had taught also survived but was involved more in the culture of contemporary society than in the churches' traditions. A gloomy analysis could see all this as a contrast between fossils and jellies.

I am not saying that in the churches no concern for the welfare of

Britain has survived. My last job was as provost of Southwark Cathedral, in an Anglican diocese covering South London. No one with any sensitivity could have failed to notice the contrast between poverty and wealth, dramatized around the cathedral: only the River Thames separated a deprived and depressed 'inner-city' area (with 'hard-left' local authorities) from the get-rich-quick City, booming after the deregulation of the 1980s. A similar contrast could be observed in Thatcher's Britain as a whole, although perhaps less vividly, and the response in the Church of England was to produce the report *Faith in the City* and the subsequent Church Urban Fund, in order to do something about the problems of the 'underclass' which the comfortable found it convenient to ignore. As long-term unemployment continued into the 1990s the ecumenical report on *Unemployment and the Future of Work* produced further ideas, both radical and constructive, demonstrating the continuing liveliness of 'social Christianity' despite the changes in the religious situation.

But these reports, and the thinking and action before and after them, had to address a social situation which made Christian commentary harder than it had been during the 1940s, when it could be taken for granted that the British public was on the side of the angels, first in the war against Nazism and then in the determination to escape from the social injustice of the 1930s.

In the 1940s and later, attractive assumptions could be made – that full employment (which had in fact been secured by rearmament) could be maintained since technology and the global market would not change drastically; that 'insurance' guaranteed by the state would cover temporary periods without a job or without full health; and that for many young people a fairly relaxed education, with as much emphasis on personal development as on the acquisition of information and skills, would be adequate. It was also widely believed that many important industries would be run better if removed from private ownership. For many Christians, including many who voted Conservative, these policies seemed to be reasonably safe and to be the consequences of the manifest duty to seek justice in society. But half a century later few can be found to defend what seemed obvious in the 1940s – and few can be found who have a clear alternative vision.

There is indeed a vision of social justice in its basic principles, and it was articulated in the 1996 statement by the Roman Catholic bishops on *The Common Good*. But the application of these moral principles to current controversies has raised great problems. Precisely because Britain has become more completely a democracy (as many Christians had learned to advocate) and has raised its material standards of living (as Christians on the whole welcomed), the poor have become a minority in the elections and the majority, while wanting 'better public services', has also wanted lower, or at least stable, taxation. The other source of income for a government, 'public borrowing', is now known to be a source of ruinous inflation. The days are gone when Christians, particularly privileged but socially responsible Christians, faced few problems when urging larger public expenditure on morally desirable purposes. It had been assumed too easily that democracy and a properly Christian care for the underprivileged would always be compatible.

I have been asked to outline the changing problems, not to propound solutions. But I must end by confessing my belief that all is not lost, although naturally I am full of an old man's nostalgia for old days. Clergymen sometimes talk as if Britain has become almost totally immoral because irreligious. I am aware of the tragedies of the divorce and crime rates, of drug abuse, etc., but it seems to me that in comparison with most of Britain's history the main change has been the disappearance of a generally accepted code of personal and social morality, caused largely by the decline of the historic churches. Morality has not disappeared: instead, Britain is a scene of many different individuals' lifestyles which are thought moral by those individuals – and of many different enthusiasms for single issues in social morality. And I cannot help recalling a vision which I could see physically on some winter mornings as I walked to Southwark Cathedral along the Thames. I saw the dawn turning the water into gold. It also shed a promising light on both banks of the divisive river. I used to reflect that within the Christian tradition, and within the goodwill of the British public, there must be some principles of social justice which could inspire policies making the years after AD 2000 better for the whole people. I am glad that I have lived to see the results of the general election of 1997, for they make more sense than any available alternative on the eve of the new millennium.

## Chapter 10

# Coming Full Circle

Richard A. Pring

There is lively interest now in ensuring that students are developed morally and spiritually as well as intellectually. Many reasons might be argued for this renewed interest. A decline of moral standards in society is reflected, so it is believed, in the lack of moral direction in schools. This view was captured in the paper given by the chief executive of the Schools Curriculum and Assessment Authority (SCAA), in which he denounced the relativism which, in his view, permeated society – and schools, in so far as they reflected society. Abiding moral truths must be reasserted against this creeping relativism. SCAA produced in 1996 a discussion paper *Education for Adult Life: the Spiritual and Moral Development of Young People*.[1] This led to the formation of the National Forum for Values in Education and the Community, which published a consultation document *Values in Education and the Community*.[2] This in turn prompted a weighty document from the SCAA, *The Promotion of Pupils' Spiritual, Moral, Social and Cultural Development*,[3] which details what teachers need to do for their children to grow up as morally upright and spiritually nourished human beings.

Much in these developments is commendable. The drive to raise standards in schools is couched in terms of competencies and skills necessary for improved economic performance; targets are set in those aspects of learning which are more easily measurable so that comparisons can be made and 'effectiveness' ascertained. But in such a context, the moral and spiritual dimension of education more broadly conceived can be neglected. The same 'brownie points' are not to be obtained in forming good people as they are in producing good 'A' levels. SCAA has, therefore, been wise to bring spiritual and moral education to the front of the education debate when it might have been ignored despite the ritualistic assertion, in the preface to all government documents on education, of 'spiritual, moral and social development'.

However, there is a conflict, rarely alluded to, between the new-found interest in moral development and the current drive to improve standards. Such a conflict could not have occurred 40 years ago without articulate opposition from the very people celebrated in this book. They had a clear sense of the aims of education which not only embraced the moral and the spiritual, but also helped define standards more generally. In the absence of such a comprehensive sense of educational aims and values, the targets to be achieved and the standards against which the learner is to be assessed are severed from a consideration of the values worth pursuing and of the sort of society worth creating. Hence, the danger of treating that which is central to education – namely, the moral and personal development of young people within a desirable form of social life – as if it were peripheral to the main educational drive.

Therefore, I make four points. First, I set out the 'official view' of the reforms in education which we are witnessing. Second, I point to the difficulties in sustaining such a view educationally – despite the fact that so many are beguiled by its apparent obviousness. Third, in response to those difficulties, I return to a consideration of the aims of education in a way that would have been comprehensible to members of the Moot. Fourth, I pick out two characteristics of those aims, namely the concern for the 'personal' and the importance of 'community' – both of which are neglected even by those who are alarmed at the indifference to the moral dimensions of education.

## The Official View of Educational Reform

A senior official of the DfEE recently explained the nature of the changes which have taken place within the education system. He said that we must 'think in business terms'. That meant that we look at those changes, as engineered by government, in terms of a 'quality circle' (see figure below). Each of these stages within the 'quality circle' might be explained thus.

(i) Define the product

(vi) Develop the partnership      (ii) Define the process

(v) Empower the client      (iii) Empower the deliverer

(iv) Measure the quality

First, as to *defining the product*, this had not previously been defined nationally. Teachers had had the freedom to define what counted as 'learning history' or 'being literate' – subject to the need to satisfy the standards set by examination boards. But these, too, had many different syllabuses, reflecting disagreement over the desirable 'product' of education. Such lack of consistency pointed to the need for a National Curriculum which 'defines the product' and specifies the targets to be achieved.

Second, as to *defining the process* it was considered important to clarify what is 'the effective school' in producing that 'product'. There has been much research which informs us of the characteristics of 'an effective school' and thus what must be done to become one.

Third, as to *empowering the deliverer* of this process, due regard must be paid to the 'stakeholders in the product' – parents, employers, the community and the schools. There is a need to empower them to 'deliver' the product. This is reflected in such innovations as local management of schools, grant-maintained schools, city technology colleges, specialist technology or language schools, reformed governing bodies, and contracts with parents. The 'stakeholders' are freed from dependence upon local authority. The role of the LEA is now to provide a service to these 'deliverers' – e.g. 'benchmarking data' on schools and setting annual performance targets.

Fourth, as to *measuring the quality*, a detailed National Assessment (a 'testing against product specification') has been created, with further instructions for 'benchmarking' and 'target setting'. Each child at 7, 11 and 14 has several numerical tags reflecting level of attainment in the subjects of the National Curriculum. Inspectors, in the light of research on the 'effective school', pass judgement on the 25,000 schools. The result of this 'measuring for quality' is that 300 schools have been designated as 'failing', one closed down and others allocated management help under the threat of closure unless there is improvement against targets set.

Fifth, as to *empowering the client*, parents have been given easily digestible information which can inform choices about schools and enable them to talk to teachers in a more informed way about the progress of their children in relation to other children. The words 'easily digestible' are important because, whatever the complexity of the educational experience of pupils, this has to be reduced to simple numerical data if parents are to be 'empowered' to act on the information.

Finally, as to *developing the partnership* in which 'stakeholders', 'deliverers' and 'clients' work together in developing the 'effective processes' for producing the 'product' (which has been defined by someone external to the 'process'), various forms of interaction are encouraged, including 'education action zones'.

## The Poverty of 'Business Terms'

What we perceive depends upon the concepts at our disposal through which experience is sieved and organized. And those concepts are embodied in a language which, although always evolving, is in large measure what we have inherited. Change the language and you change the way in which you see the world and the relationships between people. *A fortiori*, this must be true of the moral world we introduce young people to.

The language of education through which we now 'think in business terms' constitutes a new way of thinking about the relation of teacher and learner. It is a language which would not be familiar to the members of the Moot 40 years ago. It employs different metaphors, different ways of describing and evaluating educational activities. In so doing, it changes those activities into something else. It is remarkable how this has escaped so many people, affecting, at a more fundamental level than they would acknowledge, the aims of education which they subscribe to. It transforms the moral climate in which education takes place and is judged successful or otherwise. In so doing, education has come to find little room for those values which only a generation ago would have been central to the enterprise.

In this regard, I shall make three interconnected points. First, in thinking 'in business terms' the organization of education has adopted the language of management, in which teaching becomes 'the delivery of a curriculum' (designed by those disconnected from the educational encounter itself), the desirable 'product' is captured in a set of measurable targets, the learner becomes a 'client for services', teachers are beholden to 'stakeholders' who have an investment in this 'service', value lies in the difference between measurable 'input' and 'output', professional judgement cedes to 'performance indicators', the work of teachers and schools is subject to regular 'audit' according to the newly discovered causes of 'effectiveness', and, in the Orwellian phrase of the new management language, 'cuts in resources' are redefined as 'efficiency gains'.

The effect of this new language is not a matter for empirical enquiry alone, for that which is to be enquired into has become a different thing. So mesmerized have we become with the importance of 'cost efficiency' and 'effectiveness' that we have failed to see that the very nature of the enterprise has been redefined. Once the teacher 'delivers' someone else's curriculum with its precisely defined 'product', there is little room for that transaction in which the teacher, rooted in a particular cultural tradition, responds to the needs of the learner. When the learner becomes a client or customer, the relation is no longer one of apprenticeship to the community of learners. When the 'product' is the measurable 'targets' on which 'performance' is 'audited', then little significance can be attached to that 'struggle to make sense' or to the 'personal response'. The management metaphor does not embody values other than those of efficiency and effectiveness.

Second, therefore, the recent reforms in education have had little to say about the aims of education. Indeed, there is no underlying view of the educated person unless that of one who scores high against the various 'performance indicators'. That is not to say that there is no purpose behind the reforms. The driving force has been the need to increase economic competitiveness in a very competitive world. There is a need, too, to give young people the skills and the qualities necessary for gaining employment – hence, the stress upon basic skills such as numeracy, literacy and information technology. But the aim of education – what counts as an educated person in the present social and economic circumstances – is rarely explored. Of course, no document is published without reference to 'moral, spiritual, personal and social development', but this is a form of words to counterbalance what otherwise might appear to be an exaggerated pursuit of economic and social utility.

Third, the new language of education, borrowed from the worlds of business and management (the language of 'inputs' and 'outputs', of 'audits' and 'performance indicators', of 'targets' and 'benchmarks') is the language of control. Within such a language, government is able to say what children should know and how they should learn, sustained by an all-pervasive system of assessment, which leaves little room for schools to deliberate what is worthwhile or to form moral perspectives which are not captured in detailed assessment profiles. Possibly the most important *educational* tasks are those of helping young people find value in what they do and to decide, in the light of critical discussion, what sort of life is worth living, and what should be learnt to live that life. The danger is that, in making schools more 'effective' in reaching goals laid down by government, this central moral goal of education has no place.

Indeed, the metaphorical language, through which are described and evaluated the complex relations between teacher, learner and the community, shapes and transforms the moral nature of the activity. Therefore, we need to question whether, in the pursuit of greater standardization of educational output, the language of management and control, whereby efficiency can be gauged, is adequate to the moral purposes of education. Further, we need to question how far the frenetic concern for moral values arises from the poverty of the language now adopted to describe education in amoral terms and to control its outcomes.

The context, then, in which we examine the moral purposes of education today is in many respects different from that which concerned the members of the Moot half a century ago. It is one in which increased standardization and accountability has required a shift in how we see 'education', in how we conceive the relationship between teacher and learner and in how there might be room for those engagements through which moral development takes place. In such a case it is important to return to first principles, that is, to ask what are the aims of education, and to question how far the 'new language' is adequate for the task.

## Aims of Education

Recent reports which have established frameworks for 'educational reform' have provided no exploration of the aims and values which should shape and inspire that reform. This contrasts starkly with those great reports which preceded previous changes – Spens in 1938, Norwood in 1943, Crowther in 1958, Robbins in 1963, Newson in 1964, Plowden in 1967. Those reports, in addressing educational reform, set out what the aims and purposes of education were – not blandly but in detailed argument.

Since the 1960s 'education' – namely, how one forms the minds and the qualities of the next generation – has been thought not to warrant that wider philosophical and social deliberation. Indeed, such deliberation would seem to get in the way, as the problems of education are seen to be problems of management, the language of education as the language of successful business, and the perennial question, 'What knowledge is of most worth?', as a distraction from the business of getting things done.

Therefore, recent reports and White Papers have failed to tackle those questions which need to be raised. As a result, other values have taken over – quietly, unannounced – and decisions have been made which, though uncriticized, are deeply disturbing. Because the National Curriculum was too demanding, the Dearing Report (1994)[4] recommended the abolition of the humanities and the arts as requirements of the curriculum post-14. That is, those subjects which most directly deal with 'the quality of life worth living' became an option within the compulsory stage of education. Again, the Dearing Report (1996)[5] proposed, from age 16 onwards, a three-track framework of qualifications which had no basis in a consideration of the aims of education, how young people learn, what is worth learning, or how education relates to the wider society. The Dearing Report (1997)[6] similarly tackled the problems of higher education as though those problems can be couched in purely financial and managerial terms – as though there are not broader and deeper questions to be asked about the nature of a university education.

There seems to be a fear of these moral and more philosophical questions, reflecting no doubt the values of an age which is so conscious of 'effectiveness' and 'economic usefulness'. But there is a sense in which these deeper questions cannot be avoided. It always remains possible to ask 'effective for what purpose?' or 'economically useful for what sort of society?' Indeed, as we create the system for educating the next generation, it simply is not possible to dodge questions of value – questions about the quality of life which we are introducing young people to.

Education is about getting people to learn; but it is an evaluative term. It picks out those skills, knowledge, understandings, or attitudes which we think are *worth* learning. Not any learning constitutes an *educational* experience. Not any kind of learning warrants the accolade, 'educated person'. Rather is it the case that that learning is worthwhile which develops the capacity to understand the physical world, the social and personal relationships we enter into, the moral and religious ideals we are to be inspired by, and the aesthetic sensibility which gives delight. What is worthwhile goes beyond the useful. It stretches out to questions about personal identity, aesthetic enjoyment, the quality of life which 'deserves' one's commitment. And the foundation of that begins in the earliest years. It is difficult to talk about the 'effective school' without raising questions about the sort of knowledge and qualities worth nurturing as constitutive of a valuable form of life.

There may, indeed, be major differences between people about 'a worthwhile form of life', but at least we know that those differences are of an ethical kind. Different people have different views of the 'educated person'. Does such a person have to be knowledgeable in science – and if so, how knowledgeable? Does education entail awareness of those economic forces which shape one's life? What counts as an educated person is unavoidably a matter of perennial debate, and the answers will no doubt change according to economic and social circumstances. But the *criterion* of education remains constant – namely, that persons have the breadth of knowledge and understanding which, given the circumstance and state of knowledge at the time, enables them to act intelligently, critically, sensitively and reflectively in the different worlds they inhabit.

The language drawn metaphorically from the worlds of management and business is not adequate to the task of describing that 'coming to understand' which is at the heart of worthwhile learning. The standardized and measurable 'product', expected of all children, has nothing to do with the struggle to comprehend, the different and provisional ways of knowing, the forming of attitudes which are acquired in the transaction between teacher and learner. Nor can that language, concerned with the effectiveness of educational *means*, embrace the central questions about educational *ends*. That language, drawn from the worlds of business and management, requires the learners to be seen as 'clients' choosing a 'service' (and the teachers as the dispensers of a service at the behest of the 'customers'), not the learners as apprentices to a tradition of thinking and valuing, nor the teachers as custodians of that tradition, often against the blandishments of more commercial and utilitarian values.

Other metaphors are more apposite. Oakeshott[7] refers to education as an initiation into the 'conversation between the generations of mankind' in which the young are introduced to the voices of poetry, of science, of history, of philosophy. Such a metaphor reminds us that we live in a world of ideas, that these ideas have developed and are developing through criticism and argument, that there is no universal and static agreement over the best way of describing or appreciating the world, and that such changing ways of understanding are reflected in books and artefacts which become the resources upon which the teacher and learner draw. The task of the teacher is to get the children on the inside of these different 'conversations' – to think critically and intelligently (but in the light of evidence and previous deliberations) about the world in which they live, the relationships they enter into, the sort of life worth living, the sort of society worth creating.

This world of ideas comes in an *impersonal* form – in books and artefacts of various sorts. But such things are the resources upon which the teacher draws in order to help the learner make *personal* sense of the world he or she inhabits. The job of the teacher is to mediate these different intellectual and moral traditions to the particular ways of understanding of the learner. Such an interaction between the *public world* of knowledge inhabited by the teacher and the *private and inner life* of the learner cannot be standardized or reduced to precise 'products'. It is simply not that sort of thing. The learners themselves are not standardized – they come with different sets of ideas and values – and the interactions with the cultural and intellectual traditions to which they are introduced will necessarily take on different forms and be engaged in at different paces. Learning is about 'coming to see', 'struggling with ideas', 'developing an appreciation', 'finding value'. And this happens differently with different people. The school provides the opportunities, the cultural resources, the teaching guidance, the critical community for that learning to take place.

What I am referring to is not confined to the most able. The mediation of culture in its different forms can, as Bruner[8] argued, be put across to any child at any age in an intellectually respectable form – so long as one respects the mode of representation of the learner. Bruner,[9] in his 'Man: a Course of Study', centred the curriculum for all 9- to 13-year-olds around three questions. What makes one human? How did one become so? How might one become more so? The resources of the arts, social studies and the humanities were drawn upon to provide answers to these questions – or, at least, to provide the evidence upon which such questions might be explored. There is no definitive conclusion, no termination of the attempt to understand what it means to be human or to live a distinctively human life.

## Neglected Aims – the Personal and the Community

What is worth learning comes, packaged as it were, in *impersonal* terms – in the textbook, teacher's notes or media presentation. But worthwhile learning lies in the turning of that which is impersonal into something personally important for the individual. At the heart of education, therefore, is that transaction which takes place between teacher and learner, in which the learner finds personal significance in what the teacher is introducing him or her to. Such a transaction is often a struggle; it often bears fruit much later; it will have different results for each person; the outcomes cannot be predicted.

This, however, as we 'think in business terms', is dismissed as the 'child-centredness' which is at odds with the perceived necessity of a nationally defined product, of an agreed process for effectively achieving that product and of a uniform measurement of its quality. This 'making personal' – namely, the provision of opportunities whereby the young person can reflect, deliberate, test out ideas, explore different routes – is neglected. Such deliberation, although pursued in the light of evidence in the public domain, could not be expected to reach the predefined conclusions required for demonstrating school effectiveness. There is no room for such personal development where syllabuses have to be covered and outputs achieved.

I am not talking about anything esoteric. I am talking about pupils who are enabled to think about how they should live, who are encouraged to reflect on commitments worth making, who come to develop a sense of personal worth as well as respect for others, for whom moral questions are to be treated seriously, who are puzzled by challenges to received assumptions, who find challenging the exploration of what is to be valued in literature or art, who care about social and political issues. It is a matter of *seriousness* in thinking about what is worth living for. What is distinctive about being a *person* is this capacity for being serious about life, a capacity requiring the application of intelligence, moral judgement, and sensitivity, which is fostered by teachers even when much in the commercial environment militates against it, and even when it finds no place in the literature of the effective school.

All young people have that potential for 'moral seriousness'. They would, if opportunities were given, value a deeper understanding of those distinctively human problems – those universal 'areas of practical living' concerning the application of justice, the use of violence, the relationships between people, the existence of evil in its various forms (including poverty and cruelty), the sort of lifestyle worth adopting – which the humanities, the arts and the social sciences in particular have addressed. A central aim of education, through an initiation into those learning activities which are worthwhile, is to enable young people to confront, in the light of *public* understandings, issues of deep *personal* concern.

However, there remains the importance of reconciling this personal response to a wider social commitment, recognizing that individuals' identity and growth are inextricably mixed up with the communities in which they live. The search for value and personal fulfilment cannot be separated from a concern about the sort of society in which such value and fulfilment are to be found. This can be pitched at different levels.

First, the *personal* search for meaning has a public context. 'Meaning' is not a private matter. How one understands from a scientific, social, aesthetic or moral point of view is arrived at through participation in a public form of discourse. Such forms of discourse are sustained and enhanced in communities of like-minded people. Education, then, might be seen as the introduction of young people to these different communities, to the different forms of discourse, through which issues of human importance are discussed and understood.

Second, the school itself should be the kind of community where the personal significance of that which is presented in an impersonal form is explored. The best condition for a thinking child is surely a thinking community, which itself is forever deliberating the kinds of learning which are of most worth. If the learners are to explore 'what it means to be human, how did they become so and how they might be more so', and to do this in the light of literature, history, social studies, theology, then it is important that teachers are also engaged in such deliberations. The educational aims which I have spoken about, unlike the aims within the 'business plan' of government, require a particular sort of ethos – one which encourages exploration of ideas and values, and puts a premium on the serious search for the sort of life worth living.

Third, however, the fulfilment of each person's life will depend on the values which prevail within the wider community. And those values in turn will be affected by the attitudes and values of the individuals educated. Society is more than an aggregate of individuals. It is shaped by them certainly, but it shapes them in turn. Therefore, in helping children to live a distinctively human life, the teacher cannot remain indifferent to the sort of society which will, bit by bit, be formed by the learners themselves. This is more than a matter of teaching 'citizenship' or 'parenting'. Much more is it a matter of teaching a form of life, in which a concern for what is ultimately worthwhile remains a central focus, in which deliberation over matters of value are encouraged, and in which different views seriously considered are tolerated, and people of different beliefs respected. Though such a community will be pluralist in the sense of containing different ways of answering the question 'what sort of life is worth living?', there will be common values in the respect for others, the sense of human dignity, the tolerance of differences, the just distribution of basic goods and opportunities, the concern for evidence in argument. Indeed, one might go further and argue with Halsey in his Reith Lecture, 'We still have to provide a common experience of citizenship in childhood and old age, in work or play, in sickness and in health. We have still in short to develop a common culture to replace the divided culture of class and state.'[10]

## Conclusion: Coming Full Circle

The problems which united the members of the Moot in their deliberations over the aims of education were not exactly those which now need to be confronted. There was not the same thinking 'in business terms' which has so transformed the ethical frame of discussion. But the utilitarian forces which gave rise to this managerial mode of thinking were by no means absent. There was concern that the economic driving force of educational change would smother the deeper educational aim of personal fulfilment, that the focus on 'thinking intelligently' might displace, within a false dualism, 'reflective doing', that intellect might be nurtured through neglect of the feelings.

Recent reforms have justified those concerns to an extent which goes beyond the imaginings of the members of the Moot. But what they stood for – Tawney's attachment to 'community', Macmurray's 'primacy of the personal', Clarke's 'the making of souls' – remain in the practices and beliefs of many teachers. And even the policy-makers, who exercise so much control through the systems and language of management, are having their doubts – hence, the plethora of SCAA and HMI papers on personal and social development. But these papers are likely to remain irrelevant to the problems perceived unless they acknowledge what the members of the Moot argued, namely, that the whole enterprise of education (not a tiny slot on the curriculum) must nurture the personal response to the public forms of knowledge and prepare the individual for the sort of society which is worth being prepared for.

### Notes

1. SCAA, *Education for Adult Life: the Spiritual and Moral Development of Young People* (SCAA, 1996).
2. National Forum for Values in Education and the Community, *Values in Education and the Community* (NFVEC, 1996).
3. SCAA, *The Promotion of Pupils' Spiritual, Moral, Social and Cultural Development* (SCAA, 1997).
4. Dearing Report, *Final Report: The National Curriculum and Its Assessment* (SCAA, 1994).
5. Dearing Report, *Review of Qualifications for 16 to 19 Year Olds* (SCAA, 1996).

6.  Dearing Report, *Higher Education in the Learning Society* (HMSO, 1997).
7.  M. Oakeshott, 'Education: the Engagement and its Frustration', in T. Fuller (ed.) *Michael Oakeshott and Education* (Yale University Press, 1972).
8.  J. Bruner, *The Process of Education* (Harvard University Press, 1960).
9.  J. Bruner, *Towards a Theory of Instruction* (Harvard University Press, 1966).
10.  A. H. Halsey, *Change in British Society* (OUP, 1978).

## Chapter 11

# New Wine – Old Bottles? The Higher Education Foundation

John Wyatt

## Origins

Walter Moberly began his seminal work, *The Crisis of the University*, with an Olympian view: 'The crisis in the university reflects the crisis in the world and its pervading sense of insecurity.'[1] This universal summary, drawing a parallel between what we have grown used to calling a 'world' of learning and *Weltanschauung* is worth investigating again, 45 years on, in the context of this history of a group of people who cared about the crisis in both university and state. Did the institution which succeeded the Dons' Advisory Group, the University Teachers' Group, the Higher Education Group, in the years after 1980, reflect what was happening in higher education itself? It is almost banal to say that 'change' is the keyword for the sector at which we are looking. Over the centuries, universities in Western Europe have never been insulated from the effects of social change. There is an illusion, born out of their seeming permanence, that higher education is protected by some natural force from fundamental change. Plainly, that was not the case in the nineteenth century nor in the period after the Second World War. The simple statistical fact of growth in student numbers in higher education and the increase in the number of new institutions is clearly to be seen in all European countries since 1950.

The higher education institutions have not only grown, they have changed the composition of their students and staff, their forms of government, and not least added to the variety of disciplines within their prospectuses. An important, but hidden, feature of the changing scene, obscured by the apparently irreversible expansion of types of institution and the swelling of numbers, has been a significant dwindling in some areas of higher education. Sometimes the expansion of a major institution has been at the cost of a smaller specialist institution, swallowed up into the grander design. Departments judged to be too small have closed in some universities. Whole institutions have been closed for a variety of stated reasons, but all ultimately because of the late twentieth-century cover-all phrase for the unacceptable face of expansionism, 'non-viability'. Instances in the United Kingdom were the closed colleges of (teacher) education, the nursing schools, and the theological colleges. But out of the heat of this period came a phoenix-like new start. It was from the residual funds of one of the merged teacher education colleges that the Higher Education Foundation received an initial boost. More important even than money, some of the people who were closely involved in the foundation's predecessor groups viewed these college closures as serious portents. They attended a sequence of working parties and study groups to discuss ways by which a more sustained and continuous consideration of the crisis in higher education could be maintained.

I am indebted to Sinclair Goodlad, an active participant in many of these events, for the details of how HEF came about.[2] The essential part of the story is that a group of people was brought together by Roy Niblett, initially in order to report to the Church of England's General Synod Board of Education on the consequences of the closure of the Church's Colleges of Education. Out of the misery of the ending of old colleges came ideas on a new role for the Church's Colleges and then an initiative for higher education as a whole. Assisted by a grant from St Luke's Trust, Exeter, a new entity was established to continue the dialogue.

Two important features emerge from Goodlad's account of the formative period from 1975 to 1980: first, the close relationship of the signatories' Christian ideals to the aims of the new trust, while maintaining the spirit of openness – to other faiths and to other belief systems that do not accept the word 'faith' – which had characterized the predecessor bodies;[3] second, the closeness of the network of organizations from which they found their support and encouragement. There were valuable and active contacts with the people who still belonged or had belonged to the groups described in this volume. A genuinely vital line of influence can be traced through these anxious years. The result was a registered charity, a legal entity with a document summarizing something that previously had not been tightly formulated. The long-standing informal tradition had become explicit. In higher education as a whole, many implicit values were being spelled out. In venues like the Council for National Academic Awards and, as the 1980s progressed with its increasing business orientation, in mission statements and strategic plans, the unspoken assumptions of consensus became a babble of noise in the competitive market place. For the new foundation, the explicitness of its intentions was more than a legal formality; there was a manifesto in which the stated objectives of the trust affirmed the openness of the new organization to provide opportunities for a wide range of people:

> the advancement of higher and further education through promoting or providing for the benefit of the public, study and instruction devoted to analyzing and developing a greater understanding of the various underlying objectives of such education, both direct and indirect, the philosophical basis of such objectives (with particular reference to the influence thereon of Christian and other religious perspectives) and the methods whereby such objectives might effectively and harmoniously be pursued.

The trust deed was signed on 14 November 1980.[4]

In a typically generous way, demonstrating the derivation of its energy, the new foundation included within its activities the organization which in many ways had been its most direct predecessor, the Higher Education Group.[5] Until 1992, HEG continued to plan and to organize the annual Easter conference in Oxford, with HEF standing on the touch-line, assisting with secretarial support and some financial help. Then HEF took on the organization and planning of HEG's conference activities and HEG's supporters became supporters of HEF. Initially the HEG newsletter also continued by collaboration, then in another format became the responsibility of the HEF.

## Themes of the 1980s and 1990s

The essential method of HEF, as of its predecessors, has been to examine the changing structures and perspectives of higher education realistically but with a critical assessment of the values implicit in current developments. Thus in the early years there was listening and commentary to be made on the reverberations of the closures of the teacher training colleges. Shock waves were felt even in old, apparently stable institutions. Departments in universities closed; mergers were constructed. Impending 'massification' of higher education, to use Peter Scott's term,[6] generated a pressure,

even encouraged what seemed to be a duty, to increase the size of a
university or polytechnic, rather than to create new institutions from
scratch as had been the case in the 1950s and early 1960s. The
mantra murmured particularly by the HM Inspectorate and
departmental officials at the time was 'critical mass' – a metaphor
causing pain to academic scientists! Two trustees, W. A. Campbell
Stewart and Sinclair Goodlad, organized a conference in collaboration with the Department of Education on this contentious topic of
size and effectiveness of universities and colleges, under the title,
'Economies of Scale'. It was a very interesting experience to be a
member of this gathering and to observe that the officials of the
Department had to listen to what they did not want to hear. The
conference and the book that followed it[7] were demonstrations of
HEF acting as a barb, a polite and rational barb, in the skin of
official progressivism.

Study days or weekends were specially convened to approach a
particular issue of the times. A notable one was on the theme of
'Reductionism in Academic Disciplines', resulting in a publication.[8]
Other study days have drawn together people with similar interests
but diverse affiliations to concentrate on a specific topic. Recent
study days have been on management styles in universities, the
assurance of quality, culture and hierarchies in universities, and
research and its assessment. The long-established method of
collaborating for a short period with another organization has been
advantageous, not only in making the foundation better known, but
also in opening the debate to new voices and to experiences new to
the 'regulars' of HEG and HEF. One example was the weekend in
1995 at St George's, Windsor, with the Partnership Trust on 'Liberal
Higher Education'. Another was a day session organized by the
Public Management Foundation in 1993. Grander occasions were
expensive but they were arranged when it was felt that the
perception of the foundation required a spotlight on the public
stage. Professor John Ashworth, then director of the London School
of Economics, gave such a lecture, with the same title as this chapter,
in the grand surroundings of the Royal Society of Arts in 1992.

From time to time the foundation has played a more public role,
seeing its duty to make a statement on a crucial issue. The 1988
annual Easter conference was stimulated by the conference chairman, Sir Richard O'Brien to propose that HEF attempt a statement
of confidence in the purposes of higher education – a succinct
statement. Succinct statements always take a lot longer to prepare
than windy ones, so an intense period of writing and rewriting
occurred, with the aim of making a declaration rejoicing in the

education of the whole person and in the diversity of the system, as well as expressing a positive view of higher education's contribution to other worlds such as work and public service. The finished statement eventually went out to the Department of Education and to its Ministers, to civil servants, to the CBI, to vice-chancellors, directors and principals of universities and polytechnics. A useful and positive correspondence ensued. A similar enterprise arose from another Easter conference on Excellence. Dr (now Professor) Ron Barnett undertook to write a document[9] analysing the values of higher education and their relevance to the problems of a modern technological society. Recently, we have called together people leading institutions of higher education in order to prepare the foundation's formal response to the government's enquiry into higher education (the Dearing Committee of 1996–7). Here the foundation follows the path taken 34 years previously when individuals from the University Teachers' Group gave evidence to the Robbins Committee.

The third activity of the foundation has been the annual conference, a continuation of HEG's tradition. The style of the conferences has not changed greatly over the years, although those attending are nowadays likely to come from a wider range of institutions. The inheritance from HEG persists – a leisurely, thoughtful style, with not too many speakers and room for full conference discussion either in the meeting itself or in the bar afterwards and, most of all, the renewing of friendships. Most of the people who now attend are perhaps less likely to have met before, but they 'network', to use the modern jargon, when they leave. The discussions are still inter-disciplinary and peculiarly open – with no holds barred. This stands in refreshing contrast to the competitive defence of academic territories and the frequently arcane jargon in vogue in some professional academic conferences. Indeed the importance of open communication inspired one of our Easter conferences, 'Academic Community; Discourse or Discord?'[10] Participants can discuss their preoccupations in a more relaxed environment than in the large disciplinary conference with its parade of 20-minute schedules of lectures from dawn to dusk. A list of conferences of the late 1980s and 1990s, gives the flavour: Reductionism, Excellence in Higher Education, Learning from the Arts, Academic Community: Discourse or Discord?, The University Teacher: a Profession with Added Values?, Life-Long Education, the Beginning or the End of Higher Education?, The Crisis in Knowledge for Higher Education, Higher Education 2000 – University Inc.? If the modern word processor did not have a question mark on its keyboard, HEF would be in a bad way for conference titles!

Published work has been the fourth and most visible activity of the foundation, although the close working friendships, continuing in some cases for decades, have probably outlasted the books and monographs. The book on reductionism, already mentioned, is a splendid example of the conference topic which, by a gathering of essays, rumbles on and reaches ears that knew nothing of HEF and of its conference. Recently edited collections of essays have been by Ron Barnett on the theme of academic community and by Anne Griffin on post-modernism.

The newsletter of HEG became a fully fledged journal, *Reflections in Higher Education*, by 1990. This is a much more substantial, refereed document than its predecessor, with a wider circulation to libraries as well as to supporters of HEF. The American Society for Values in Higher Education exchange their journal with HEF. Professor Stephen Prickett, in the period when he was chair of HEF, connected with the American society which has similar intentions to the foundation and it has been a pleasure to greet members of the Society at three recent Easter conferences. Despite the formalizing of the journal, it still continues to give an opportunity for highly individual thoughts to be published. Contributions express opinions as well as analyse situations. Kite flying is a feature, so long as they are high-flying kites!

Thus far a reader might be forgiven for the assumption that all is well and, in a Whig progression from chaos to the well ordered society, it will get even better. There are, however, troubling signs of battles yet to be fought. In the first place, HEF's activities may at best be restricted and at worst terminated by shortage of finance. The challenge has to be thrown down and spoken with bluntness – is the academic world of today one that neither values nor makes time even to debate the kind of animal that is HEF?

The support that HEF has relied on in the past has frequently been in the form of time given generously by already busy academics. Some key figures have been senior enough to be in control of their own diaries and therefore able to devote time and occasionally facilities such as meeting rooms to the furtherance of the trust's business. The academic scene in the 1990s is busier, even harassed, and few academics of any level of seniority have time to spare from teaching, from research, or (more demanding in time than anything) from administrative and managerial tasks related to raising finance. Academic institutions have less slack for time to be spent on affairs that do not appear to bring in money. A more persistent problem for HEF is the passage of time. The Dons' Advisory Group, the Frontier Council and the other organizations described in this book formed a closely knit group of people who remained in touch over many years. Original members welcomed new members arriving from different organizations or institutions. I was one of those new members in the early 1970s and felt warmly included. I fear that, although the welcome is still as generous as ever for new lecturers, there has not been anything like the same replacement by them. This is partly owing to demographic profiles and partly owing to the changed circumstances of work in higher education – and this is where I make an attempt, a personal jeremiad, to analyse the angst of the millennium!

## What Exactly is the Crisis and Whose Crisis is it?

The last 25 years of publishing have seen many bookshelves groan, but few sectors of the written word can rival the expanding texts on what is wrong with modern life and particularly with modern education. These have been the years of prophets wandering the land crying that desolation is round the corner. The problem with pioneers of doom for the higher education sector has been that, every five years, events prove that forecasts of things to come have been underestimations. A valuable perspective is to compare the perception of the threats to the integrity of the idea of the university in 1945 and in the year 2000. After the Second World War, writings on the nature of the university and on the hope of a new start had a common picture of the 'enemy'. The experience of the totalitarian regimes of the 1930s and the 1940s, together with the sobering realization of the impact of science on total war, gave an immediate sense of what the abyss looked like. What then is the 'enemy' at the end of the century?

First, it is important to eliminate those aspects of modern university life which are irritating but do not destroy the roots of higher education. Growth of student numbers and the increase in institutions of themselves should not be automatic targets. The improvement in the age-participation rate, the increased proportion of women and of mature students in higher education are instances of success in achieving the ambitions of the 1940s and 1950s. The detail within these undoubted advances – the continuing low proportion of students from lower socio-economic groups, the reduction of financial support for students so that many are not actually full-time students at all, the relative reduction in capital equipment funding and so on – is another matter altogether and I have no doubt that HEF and bodies like it will continue to make known that expansion costs more than money. Nevertheless, growth is not the enemy, unless one espouses an unthinking allegiance to 'More means worse'. Similarly, the cynosure of teaching quality is surely not to be rejected as a dangerous interference with civil or academic freedom. In the light of increased numbers and a new generation of students, attention to how we teach is not optional. Attention to the way universities are managed also deserves some thoughtful understanding, despite all the jargon of management techno-speak. Universities and colleges require the best value from every pound they receive, but they have not always been shining examples of care and good employment for their staff, particularly for the support staff. The records of HEF meetings show that the effects of rapid expansion and managerialism have not escaped trenchant critical discussion, but there are deeper concerns lying in strata below the surface of the times.

## The University at the Centre or on the Margin?

An important shift in the locus of the university in modern society has been diagnosed by Peter Scott in two books, *The Crisis in the University* and *The Meanings of Mass Higher Education*.[11] Scott surveyed higher education from two vantage points, first as an editor of an influential weekly journal and second as a member of a university senior management team. He was also a speaker at one of the HEF Easter conferences where he shared with delegates themes from his books. Scott is forced to note with increasing concern a progressive marginalization of the university. What follows here is my personal gloss on his cool analytical survey.

At a superficial level, the university appears to be essential to a modern technological society, providing a high-quality work force and new and advanced technologies giving advantage in competition, but this is only part of the truth, for there is parallel growth of new research institutions which are not part of higher education. More significant, particularly for disciplines which are judged to contribute no economic benefit to the nation or for the types of research and enquiry which are 'pure' and seemingly 'useless', there has been a shift in a relationship with the state, part directed and part an informal drift. The university, along with other public and social services, is now deemed to be like any other economic institution, a market-place stall, trading in measurable, technically judged items on a contractual basis. Like other institutions which for so long seemed to have their place in society guaranteed because of the social reforms of the six years after 1945, the universities since 1980 have had to adjust the boundaries between public and private. They have been transported into a consumer valued system. How much more marginal can they become? In a Brave New World will information technology render the concentration of knowledge in expensive institutions redundant? Will government or multinational corporations abandon the universities and establish alternative centres for the supply of labour or for research enquiry?

External forces can not be blamed for all the dilemmas of academics. Some problems arise from the very devices which the universities have adopted as coping mechanisms. An example would be the exclusion of disciplines because of theories of economic size and value. Another is the stress consequent on over-enthusiastic recruitment, either of home students or of overseas students. Assessment fatigue and diminished imagination are well-known symptoms of a quest to prove quality ratings. These ills are easy to identify and deserve open self-criticism and reform. There is a more insidious enemy within, which has perhaps more permanent and complex effects on the nature of the academic community. This has little to do with any government, for it is a phase in the history of ideas – the circulatory system of the academic body.

## The Real Enemy

Since 1960, successive revolutions in interpretations of the nature of knowledge have broken on the beach of the universities. Wave after wave of master theories (Marxism, post-Freudianism, feminism) dominated the debates of the late 1960s and 1970s and still continue in new forms today. Alongside these over-arching explanations of the way people have interpreted the world, that designate some perceptions as true ways of knowing and others as trivia or heresies, has been a counter movement or set of movements that reject 'grand theory'. Both the grand theories and their critics, post-structuralism and post-modernism in their many manifestations, have this in common for the modern university: they challenge long-held assumptions about the previously debated but fundamentally unchallenged basis of the discipline divisions and of the definitions of the nature of the material with which academics work. The debate has appeared to academics to be in their legitimate arena but it has been far from exclusively academic. The mass media play a vital role in circulating, and often initiating debate on post-modernist explanations of life. New forms of knowledge and new social 'goods' are generated by agencies separated from society's traditional home for knowledge. Once again the university is not the only centre of intellectual energy for civil society, and indeed it may well be seen from within and without as an institution at odds with the mainstream of life.

The modern academic who believes she or he is faced with an assault on the accepted nature of knowledge has three choices: to turn to areas of work which are valued because they bring in lucrative contracts from industry or government, to join the parties which destroy the accepted foundations, or to despair quietly and perhaps even cynically 'get on with the job' (which inevitably means coping with the increasing numbers of undergraduates who still paradoxically regard a university experience as a value). This scenario helps to explain why the kind of debates that HEF encourages, about value, about a liberal education, and about the individual's response to his or her disciplines of study, is hardly in the ascendant for the majority of academics. The words I have just used – values, subject disciplines, individual response – are the language rejected by the clerks muttering treason. Particularly, but far from exclusively, in arts, social sciences and education faculties, the low morale of the teachers and researchers is as much about the insidious feeling of becoming marginal to the main purpose of the large university as about work load and managerialism. Excluded largely from the club of the financial entrepreneurs, dismissed by the inner circle of social analysts of whatever -ism is in the driving seat, some academics and indeed some whole discipline areas can experience a sense of homelessness, an uneasy acquaintance with a new enemy.

The antidote to despair is not a new medicine or the introduction of a revolutionary way of perception. It is the essentially human impulse to satisfy curiosity. Some curiosity, at the level of learning in higher education, is undoubtedly instrumental, but there is also at this level an eternal quest for meaning which has no immediate connection with changing the physical circumstances of life, perhaps no connection at all with an outcome narrowly defined, other than a seeking for 'personal knowledge'. Mature students display this type of curiosity when they return to study, perhaps after years of living with and using a different kind of knowledge. Equally, young students continue to enrol on courses which do not deliver a meal ticket at the end. These impulses for knowledge have deep roots in human nature across all cultures, but it is not unfair to return at this point to the link between HEF and its Christian origins, for Christians make affirmations about 'meaning' in knowledge.

The continuing question is posed, 'What is the Christian's role in higher education?' The word 'continuing' is used deliberately, for I do not see the issue as a prerogative of the end of the century. It was the same question for J. H. Newman in the 1850s as he began to prepare the set of statements later to emerge as the seminal *Idea of a University*.[12] The same concern was shared by Walter Moberly and the members of the groups celebrated in this book in the period 1945 to 1965.[13] Neither Newman nor Moberly proposed a seminary solution isolated from the mainstream universities of their time. They both aimed to create an influence of Christians within a continuing and changing vehicle travelling towards truth, a vehicle which was secular, varied and plural.

The Christian doctrine of the wholeness of the person has to be reaffirmed in the face of the tendency to put it to one side in many academic processes and activities. The potential for a narrow and specialist view of the human condition is greater than at any time before as subject specialisms divide and research becomes more and more particular and classified into subdivisions. The subject department and the research 'unit' embody and endorse the classification of knowledge. Thus HEF's determination to bring people together from different disciplines and institutions and to recognize their contributions to the whole is a vital enterprise.

There are local and particular problems for the Christian seeking to locate his or her belief in a university setting. Gradually and without much protest one form of support, both academic and personal, has declined in a way that Newman certainly could never have imagined and Moberly never contemplated. The formal study of theology has been markedly reduced in the British university system in the last 20 years, the victim in many universities of attrition by definition as 'uneconomic units of resource'. The closing of a theology department is not just the silencing of a set of voices in an academic senate or the abrupt termination of a library section. The informal support for Christians and for people of other faiths in all subject departments disappears, as well as the opportunity to conduct inter-disciplinary studies which include theological dimensions. Where there is no basis for research and postgraduate study, the religious dimension of studies in the arts is obviously weakened, but scientific and technological studies are also deprived. One brighter lining to this cloud is perhaps the live interest in religious studies and in inter-faith enquiries which have developed in some notable centres of excellence in the United Kingdom.[14]

HEF has many records of optimism and of positive discussions and we have to ask now how the foundation may help teachers and researchers to flourish despite the risks and threats. At the end of *Crisis in the University*, Moberly made one vital proposal, that there should be regular meetings of people who would affirm values and maintain a flame for the new generation.[15] Such groups are brought into being by acts of will. The sheer determination of founding fathers like Roy Niblett enabled HEF to be born. Acts of will continue to be required even to keep institutions as large as colleges and as small as voluntary organizations alive. I believe that this power to persist with an ideal is the same power that keeps alive a scholar's determination to keep enquiring through frustration and reversals. The motivation is curiosity, but curiosity combined with faith. That remark is an invitation to an *envoi*.

One of the frequently observed 'extras' of an HEF meeting is that, advised by those around you, you depart with a list of books to read. In this time-honoured fashion therefore I recommend a book which speaks to our modern condition of the teacher's and scholar's task. *In Pursuit of Coleridge* by Kathleen Coburn, the editor of Coleridge's Notebooks, tells of the long, hard, often frustrating search to find the long-lost notebooks and lecture notes and the delicate task of making them available for future generations of students. One quotation describes the scholarly and personal dialogue over many years with a close friend: 'In harmony, in argument, cheerfully, furiously, we knocked our heads together; for there was in it all that combination of zest for solutions, daemonic concentration and personal affection that makes such working together one of the most honest privileges and some of the best fun in the human world'.[16] HEF has been for so many of us 'one of the most honest privileges and some of the best fun'.

## Notes

1. Moberly, *The Crisis* (see ch. 6, n. 2), p. 15.
2. S. Goodlad, 'The Higher Education Foundation and the Higher Education Group: A Brief Account of their Interrelationship', *News-Letter* (July 1983), pp. 25–34.
3. The combination of Christian commitment with 'openness' in dialogue was characteristic of the groups described in Part II.
4. The first trustees included a vice-chancellor, three principals of higher education colleges, a retired vice-chancellor, four professors, two university lecturers, and a retired headteacher.
5. For the HEG and its predecessors, see above, ch. 8.

6. P. Scott, *The Crisis in Higher Education* (Croom Helm, 1984).
7. S. Goodlad, *Economies of Scale in Higher Education* (SRHE, 1983).
8. A. Peacocke, (ed.) *Reductionism in Academic Disciplines* (SRHE, 1985).
9. R. Barnett, *Responsiveness and Fulfilment: The Value of Higher Education in the Modern World* (HEF, 1989).
10. The proceedings of this conference were later issued in R. Barnett (ed.), *Academic Community: Discourse or Discord* (Jessica Kingsley, 1994).
11. Scott, *The Crisis*; *The Meaning of Mass Higher Education* (SRHE/Open University Press, 1996).
12. J. H. Newman, *The Idea of a University Defined and Illustrated* (Oxford University Press, 1976).
13. See ch. 6 for Moberly's own experiment in giving these ideas substance at Cumberland Lodge.
14. The popularity of courses in psychology of religion and, more broadly, in the human sciences points in this direction.
15. Moberly, *Crisis*, pp. 309–10.
16. K. Coburn, *In Pursuit of Coleridge* (Bodley Head, 1977), p. 123.

*Chapter 12*

# A Free Society Today?

Duncan B. Forrester

## Building Jerusalem? Christians and the Welfare State as a Free Society

At the heart of 'war aims' in the Second World War was a broad and generous understanding of freedom, with freedom from want at its heart. As a result of the poverty, unemployment, suffering and distress of the Depression years there was a widespread conviction that freedom in the truest and deepest sense could not be realized until people had a kind of material and job security that had not been available for multitudes. A proper system of social security and full employment were increasingly strongly believed to be the necessary foundations for a free society. The Depression had left a deep scar on the consciousness of the British working class, and many people who were themselves relatively prosperous shared the determination that the sufferings of the 1930s should never return and that prosperity and security should be more equally shared. By contrast with the Depression, hardships and sufferings as well as resources had been more equally shared during the war; people discovered a new sense of shared purpose and of interdependence, and in this a new experience of freedom. No one group bore a disproportionate share of the costs, as had the poor in the 1930s, and few were able to profit at the expense of their fellows. Social barriers were to a notable degree breached, and people knew themselves to be 'members one of another'. This new sense of mutual accountability and community was also experienced by many as a new quality of liberty, which they were determined to retain and develop in the post-war period.[1] The seeds of a new, more just, equal and free social order were being sown.

Christians very widely embraced this new social vision with

210

enthusiasm. In 1942 William Temple, the archbishop of Canterbury, greeted the publication of Beveridge's report on *Social Security and Allied Services*, the keystone of planning for post-war reconstruction, by declaring that this was the first time that an attempt had been made to embody the whole spirit of the Christian ethic in an Act of Parliament! It is not hard to show that Christian social thought in Britain in the 1930s and 1940s contributed significantly to the shape of post-war reconstruction and gave powerful support to the welfare settlement that was put in place with the election of a Labour government in 1945. The influence of William Temple on wartime planning for reconstruction is generally recognized. This book has focused attention on a range of thinkers in the 'Oldham circle' who worked with Temple and carried his message after his death. Some were major public figures whose thought influenced policy formation and whose support, and that of the academic and ecclesiastical constituencies they represented, was vital for the implementation of the new measures. More secular figures of great eminence and influence, such as J. M. Keynes and William Beveridge and many others, interacted closely with the circle around Oldham and *The Christian News-Letter*, and took the ideas emanating from that group with great seriousness. Keynes, for instance, made copious and positive comments on the proofs of Temple's *Christianity and World Order*, in particular suggesting that Temple should have put more strongly the necessity of a theological contribution to economics, and he warmly endorsed the general approach of Temple's significant little book.[2]

Temple's *Christianity and Social Order* (1942), together with T. S. Eliot's *The Idea of a Christian Society* (1939) and John Baillie's *What is Christian Civilisation?* (1945) amounted to a sort of blueprint of the kind of post-war society that would be desirable in an increasingly secular and post-Christian age. Eliot was the closest to presenting a vision of the restoration of Christendom; the others spoke quite clearly about Christian contributions to a society that was recognized as pluralist. Temple on education, for example, was concerned, it is true, with the place of Christian education and religious observance in the life of the school, but his major interest was in the quality of education and the contribution that the school system might make to the development of a community in which there was a shared sense of responsibility for one another and in which Christian values found expression in a non-sectarian way. For him, 'the aim of a Christian social order is the fullest possible development of individual personality in the widest and deepest fellowship'.[3] This objective would be achieved through the realization of a series of guidelines for government which Temple believed were rooted in the Christian faith, and which he hoped might be implemented in post-war Britain. They deserve to be quoted in full:

1. Every child should find itself a member of a family housed with decency and dignity, so that it may grow up as a member of that basic community in a happy fellowship unspoilt by underfeeding or overcrowding, by dirty and drab surroundings or by mechanical monotony of environment.

2. Every child should have the opportunity of an education till years of maturity, so planned as to allow for his peculiar aptitudes and make possible their full development. This education should throughout be inspired by faith in God and find its focus in worship.

3. Every citizen should be secure in possession of such income as will enable him to maintain a home and bring up children in such conditions as are described in paragraph 1 above.

4. Every citizen should have a voice in the conduct of the business or industry which is carried on by means of his labour, and the satisfaction of knowing that his labour is directed to the well-being of the community.

5. Every citizen should have sufficient daily leisure, with two days rest in seven and, if an employee, an annual holiday with pay, to enable him to enjoy a full personal life with such interests and activities as his tasks and talents may direct.

6. Every citizen should have assured liberty in the forms of freedom of worship, of speech, of assembly, and of association for special purposes.[4]

Temple presents these objectives as derived from the Christian faith, and a kind of explication of the 'Principles of Peace' suggested by four religious leaders in a notable letter to *The Times* on 21 December 1940. They should command the allegiance of every Christian and indeed of all people of goodwill. They were not, Temple believed, the sort of technical issues in which there is bound to be legitimate difference of opinion – such matters he relegates to an appendix, as his personal views rather than the teaching of the church.

At the heart of the post-war settlement and the Christian contributions towards its formulation was the search for community. 'Everybody knows', said John Baillie,

that, whether we like it or not, the life of our country, and the life of all the Western nations, is going to wear after the war a complexion very different from that of the life so familiar to us in pre-war days. .... Weary of a day when every man was his own master, men are seeking new forms of community.[5]

The 1942 Report of the Church of Scotland Commission for the Interpretation of God's Will in the Present Crisis, chaired by Baillie, devoted a long section to the discussion of 'True Community'. The 'long reign of individualism' was over, it was argued, and there was a returning spirit of community. Liberal individualism had offered new freedoms, but it had been corrosive of old and deep ties of solidarity. The tide had now turned; totalitarianism was a daemonic, because narrow, understanding of community, demanding total, unqualified devotion to a particular race, soil or blood. The church must denounce the 'idolatrous wickedness' of such distortions of community and its consequences in the oppression of other races, and in particular the 'brutal anti-Semitism' of Nazism. 'Total devotion', the report suggests, 'can properly be claimed only for a community which is in its own nature total and universal.' Thus,

> If the world's only hope lies in the discovery of some form of community which, being at the same time more than national and more than merely human, can offer mankind a stronger solidarity and draw to itself a more wholehearted devotion than even the youth of the totalitarian organisations can claim to possess, then to the Church's hands has the required solution been committed. For there is only one such community – namely, the Christian Church itself.[6]

Thus the Christian faith, they argued, provided insights into the nature of community – and, more important, a real if imperfect model of true community. Like Temple and most of the others, Baillie bought into a mild form of collectivism, and assumed that this did not involve an unacceptable surrender of freedom; indeed, new styles of economic and social liberty (what Temple called 'positive freedom') would only be possible in the new system which they were determined to establish. And this new sense of community demanded the establishment of a welfare state and a planned economy.

The Christian social thinkers studied here were very close to the heart of the establishment, intellectuals from privileged backgrounds with a lively sense of social responsibility and the importance of the task of leadership, imbibed or reinforced in private schools and the older universities. They had dual intellectual roots, in the Christian tradition and in philosophical idealism, each of which reinforced their implicit assumption that they were responsible for working out, like Plato's Guardians, what was good for society and for other people. Heirs of a long and noble tradition of aristocratic Christian commitment to social reform, their self-understanding is captured in Karl Mannheim's account of the intelligentsia. He argued that in most cases people's behaviour and opinions were determined by the interests which related to their place in society. Intellectuals, however, were to a great extent a free-floating social group, detached from classes, and able to transcend class interests and thus (like Plato's Guardians) capable of taking a more objective view. On this basis it was possible to have a great deal of confidence in the impartiality and objectivity of the élite, and also to believe that they were capable of understanding what was good for other people, sometimes even when this differed from what the people concerned felt they wanted.

This rather patrician approach was deeply entrenched in the British Christian mind. The assumption that some people by virtue of their intellect or faith are capable of knowing what is good for others better than they can themselves is, however, responsible for some of the problems that developed in the decades of the welfare state project after 1945, and for some of the methodological dilemmas in recent Christian social ethics. It is hard for such an élite to envisage or advocate radically changed power relationships, or take active steps to empower the marginalized. Nor is it easy for them to be adequately critical of their own motives or those of their own kind. In a famous passage, John Macmurray demystifies government:

> Leviathan is not merely a monster but a fabulous monster; the creature of a terrified imagination. If we track the state to his lair, what shall we find? Merely a collection of overworked and worried gentlemen not at all unlike ourselves, doing their best to keep the machinery of government working as well as may be, and hard put to keep up appearances.[7]

There is, of course, truth here. But it is also true that 'overworked and worried gentlemen, not at all unlike ourselves', were the backbone of those who enthusiastically implemented the Holocaust under Hitler – the 'ordinary Germans' of Goldhagen's horrifying book.[8] It is easy for church leaders, theologians and intellectuals to see their role as doing good to others and defining what is good for them. This is, of course, a thoroughly top-down process, classically paternalist. It does not adequately recognize that church leaders and professionals and intellectuals have their own interests, and often these interests, usually unconsciously, give a skew to their judgements. It is no easier for church leaders and theologians than for others to be altruistic, and their claim to be surveying reality from a mountaintop of objectivity is usually largely spurious. For these reasons, well-intentioned schemes of welfare devised by intelligent and caring people and imposed in a paternalistic way often go seriously wrong. Power is sometimes abused, and welfare schemes turn out often to do more for those already prosperous than for the poor.[9]

But at least some of the thinkers in the Oldham circle became sharply aware that this élitist ideal of the intelligentsia was sharply at variance with mass democracy. They agonized over this issue. How could the new 'masters' exercise power without the necessary training and experience? Discussions in *CN-L* by Cole, Middleton Murry, Demant and others reflect vividly the dilemma in which Christian social thinkers, deeply imbued with a patrician sense of responsible leadership, found themselves. Could they nurture the seeds of a truly free society while playing a less conspicuous role themselves? They believed they had found a partial answer in the concept of small-group democracies as the foundation for larger and more participative power structures. The clue, as Temple had said, lay in a new culture. Yet the new freedom had to be planned. The post-war consensus assumed that freedom depended on planners and planning, invoking the full power of the state. With prophetic foresight, several of the 1940s Christian thinkers feared that the new 'planning State' would be instinctively inimical to all lesser forms of association, but it was hard for them, drawing on the resources of Christian idealism, to envisage an alternative. There continued to be a fundamental tension between two concepts of freedom: through direct personal relationships (e.g. Buber and Macmurray) or through diktat. And yet the beginnings of what would today be called a communitarian approach to the deployment of power and wealth can be discerned in the discussion.[10]

## 'Positive' or 'Negative' Freedom?

F. A. Hayek took up the problem from a different perspective. His little book, *The Road to Serfdom*, aroused much controversy when it was published in 1944, but few people took its argument very seriously, and it was commonly dismissed as a rather hysterical piece of apocalyptic. Hayek's thesis was that central economic planning and control was inherently subversive of the free society. Any step in the direction of socialism, nationalization or social engineering was a move towards the very totalitarianism against which the Allies had waged the war. Freedom in the classical liberal individualist sense, Hayek argued, must not be sacrificed on the altar of social justice, equality or economic freedom. Karl Popper pursued Hayek's argument in a rather different direction. He argued in *The Open Society and its Enemies* (1945) that all grand rational schemes for the improvement of society (he concentrated especially on Plato, Hegel and Marx) were inherently and unavoidably oppressive and destructive of the freedom that was most vital if there was to be a decent life for human beings, economic prosperity, and an acceptable form of social order.

Hayek and Popper were joined in their critique of collectivism and their attempt to rehabilitate a liberal idea of freedom by a variety of thinkers, among whom was Michael Polanyi who stressed the necessity of a free society as the condition for the proper development of knowledge and understanding.[11] For nearly 30 years this variegated school of neoliberals was largely in the wilderness, excluded from power, and regarded as rather marginal and deviant in academic life. Then, in the late 1970s, they found themselves on the crest of a wave, becoming popular and influential just as the Marxist dictatorships in Eastern Europe were breaking up, as if to demonstrate the validity of the neoliberal critique.

For our purposes the nub of the neoliberal argument is that only at the cost of freedom can a planned economy and social justice be realized. The neoliberals believe that those thinkers who argue that there is a need to supplement traditional civil liberties with 'economic freedom' and 'social justice' have simply misunderstood the situation, and have unknowingly started down the road to serfdom. Small face-to-face societies – what Hayek calls 'teleocratic' societies – may be held together by shared values and common goals; but any attempt to impose such shared values on a large and complex modern society destroys its prosperity and its freedom alike. The Baillie Commission's analogy between the church as congregation and the kind of society we should seek is, according to the neoliberals, systematically misleading and dangerous. You cannot impose the values and virtues which are appropriate in a small face-to-face community on the 'Great Society' without destroying its dynamic, its prosperity and its freedom. There is here, of course, a resurgent individualism at work, and also a narrow account of freedom. This latter is the 'negative liberty' of Isaiah Berlin's renowned inaugural lecture.[12] In the classical liberal account my freedom consists in absence of interference from others. The necessary limits to this negative freedom largely arise when one person's freedom infringes the freedom of another, or when the state requires the resources to defend the community or enforces the necessary rules that enable the maximization of individual liberty.

Neoliberals after the school of Hayek reject notions of 'positive freedom', regarding them as destructive of liberty by enforcing values and norms on people, often with the highest of motives. The image of society they see as linked to positive freedom is the barracks, where the whole of life is directed to the achievement of common goods. The kind of common purpose that bound people together in Britain during the war could not and should not, the neoliberals argued, be sustained in peacetime because it demanded the sacrifice of the fundamental principles of the free society and in the long term was subversive of liberty.

Christians, however, might well feel uneasy about the adequacy of Bertrand Russell's famous negative account of freedom – 'the absence of obstacles to the realisation of desires'. For the liberty of the children of God consists in finding freedom and fulfilment in the service of God and the neighbour. This kind of liberty is essential for the upbuilding of healthy community life. And if the church is presented, as it was by Baillie, as a kind of model of the free society and true community, it can only be so in as far as it is orientated towards the goal or telos of the reign of God. There seems therefore to be a Christian predisposition towards 'positive liberty' and an inbuilt suspicion of the adequacy of 'negative liberty'.

## The Free Society Today

Many of us, I suppose, were struck by the impoverishment of British political discourse revealed in the course of the 1997 election campaign. Politicians operated almost entirely in terms of slogans and soundbites. Issues believed to be sensitive, or likely to worry or alienate any group of voters, were sedulously sidelined and forgotten. Reforms and improvements were presented as far as possible as involving no cost. Apart from the Liberal Democrats, no one suggested increasing personal taxation in order to benefit the community. Issues like poverty, world development, disarmament, redistribution seemed to have disappeared from the agenda. There was precious little talk of visions of the future of British society, and hardly a suggestion that sacrifices now might be required from some for the sake of others, or now for the sake of a better future.

Two processes seemed to come together in that lacklustre election campaign. On the one hand, it demonstrated that Daniel Bell's 'End of Ideology' had in fact arrived after many premature announcements. The collapse of the Marxist regimes of Eastern Europe had left behind a profound distrust of ideology and grand overarching theories, including neoliberalism, partly for the very good reason that they are so effective at concealing what is really going on, disguising corruption and self-interest by 'the illusion that the system is in harmony with the human order and the order of the universe' (Havel).[13] For the moment, at least, nothing has taken the place of the old comprehensive ideologies, which for all their defects and problems were at least sometimes able to constrain selfishness and locate political activity within a larger horizon than horse-trading.

The end of ideology is also the context within which we have to understand the strange renaissance of political religion in Britain, and the powerful phenomenon of conviction politics which emerged first with Mrs Thatcher, and is continued by Tony Blair in rather different form. We have today the resurgence of the Christian Socialist Movement, and that redoubtable Anglo-Catholic MP, Frank Field, arguing that the fundamental defect of the welfare settlement of the 1940s was that it was based on a simplistic and over-sunny account of human nature. A Christian understanding of human nature which takes both the *grandeur* and the *misère* (Pascal) of the human condition on board would provide, he suggests, a far better, because truer, basis for welfare provision and policy.

In this situation, the churches feel a special responsibility to contribute to public debate and to try both to enrich it theologically and to root it in the kind of realities which the church as people knows at first hand. And the great British public looks to the churches and to theology with almost unprecedented expectancy to make constructive and significant contributions to public debate. Two quite closely related, but distinct, documents appeared during the 1997 election campaign as conscious attempts to influence the agenda and enrich the discourse of electioneering: the English RC bishops' paper on *The Common Good*, and the CCBI report of an enquiry into *Unemployment and the Future of Work*. The first is purely Roman Catholic in provenance, but consciously addresses a far broader audience. It draws on a coherent body of social teaching which it believes to be public truth, capable of commending itself to many who are not Catholics or Christians. The second report was commissioned by the Council of Churches for Britain and Ireland and published in 1997. This is, of course, an ecumenical document which has its roots in a more complex, variegated and confusing tradition of social theology. These two significant reports suggest that the tradition of Christian reflection on the state of British society is still vigorous. The tradition rooted in the 1930s and 1940s of seeking a society in which freedom flourishes in the context of a special concern for the weak and the poor and the underprivileged is alive and well. There is a willingness to learn from the mistakes and failures of earlier decades, and to respond to or incorporate some of the emphases and insights of neoliberalism, rather than simply reiterate the positions established in the 30s and 1940s. The search is for a just and caring society in which human beings and families and groups can flourish in freedom, Oldham's 'free society' which 'has a particular kind of unity – namely, the unity of people who have developed a sense of responsibility for each other and for the future'.[14] The shape of that society, and its problems and tensions, will be different in the twenty-first century from what they were in the 1940s. But Christian thinkers and Christian leaders have a continuing responsibility to contribute towards the discussion of the free society, and to learn from the insights and from the limitations of the Christian thinkers who wrestled with these issues in the 1930s and 1940s. Tensions between individual autonomy and collective fulfilment, between the market and the common good, between democracy and efficiency, will remain. The goal continues to be, in Niebuhr's phrase, the 'impossible possibility' of a responsible democracy in which both freedom and social justice are recognized as the joint pillars of a proper conviviality.

## Notes

1. See my *Christianity and the Future of Welfare* (Epworth, 1985), ch. 2.
2. Keyne's comments are cited in F. A. Iremonger, *William Temple* (Oxford University Press, 1948), p. 438.
3. W. Temple, *Christianity and Social Order* (Penguin, 1942), p. 74.
4. Ibid., pp. 73–4.
5. In J. G. Riddell and George M. Dryburgh (eds), *Crisis and Challenge* (Church of Scotland, 1942), appendix.
6. *God's Will for Church and Nation: Reprinted from the Reports of the Commission for the Interpretation of God's Will in the Present Crisis as Presented to the General Assembly of the Church of Scotland during the War Years* (SCM Press, 1946), p. 23.
7. John Macmurray, *Persons in Relation* (Faber, 1961), p. 200.
8. D. J. Goldhagen, *Hitler's Willing Executioners: Ordinary Germans and the Holocaust* (Random House, 1996).
9. On this see the work of Julian Le Grand since his groundbreaking *The Strategy of Equality: Redistribution and the Social Services* (Allen & Unwin, 1982).
10. This paragraph is much indebted to Dr Marjorie Reeves's comments and suggestions.

11. See especially Polanyi's *The Concept of Freedom* (1940), the ideas of which are further developed in *The Logic of Liberty* (1951) and in his 1951–2 Gifford Lectures, published as *Personal Knowledge: Towards a Post-Critical Philosophy* (1958).
12. Isaiah Berlin, *Two Concepts of Liberty* (Clarendon Press, 1958).
13. V. Havel, *Living in Truth* (Faber, 1987), p. 39.
14. *CN-L*, L72, 12 Mar. 1941.

*Chapter 13*

# Britain and the World Today: A New Moot?

Keith W. Clements

## To Win or Lose it All

Looking back to a previous generation of creative thinkers can on occasion be demoralizing rather than inspiring. We are apt to envy the confidence and competence with which they seemed to tackle the issues of their day, and our own hesitancy and confusion stand out in even greater relief against the distant backdrop of their achievements. It was therefore almost with a sense of relief, as well as being rather intrigued, that while researching among the papers of J. H. Oldham recently, I found that on the inside cover of his pocket-diary for 1945 he had penned the lines from the ill-fated marquess of Montrose three centuries earlier:

He either fears his fate too much,
Or his deserts are small,
That puts it not unto the touch
To win or lose it all.

Oldham was not a betting man, nor given to dramatic gesture. But throughout his writings, lifelong, the word *adventure* runs like a refrain. Whether at his desk in Edinburgh House, or in the gentlemanly ambience of the Athenaeum, or in weekend conversation at Bishopthorpe Palace, or in the wartime meetings of the Moot in quiet retreats in Oxford, he was always interested in the *new* challenges emerging in the present situation both in Britain and the wider world. The fact that he never seemed to panic did not mean he did not believe there was a crisis. Often he discerned crisis long before others did. But his characteristic reaction to crisis was to study the situation even more thoughtfully, and to ask what light could be shed on it from Christian faith. The facts had to be studied thoroughly and patiently, with the aid of the best human science, and reflected upon with the most rigorous theological and philosophical help. It was thus that he reacted to the crisis in British colonial policy in Africa in the 1920s, and the corresponding challenge to Christian missions in that continent; to the growing threat of totalitarianism in Europe in the 1930s and the ecumenical responses to it which culminated in the 1937 Oxford Conference on Church, Community and State; to the widespread sense of impending collapse of Western civilization during the Second World War; and then, immediately that war was over, to the frightening new world of atomic warfare.

Meeting these challenges in this way was always for Oldham the great adventure. If not a gambler, he knew that facing crisis did mean hazarding much that had hitherto been valued and cherished. His approach was undergirded by a deep personal faith in the lordship of God over all history. To faith, the *end* could never be in doubt for it was in God's hands. But here and now, great issues really were at stake. And not the least of risks were to be faced by Christianity itself. Traditional Christian thinking and practice were being called in question precisely by the truly missionary nature of the church, and had to be risked if that church and its gospel were to remain a force within the world rather than simply existing as a backwater to it.

## A Genuine Retrieval

Oldham is of course only one, though one of the most crucial, of the figures featured in this study. I represent him in this way because it is important that we consider carefully *how*, and with what precise aims and motives, we attempt to retrieve such a pioneer and his contemporaries. We may, after all, simply be wishing to re-enact what we imagine were their assured roles as arbiters of the social good, by way of compensation for our own feelings of frustration at being marginalized from the main currents of influence in society today. Or, coming away from an inconclusive group discussion or conference on faith and ethics in relation to modern society, we may long for the calm, collected rationality of a Temple, or the single trenchant insight of a Niebuhr, or the sanctified earthy wisdom of Oldham himself, to answer all our questions.

If so, we are chasing mirages. Many of the Christian social thinkers considered in this volume would hardly recognize themselves in the caricatures of assured wisdom which we are apt to draw. Yes, there was a certain air of assurance in what they had to say – in Temple, particularly, with his assertion that the church's task is, first, to announce the great overarching principles which should inform social order, then, second, to point out where actual social life is violating these, and then leave it to individual citizens to apply the ethical insights accordingly. But even Temple, archbishop though he was, did not speak from the Olympian (or Sinaitic) heights of lonely genius or inspiration. His *Christianity and Social Order* could not have been written without the informal teams of thinkers he had collected on issues such as unemployment since the early 1930s.

Still more instructive is the case of Oldham and his 'Moot', that 'think-tank' of such varied characters as T. S. Eliot, Karl Mannheim, Walter Moberly, John Baillie, John Middleton Murry, H. A. Hodges, Alec Vidler and others. Reading the verbatim minutes of the Moot is a rewarding experience, as one hears almost first-hand the flashes of insight and sees taking shape before one's eyes what came to birth in Mannheim's writings on freedom and planning, the wisdom of Baillie and the argumentativeness of Middleton Murry. It is also sometimes a tedious business, especially in the interminable debates to which the Moot, particularly in its early years, subjected itself on *how* it should actually influence society and preserve Christian values at a time of critical change. Here were thinkers as frustrated as any group today when they looked at the deficit between their thinking and their power to change society's direction. The conclusion to which they eventually came was that the fruits of their shared thinking could largely be mediated only through the roles they already had, as literary editors, writers, academics, administrators and church workers – largely, but not, of course, completely. *The Christian News-Letter*, edited by Oldham, of which an account is given above,[1] together with some of its associated books, gave an important public outlet to a good deal of the Moot thinking. Moreover, *CN-L*, attracting as it did both readers and contributors from all walks of life and from many points of view, itself became a kind of popular 'Moot' in extension.

A retrieval of that generation's approach must therefore attend to two features displayed in their work: their conscious acceptance of risk in venturing into new areas of enquiry, and their patient, painstaking collaboration in groups and networks. Too often, reflection on social and international issues, whether by Christians or by others, begins with the unspoken premiss that the answer really is known already and the only problem is how to express and communicate it. It was John Macmurray who once said that the wish to know the truth is the wish to be disillusioned. That, of course, is what we habitually do *not* want. We prefer to analyse the world, endlessly and brilliantly, reshaping it intellectually in order to fit our preconceptions, whether cultural, theological or philosophical. By contrast, for example, it was the genius of Oldham to notice what was happening in colonial Africa and to realize that the established thought and practice both of Western governments and Christian missions needed drastic rethinking. He called for a vast relearning exercise on Africa in which colonial administrators, anthropologists, scientists, educators, language experts and missionary leaders could collaborate, and his vision bore fruit in the establishment of the International Institute of African Languages and Cultures. His riposte to the comfortable, paternalistic white view of Africa, expressed by Jan Smuts in his broadcast talks in 1930, was devastating: less by opposing ideology to ideology, than by simply exposing how naïve and ill-informed was Smuts on many of the realities of the continent he claimed as his home.[2]

Similarly, the preparations for the 1937 'Life and Work' Conference at Oxford involved the participation of numerous study groups and contributions from social scientists, political thinkers and theologians in many parts of the world. No less than the reports of the conference itself, the preparatory volume *The Church and its Function in Society* by Oldham and W. A. Visser't Hooft, emerged from that long and at times highly contentious process. But scarcely was the conference over than Oldham was already looking for the next question to be faced: that of preserving the humanity of the human person, and especially his or her freedom, in a society which – especially under wartime conditions – was increasingly a *planned* society. Hence the 'Moot'.

If today we are serious about learning from that generation of thinkers, there must be sober reflection on whether we are prepared for similar exercises of enquiry involving long-term, collaborative inter-disciplinary work on basic, structural issues in society. We may not yet have realized just how unpropitious are our social and cultural conditions in present-day Britain for this approach. Elsewhere I have written at greater length on the factors which in my view militate against it.[3] Our culture, media-obsessed and media-driven, prizes publicity over against underlying reality. It encourages a pseudo-technological perception of the world as a set of 'problems' to which neat 'solutions' need to be found and applied. And it wants quick results. These features have not only come to determine much of the quality, or lack of it, in political life and debate. They have also taken over much of the churches' approach to social and international issues. The relentless pressure is on for bishops to make instant comment and for church assemblies to pass resolutions at the drop of a hat – and then wait for whatever issue next hits the headlines. Of course there is a requirement for the churches to have a public voice on urgent issues of the day. But their thinking needs continual resourcing and undergirding if prophecy is not to be reduced to mere commentary.

Granted, from time to time denominational or ecumenical working groups are set up to carry out a study and to produce a report. On occasion these have carried real weight and influence, for example *Faith in the City*,[4] or the recent ecumenical report *Unemployment and the Future of Work*.[5] Working groups set up by churches often, however, have to operate under extreme pressure of time and of limited resources. Often, too, those who serve on them find that they need more information, analytical tools and theological and ethical insight than they themselves have. What of university departments? Academics in Britain today habitually express frustration at being hardly able to keep up with their own teaching and research under the increasing administrative burdens they carry, let alone make themselves available for wider creative work. One highly placed teacher in a theology department recently remarked to me that a few years ago he dreamed of writing another book; now he dreams of reading one.

It is not that there is little Christian comment and reflection on societal issues today. But most of it is in individual, monographic form, lacking the edge and spice produced by multidisciplinary encounters. Perhaps the nearest in spirit to *CN-L* today is the occasional SCM Press *Trust*. The latest number (September 1997) at the time of writing comprises two excellent pieces by Chris Arthur and Ian Hargreaves on the role of the media in contemporary society. But such a vital topic needs to be explored in round-tables of many more people with real stakes and responsibilities in the media: producers, writers, journalists, politicians, educationists, together with some non-specialist representatives of 'the viewing public'.

There are, however, some signs of hope. New College, Edinburgh, has its Centre for Theology and Public Issues. Queen's College, Birmingham, has set up a Research Centre, and is also home to the newly founded George Bell Institute. The Council on Christian Approaches to Defence and Disarmament has stimulated reflection of an excellent quality on issues such as the arms trade, international intervention in conflict situations, and comparison of Christian and Muslim teachings on war. The value of such bodies is that they are of sufficient standing to call on relevant expertise, sometimes through being closely related both to universities and the churches, yet with a real degree of independence. It is in finding the right balance of both security and freedom that there lies the key to sustained, experimental, creative thinking: a large enough guaranteed space amid the debilitating cultural factors to which I alluded earlier. It also has to be said that most of these institutions, being relatively unglamorous, are desperately short of funding – and in an age when a successful and well-known novelist is prepared to found a chair in religion and science at Cambridge.

## Britain in the World

We may take one example of an area in need of renewed and serious reflection. As Marjorie Reeves has shown earlier,[6] one of the striking features of the *CN-L* was its continual wrestling with the future role of Britain in the world. In one sense, this preoccupation was not surprising. Britain was at war in an epochal struggle which was not only about her own survival, but which would decide the future of Europe, and of much of the rest of the world, in the issues between democracy and totalitarianism. At the same time, Britain was still a major imperial power, albeit being rapidly eclipsed in significance by the United States. Many of the Christian social thinkers of the 1930s and 1940s still assumed a dominant world role for Britain, while being aware that the days of the empire as they knew it were probably numbered. But this awareness of the importance of the question was not just a product of immediate circumstances and inherited attitudes. It was also born out of that deep sense of mutuality in human relationships, the need to build genuinely communal values even on the international level. How, on the one hand, to accept the *fact* of colonial power, and on the other to act with a real responsibility for the advancement of Africans and their *paramountcy of interest*, was the challenge which Oldham had identified since the 1920s.

Dean Acheson's comment, that Britain has lost an empire but has yet to find a role, became a cliché almost overnight. It irritated those who felt that the largely dignified and peaceable manner in which Britain gave up (rather than simply 'lost') its empire was itself a major contribution to the world scene of the second half of this century. Be that as it may, it is the case that Britain's loss of actual power in world affairs has not been accompanied by any real reflection on what her responsibilities now are and how they are to be exercised. This became all too obvious in British governmental attitudes to Europe in the 1980s and 1990s. From her imperial past, Britain has inherited an attitude which assumes that the only worthwhile relationship to the wider world must be a dominating one. If one cannot dominate that world, then one should try to ignore it. Or at best, one should put on a show of bulldog aggressiveness and defensiveness by turns and claim to have done one's best 'for Britain's interests'.

It may be that the change of government in Britain in 1997 heralds a real shift in attitude. But it is an enormous psychological leap which still has to be made by Britain (or, perhaps more specifically, by the English) if the assumption of a bleak choice between dominance and retreat is to be overcome, and if the value of *partnership* with our European neighbours is to be accepted and affirmed. It involves a shift from asking the question 'How can Britain still control – or pretend to control – the world around us for Britain's benefit?', to asking 'What is really distinctive about Britain today, and how can that contribute to a Europe at peace with itself, and a Europe making for a just world order?' It will be marked by a change of language which signals the recognition of contemporary realities: we are no longer *separated* from the continent by the sea, but *joined* to it by the currents that sweep our pollution to Scandinavia.

The legacy of flags and songs, and of nostalgia for Britain's finest wartime hour, keeps us trapped in trying to replay the old imperial script which, far from demonstrating a real loyalty to country, studiously ignores looking at what really is loveable about Britain today,[7] what is valuable in our experience and what its significance may be for the wider scene. And it is in the churches, whatever their shortcomings, that much of this significant experience is located. The churches today may be thin on the ground, but the important thing is that they *are* on the ground, in all sorts and conditions of life, from rural villages to the inner cities (and one of the *great* stories of the churches in modern Britain is how, even if only by their toe-nails, they have stayed with the inner cities). They are also 'in Europe' in a significant way. For example, in June 1997 there was held in Graz, Austria, the Second European Ecumenical Assembly, sponsored jointly by the Conference of European Churches and the Council of Catholic Bishops' Conferences in Europe. Seven hundred official delegates from all the Christian traditions of Europe – Protestant, Anglican, Orthodox, Roman Catholic, Pentecostal – and from all parts of Europe, from Portugal to the Urals, from Arctic Norway to Crete, gathered to study, debate, celebrate and pray about the theme 'Reconciliation – Gift of God and Source of New

Life'. Ten thousand more unofficial participants, many from Eastern Europe, testified to the widespread groundswell of yearning for a truly new Europe, a hope outliving the collapse of the euphoria which greeted the end of the Cold War at the end of the 1980s.

From a British perspective, two features marked this event. One was the studied indifference displayed by the British media, in marked contrast to continental press, radio and television. Even the religious media in Britain affected a marked lack of interest, summed up in the attitude of the editor of one major church weekly who stated that 'Europe is a turn-off'. The other feature was the discovery by some of the many British participants that they had something special to share. There was much talk at Graz about the need to affirm the pluralistic culture and multifaith nature of Europe today, in face of the forces that would destroy it, seen at their worst in the fate of the former Yugoslavia. In the discussion groups and forums, it was precisely the British participants who discovered that it was they who brought with them the actual experience of Christians living as black and white together, and of living alongside Muslim neighbours. What others talked about as a 'problem' or a 'challenge' facing Europe, British church people talked about as an aspect of their daily lives – not least because some of them were themselves black (most of the black Europeans at Graz were from Britain).

Britain still needs more than many admit to re-examine its role in Europe and the wider world. At the same time, Britain is also in possession of greater resources than many recognize to be able to make a positive contribution. If I have a dream, it is for a contemporary kind of Moot to be created (and of course funded!) in which people of varied experience and outlook, yet aware of both these facts, could be given the space and freedom to debate, to imagine, to re-envision what Britain-in-the-world might look like the far side of the year 2000.

## A 'Moot' Today?

The strength of a group such as Oldham's Moot was that it comprised highly gifted people, experts or creative thinkers in their own fields, who had the opportunity for sustained conversation and debate over a long period of time in complete freedom. Free from the pressure to produce according to a strict timetable, it was in fact highly productive because it allowed ideas to germinate and grow at their own pace, sometimes painfully. Not beholden to any church, political party, publishing house or university, it nevertheless had a deep sense of accountability to the churches and institutions from which its members came. Meeting incognito (its minutes and papers were always marked 'Confidential') its thinking, when judged right, did become public through the *CN-L* and other means.

The prime need now is not to attempt the formation of another 'Moot' following the exact pattern of its meetings and composition of its kind of membership; nor to reproduce the kind of study-groups fed by papers from famous theologians, as led up to the 1937 Oxford Conference; nor to expect an archbishop to sketch a new vision for Britain and the world within a best-selling paperback. The prime need is to ask how and where that *quality* of exploration, independent and free on the one hand, yet supported by and responsible to a number of institutions on the other, might be fostered today.

'Networking' is a phrase of the 1990s, perhaps over-used, to describe what might be nothing more than one organization exchanging mailing lists with another, or the possibilities of distributing and receiving vast quantities of information (relevant or not) through the electronic Internet. And in some cases it is the 'net' rather than the actual 'working' which seems most evident. But its best uses do refer to a vital feature of any intellectual engagement with contemporary issues which wishes to be fed and enriched by thinking and perspectives from outside the group. Any group, to be creative, needs to have diversity. Equally, to be cohesive, its size must be limited. It cannot deal with all problems in the world, indeed its purpose will be to focus on just some. But the work of one such group can be immeasurably strengthened by a live contact with another group which may be majoring on some quite other topic and with a different scope. Groups are much more likely to function well and creatively if they include one or two members who are also members of other such groups.

During the period under review, a first-class example of such inter-group networking was provided by the connection between the Moot and the Church of Scotland's Commission on God's Will in a Time of Crisis.[8] The point of contact was John Baillie, who chaired the commission and was one of the longest-standing members recruited by Oldham into his Moot. From the Moot, Baillie received the stimulus of a breadth and incisiveness of sociological analysis and ethical reflection which he would never have received purely in his church's commission. In turn, that commission was facing particular social and moral issues (employment, industrial relations, military service and pacifism etc) in a much more concrete way than the Moot. Baillie thus brought a wider perspective to the commission, and often brought the Moot down to earth.

One of the features of an increasingly fragmentary (or 'post-modern, if one prefers) society and culture is the seeming incapacity of any of the particular interest-groups to offer themselves as a point at which an attempt might be made at bringing together the various perspectives in encounter, dialogue and joint reflection. Some will argue that this has simply to be accepted, if not actually welcomed, as a given feature of our time and place and that our ethical thinking will have to abide by it, whether we like it or not. This however raises major questions for a body like the Christian church which knows that it exists as local communities in particular contexts (not to mention individuals seeking to live out their discipleship in very particular circumstances) *and* as a universal fellowship of the *oikumene*, the whole inhabited earth. The problem has recently been explored in the World Council of Churches' study on 'Ecclesiology and Ethics'. As the report of one of its consultations states:

> We face post-modernism's penchant for the deconstruction of all large systems of thought as well as the power structures legitimated by them. On the one hand, such deconstruction very properly attacks the pride of certain great syntheses of the Western academic world, syntheses that assume, for example, that objectivizing human sciences are forms of discourse superior to the 'subjugated languages' of the poor and dispossessed. But on the other hand, such attitudes can be seen as demolishing, or at least undermining, the very notion of an ecumenical vision as itself a kind of global synthesis. Just at the moment where we are trying to give ecumenism a new comprehensive meaning which might clarify the calling of the World Council of Churches we find ourselves living in an age whose thinkers seek to dismantle all such large ideas. Our emphasis on formation, with its preferential option for the immediate and local, seems in tune with the prevailing philosophical temper. But the very word *oikumene* seems to violate this post-modern preference for particularity, evoking as it does the notion of the unity of the human race in the household of God. Can we still convincingly speak 'ecumenical language'?[9]

Oldham and his like-minded contemporaries would enter this debate by reminding us that if post-modernism wishes to deconstruct *society* and *community*, at whatever level, then so be it – but that is the reverse of what Christian social ethics is about. The prevailing philosophical climate may look askance at the notion of 'middle axioms' which Oldham and W. A. Visser't Hooft set out at the time of the 1937 Oxford Conference, and which was taken up in a major way by, for example, the Baillie Commission in the Church of Scotland. But it is also significant that the concept has been taken up again with some enthusiasm by, for instance, the South African theologian Charles Villa-Vicencio. In a context of *nation-building* in the aftermath of the destructive years of apartheid, there is a vital need for some binding, unitive principles which will define certain medium-term goals, embodying key human values, which can draw the adherence of people from a variety of cultural, political and religious backgrounds. As Villa-Vicencio puts it:

> At the centre of this theology is the integration of an ultimate vision which disturbs the *status quo* that emerges at any given time, while promoting concrete proposals which provide the best possible solution to the specific needs of the time. Such a theology can only emerge from a thorough and careful understanding of the nature of the society it is seeking to address. In this sense, it is marked by contextual particularity, while drawing on historical and global insights as a basis for providing a thoughtful and critical social ethic.[10]

Far from themselves succumbing to the process of fragmentation by retreat into the religious ghetto, it is precisely here that there lies a crucial role for the churches: not as supreme ethicizers over society, but as those communities which serve society by helping to facilitate a broader and deeper moral exploration.

Assuming for the moment its desirability, is such a venture possible today? This requires the churches, other faith-communities, academic institutions, advocacy groups, local community-action groups and others to enter into alliances of free enquiry about the shaping of modern society. Is it naïve to hope for the formation of a new kind of Moot, or think-tank, or a network of such groups? The basic criteria for membership of such an alliance would be a belief in the necessity of restoring and maintaining the ethical component in public policy and decision-making, with the no-less-deep conviction that, at every level, learning to *live together* is the only way forward if humanity is to have a future. It will mean risk by all concerned, as they put their natural wishes for their own programmes and prestige at hazard for the sake of the greater good of the whole. It will also mean risk for those individuals, foundations and businesses who might be invited to be the benefactors of such an enterprise. But then, in a world of increasing uncertainties, faith still remains to be put to the test, to win or lose it all.

## Notes

1. See above, chs 2 and 3.
2. J. H. Oldham, *White and Black in Africa* (Longmans, Green, 1930).
3. K. W. Clements, *Learning to Speak: The Church's Voice in Public Affairs*, (T. & T. Clark, 1995).
4. *Report of the Archbishop of Canterbury's Commission on Urban Priority Areas*, (Church House Publishing, 1985).
5. *Unemployment and the Future of Work: An Enquiry for the Churches*. (Council of Churches for Britain and Ireland, 1997).
6. See above, ch. 3, s. 5.
7. Cf. K. W. Clements, *A Patriotism for Today: Love of Country in Dialogue with the Witness of Dietrich Bonhoeffer* (Collins, 1986).
8. See A. Morton (ed.), *God's Will in a Time of Crisis: A Colloquium Celebrating the 50th Anniversary of the Baillie Commission* (Centre for Theology and Public Issues, 1994).
9. T. F. Best and M. Robra (eds.), *Ecclesiology and Ethics: Ecumenical Ethical Engagement, Moral Formation and the Nature of the Church* (WCC Publications, 1997), p. 77.
10. C. Villa-Vicencio, *A Theology of Reconstruction: Nation-Building and Human Rights* (CUP, 1992), p. 275.

# Conclusion

Although the essays in this book have been independently written, they have thrown up certain general themes and principles. It may be useful to list these:

1. The needs of human beings and their societies cannot be addressed successfully by the application of any ready-made ideology, political or religious. Their complexity calls rather for open dialogue between people of diverse experience and thought who do not work confrontationally from prepared positions, but can and will engage in a real meeting of minds with those who differ from them.

2. Behind this insight on method lies a concept which had its source in John Macmurray's philosophy. Whether acknowledged or not, his key idea of the person-in-relationship, rather than the atomistic individual, as the reality of human society exercised a pervasive influence in the period *c*. 1930–*c*. 1970.

3. This finds particular expression in Archbishop Temple's prophetic statement (quoted by others) that the crisis in a fragmented society was primarily cultural, in the sense of the way people live together. It cannot be radically addressed by applying 'moral plasters' of exhortation nor even directly by central political *diktat*. Integrity, responsibility, compassion and other social virtues are learned through role models in a supportive group.

4. From different angles writers develop this theme in terms of the crucial need for small, 'on-the-spot' democracies of all kinds, from political to artistic and religious. G. D. H. Cole wrote movingly of 'Democracy Face to Face with Hugeness' and the need of 'ordinary people' for 'manageable societies'.

5.   Educators (or communicators) are everywhere and their stance is crucial. Various writers reflect on the knife edge which teachers of all kinds must walk between the propaganda of the totalitarian and the total relativism of the ultra-liberal. Sir Walter Moberly denounced 'negative neutrality' but defined 'positive neutrality' as a constructive position, similar to the 'human explicitness' later called for by the University Teachers' Group. The Auxiliary Movement of the SCM went further in advocating 'education for commitment'.

6.   Faced at that period with the stark alternatives of *laissez-faire* liberalism and the central planning of the totalitarian state, a warning note was struck several times concerning the instinctive hostility of the central authority towards any competing forms of local democracy. Nevertheless, thinkers of the 1940s and 1950s sought to grasp the nettle of finding the right combination between the necessary central planning of a new order and devolution to vigorous local initiatives.

7.   Behind this thinking lay the conviction that, on their pilgrimage to a heavenly citizenship, Christians must be fully secular in their earthly citizenship.

Somewhere in the late 1960s and early 1970s the cultural climate began to change. Widespread concern for fundamental values in society and in its educational procedures seemed to evaporate. There was a failure of nerve. Subtly the sweeping influence of managerialism began to shift the focus from organic relationships of persons to the mechanisms of controlling individuals. The line between the church and the world hardened: 'frontiersmen' were now seen as a bit odd. For a range of reasons many of the experiments in 'thinking together' described in this book had petered out or were greatly diminished. As the grand vision suffered deconstruction, people – young people especially – sought security in devoting themselves to single issues. The pressures of specialisms increased and people had little time or enthusiasm for shared reflection, for cross-dialogue or for ecumenical and inter-disciplinary 'meeting' (in Oldham's sense). The shift was gradual but profound. Perhaps we did not realize its extent until the blinding revelation of the famous pronouncement: 'There is no such thing as Society.' Was that the point from which we started on a return journey which is also a new journey into the future?

# Index